HOPE

BY TERRY FOX

HOPE

BY TERRY FOX

EDITED BY BARBARA ADHIYA

BURMAN BOOKS

MEDIA CORP.

Published by ECW Press and Burman Books

ECW Press
665 Gerrard Street East
Toronto, ON M4M 1Y2
416-694-3348 / info@ecwpress.com

Burman Books
260 Queens Quay West
Toronto, ON M5J 2N3
info@burmanbooks.com

Friesens Corporation, in business in Canada since 1907, is honoured to support the Terry Fox Foundation and its work through the donation of this book and to continue working in partnership with Canadian publishers like ECW Press, who designed and published this celebration of Terry Fox.

Editor: Barbara Adhiya
Cover photo: Gail Harvey

LIBRARY AND ARCHIVES CANADA CATALOGUING IN PUBLICATION

Title: Hope by Terry Fox / edited by Barbara Adhiya.

Names: Adhiya, Barbara, editor.

Identifiers: Canadiana (print) 20240390695 | Canadiana (ebook) 20240392159

ISBN 978-1-77041-681-9 (softcover)
ISBN 978-1-77041-801-1 (hardcover)
ISBN 978-1-77852-339-7 (PDF)
ISBN 978-1-77852-338-0 (ePub)

Subjects: LCSH: Fox, Terry, 1958-1981—Anecdotes. | LCSH: Fox, Terry, 1958-1981—Friends and associates—Interviews. | LCSH: Cancer—Patients—Canada—Anecdotes. | LCSH: Runners (Sports)—Canada—Anecdotes. | LCGFT: Anecdotes. | LCGFT: Interviews. | LCGFT: Biographies.

Classification: LCC RC265.6.F68 H67 2024 | DDC 362.19699/40092—dc23

This book is funded in part by the Government of Canada. Ce livre est financé en partie par le gouvernement du Canada. We also acknowledge the support of the Government of Ontario through the Ontario Book Publishing Tax Credit and through Ontario Creates.

PRINTED AND BOUND IN CANADA

PRINTING: FRIESENS   5   4   3   2   1

CONTENTS

FOREWORD

Like many Canadians, I learned about Terry Fox in elementary school. I knew he tried to run across Canada, how he wanted to find a cure for cancer, and that we were raising funds to support his dream. Being so young, that was all I remembered. When I joined this project, I began to read more about him and realized he actually ran "a marathon a day." I was shocked by that simple fact. How did I not know that? Embarrassed that I didn't really know his story at all, my deep dive into everything Terry began.

Terry Fox was an ordinary teenager, dreaming of competing on the athletic stage internationally and then becoming a teacher and a coach, passing his knowledge on to students. Quite suddenly, all of that changed. At eighteen, he was diagnosed with osteosarcoma and learned that within days they would have to amputate his leg. He would then have to undergo harsh chemotherapy treatment for the next year and a half with only a thirty percent chance of surviving.

Terry's dream for his future was shattered in an instant. But he decided not to focus on what he had lost — he was going to focus on all he had to gain. Instead of despair, Terry chose hope. This hope was the foundation upon which he fought through his cancer and continued to be an athlete. He did not see himself as extraordinary; if anything, he most often spoke about how he was no different than anybody else. He'd worked hard to be a good student and an accomplished athlete — he wasn't going to give up now.

Sometimes, the hardest challenges we face can be doors to great opportunities. Devastating but also life-changing. Terry's upbringing had instilled the ethos of hard work, and he put all his effort into everything he did. He survived his initial battle with cancer thanks to a new drug discovered through progress in research. He saw others, however, who were not as fortunate. He felt deeply that he had to do something to help continue to advance this research, and this challenge gave his life a new meaning — a new purpose.

On April 12, 1980, at age twenty-one, Terry began his run across Canada from the East Coast to raise funds for cancer research and, hopefully, for a cure. Although Terry tackled running a marathon every day for 140 days, he could not have achieved his goal without the support and actions of his family, friends, and strangers across the country. He made believers out of everyone. He led the call to action by example, and not one person who watched his Marathon of Hope would say they weren't changed by him. There was no doubt that this young man, his spirit full of hope, would make it across the country running with only one leg. He greeted people along the way, sharing his story but also listening to their stories of grief and survival. With his perseverance and endurance, he entranced whole crowds, speaking his truth with purity and authenticity. He touched their souls and their humanity with his demonstration of selflessness.

The story of the Marathon of Hope has been told many times in books and movies, in schools across Canada and in communities around the world who participate every year in the Terry Fox Run. In reading segments of his journal, I wanted to know how it was possible that an ordinary man could accomplish such an extraordinary feat. How does someone get up and run consecutive marathons in the cold, rain, sleet, or heat day after day?

In 2023, our team dove into thousands of artifacts and connected with the people from Terry's youth, his support teams, communities, friends, and family, as well as those who were so moved by their experience forty-three years ago that it changed them forever. In interviews with me, they recalled how inspired and intensely moved they were by who Terry was and what his determination, courage, and sacrifice taught them. Strengthened by their connection to Terry, they learned to bravely face any challenge in their life with hope. Some had never before spoken publicly about their experience with Terry, and through them, I discovered new stories, pictures, and letters. The story of the true Terry emerged: his humanity, his character, his mischievous nature, and his steadfast integrity.

How he got up every day became clear. Besides his innate character, Terry became the strong person he was because of his relationships, each having a place and purpose in his life. He may not have won his final bout with cancer, but he did overcome his challenges and achieve his dream with the help of others along the way. All of us can reach our goals, overcome and conquer what may feel impossible by incorporating some of the same elements that he did: having hope and staying positive, keeping the company of family and friends, finding support in others, taking guidance from mentors and coaches, being part of a community, embracing selflessness and service, finding inspiration, doing the hard work with discipline, and never giving up.

As Terry said, "Anything is possible if you try."

Barbara Adhiya
November 2023

The Fox family participates in a group head shave to support fundraising efforts.
Courtesy of Martha McClew, Terry Fox Foundation

INTRODUCTION

FRED FOX

Brother, Terry Fox Foundation spokesperson

Fred answers the door and welcomes me into the home of Martha McClew, who is hosting him while he's in Toronto, Ontario. He is on tour once again, speaking to students, media, and communities, representing the Terry Fox Foundation, and sharing the hopes and stories of his brother Terry. Dressed in his Terry T-shirt and shorts, he leads me to the office on the main floor with a desk, full bookcases on the walls, and two comfortable sitting chairs nestled on either side of a table, where we sit to chat about his family.

The Fox children were born in Winnipeg, Manitoba, and as such they were made of tough, prairie-winter stock. Both their parents, Betty and Rolly, worked hard and taught their kids how to have a strong work ethic. They had to help around the house, do the dishes, cut the grass, and be active. If they were going to wrestle with Rolly, as he and Terry often did, then they had to accept that even if they ran crying to Betty, Rolly would never let up.

Betty used to share a story of Terry in his highchair stacking blocks that Fred continues to tell as well. Even if the blocks fell, Terry kept stacking them until he had them all standing up. He didn't get mad; he didn't throw them, just kept at it until he got it. Betty was also tough in her own right.

> Mom would often say to us when we were younger [that] we had to finish everything we started. It didn't matter what it was; it might have been a colouring book. Even if we were making a mess of it, we still had to finish the picture we were colouring before we turned the page, and I think Terry applied that to lots of things he did, whether it was sports or schoolwork or anything.

She was the athlete in her family, playing ice hockey, baseball, and other sports against her brothers. Facing them, she knew she couldn't back down. All her kids were involved with sports, and that came from her.

The Foxes were a tight family. Fred didn't see himself as Terry's older brother because they grew up so close together, only fourteen months apart in age. One day, when Fred returned home after work, the house was quiet. He knew something wasn't right. It was normally a busy, full house with his siblings still in school and living at home and his mom starting dinner every day at 5:30 p.m. Five minutes later, one of his close friends arrived at the house. Betty had sent him, wanting someone to be there for Fred when he came home. Then the phone rang, and it was Betty saying that they were all at the hospital and Terry had been diagnosed with cancer. The news hit the family hard. Fred can't recall specific details anymore, other than being in a small room with the family later on as orthopedic surgeon Dr. Michael Piper shared the next steps.

They didn't know what cancer was, and they were taking it all day by day. It was Terry who was dealing with it better than anyone, as though something clicked in his head right away. He knew he had to pivot.

> Terry faced all kinds of different challenges as a kid. Now, this was just something else. The night before his surgery, his amputation, I had visited him in the hospital, and it was just him and I. I kind of said to him, "This is the shits. Why do you have to have cancer? You're playing basketball at Simon Fraser University. You're working towards your university degree. Why you? Why? All your dreams are coming true." And he'd already had four days or whatever to think about it, and his answer was "Why not me?

I've been told all my life, I'm not the best or smartest or biggest. This is just another challenge I have to overcome." So, he had already figured out that he was gonna do what he could to make it better.

When Terry began training for the Marathon of Hope, Fred wasn't living at home anymore. He knew Terry was participating in wheelchair basketball games and competitions and running often. The family thought it was in preparation for the Prince George race, a goal Terry had set for himself. Terry hadn't told many people of his plans to run across the country to raise money for cancer research. Fred thinks probably only Doug Alward (Terry's close friend) or Rika Schell (his girlfriend) knew about the Marathon of Hope at first. But once more people learned of his plan, it wasn't a surprise to anyone. That was Terry: big dreams, dedication, follow-through.

Fred was at the airport with his now wife, Theresa, and the rest of the family to send Terry off to Newfoundland to begin the Marathon. It was a difficult moment, with Betty having the hardest time as she and Terry were so close. If his parents had any concerns, they didn't share them with Fred, and he didn't know the doctors had warned Terry and his parents about the weakening of his heart from the cancer treatments. They kept all of that to themselves. Fred watched the first days of the Marathon on TV, but there was little coverage after that. His parents would get some phone calls and receive postcards from the first four provinces, but Fred didn't hear much during that time. It wasn't until later in life, when he went out to drive Terry's route in Newfoundland, that he realized how many hills there were and how rough the terrain was. Add in the cold maritime

April 7, 1980: Terry smiles at the airport before departing for St. John's, Newfoundland, to begin the Marathon of Hope. It would take him and Doug ten flights to reach their destination.

Courtesy of Doug Alward

weather in April, and he realized just how hard it must have been. But Fred says Terry's reason for doing it was what kept him going.

Terry shared this in his journal and in the letters he sent out asking for support. He couldn't forget the people he left behind in the hospital wards where he had his amputation. He knew they were suffering, and he remembered his suffering. That's why he didn't want the run to be named after him. It was the Marathon of Hope, not the Terry Fox Marathon. It's what got him up every morning. He didn't want to let anyone down.

> He did meet people with cancer along the way. And he probably took a lot of that, how they were feeling and everything, on his shoulders and began to feel that he really couldn't stop now. People are probably thanking him [along the way] for what he's doing and raising money. And so there was that extra pressure on him. He met that little girl [Annie Marie von Zuben], who gave Terry flowers, and Greg Scott. That's what it was all about for him. We've all seen the video footage of him speaking about that day, and he was very emotional about it because it meant everything to him. That's why he was doing it.

Fred was able to see Terry on his Marathon twice. First, he flew a red-eye and arrived the morning of July 9, 1980, to meet his parents and sister, Judy, to surprise Terry in Whitby, Ontario, a suburb just outside Toronto. Two days later, Fred joined Terry, their brother Darrell, Doug Alward, and Darryl Sittler, running down University Avenue to a massive reception awaiting them at Nathan Phillips Square in Toronto. Then in August, Fred had a couple of weeks of vacation, so he and Theresa drove from Coquitlam to Northern Ontario and arrived in the Wawa/Montreal River area on August 15, the day before Terry ran up Montreal River Hill — a difficult incline that had been on everyone's radar for days.

Driving around, they tried to join up with Terry and the Marathon crew but couldn't find them. They were near Wawa, and it was getting dark, so they asked the locals if anyone had seen Terry, and people excitedly said yes, pointing in various directions. They finally found the group a ways off the highway on a quiet logging road — they were getting so famous at this time that it was the only way to stop and have some privacy. Fred had some time to catch up with his brothers. The morning after, some locals arrived and gave Terry a special shirt, proclaiming he would conquer the Montreal River Hill, a buzz of anticipation in the air.

There are four statues in Vancouver at BC Place — it's Fred's favourite memorial. It starts with a small statue of Terry that gradually gets bigger and bigger with each statue.

> When you're out in the middle of nowhere in Northern Ontario and Terry's climbing hills, you would stand on the highway waiting for him to come, and in the distance, he would be this big. [Fred demonstrates with a small space between his thumb and forefinger.] And then, as he got closer and closer to you, he got bigger and bigger and bigger. It's exactly how I remember seeing Terry. Those four statues getting bigger and bigger as he gets closer.

In 2011, BC Place unveiled its Terry Fox memorial, depicting Terry in four statues that appear to be running towards you, growing with each step. The statues were designed by artist and author Douglas Coupland.

Photo by Barbara Adhiya

> It was amazing to see him do that. He had a water break
> and he had run [through] it to get to the top of that climb,
> so nothing was going to stop him.

I ask Fred if he noticed anything at that time about Terry or if there might have been some trouble already brewing. Fred clears his throat and says he knew we'd get to this point of the story. As he shares his reflections on this time, his voice gets raspy and thick with emotion.

> Theresa and I talked about it one night. We were there after
> a long day of running and water breaks. I was sitting in the
> van with him, and he was coughing. Then we were having
> supper at a campground, sitting around the picnic table,
> and he had a bad cough. We just thought he's running every
> day, you know? He's tired, and maybe it's a cold or some-
> thing like that. So, never ever thought that it would be what
> it was. It's one of those things that had I been old enough,
> or maybe been able to recognize something like that — but
> we didn't know what that would mean. We've all specu-
> lated. We might not have known, even though he had a
> bad cough and all that. But it's pretty clear that he probably
> knew something was going on, which is harder. It is harder
> to deal with knowing that he knew.

On September 1, Fred was with his parents heading home from a fund-raiser in Chilliwack at the Canadian Forces base. Rolly was driving, and he turned on the radio for the news. The very first thing they heard was that Terry was in hospital in Thunder Bay. They thought maybe it was the tendonitis that he had been dealing with for a few days. As they approached the house, they heard the phone ringing, and Betty went running inside. It was Terry — his cancer had returned. Family friend and volunteer Doug Vater jumped into action and got Betty and Rolly on a plane right away. Fred stayed home with Judy, as she was only thirteen, and they watched the situation unfold from home on the TV.

His memory is vague after that because so much was happening. He remembers bits and pieces from seeing photographs, but it's hard to differentiate between memory and what was shared by the media in the following days. He remembers manning the phones at the telethon CTV hosted just a week later to keep fundraising for the Marathon.

> When he had to stop, Canadians reacted and made donations and responded to what Terry wanted them to do in the first place. I think he actually thought he would get back out there and finish his run. He really thought he would, even though he knew how serious this second diagnosis was. But he never until later on, of course, gave in to the fact that he wouldn't be able to get back out there again. But he was happy that people were supporting him the way they were.

Losing Terry on June 28, 1981, was incredibly difficult, as any of us can imagine and relate to in grief. Fred and Theresa's wedding was planned for five weeks later, which was an additional challenge. Although they had gotten engaged at the end of the previous year, knowing Terry's diagnosis and that things weren't going to work out, they hadn't gotten the chance to ask him to participate.

> We weren't going to cancel. We got married on August 8, and Terry wasn't there. It was always my intention. And Terry was supposed to be there. He was supposed to be my best man. You see in our wedding pictures that he was missing because on Theresa's side, there was Judy and [Theresa's] sister. And then my side, there was only Darrell standing there. So, it was very, very hard. [Even so,] it was the best thing at that time to have happened to our family. We had a small wedding; we got married in my mom and dad's backyard. There were only maybe fifty family and close friends, and upstairs above the hotel — there were some banquet rooms — we had a small, little reception up there. And it was the best thing for our family because we could have fun and celebrate and dance, and it was the best time we've had in months, in a year probably at that point.

July 2, 1981: Fred, Betty, Rolly, and Darrell Fox leave Terry's funeral.
Photo by Frank Lennon via Getty Images

The funeral was also full of mixed emotions for the family because it was a big televised affair, and they weren't comfortable being in the public arena.

> It's, of course, what Canada wanted, to be involved and see and all that. Terry probably wouldn't have wanted that kind of a spectacle. It was difficult. I mean, again, it's something you blank out. I've [recently] seen pictures of Terry being carried out of the church afterwards and to the hearse. One thing I do remember about that day is the entourage of vehicles heading up to the cemetery and people lining the street. It was amazing, but yeah, I guess it's for Terry in an amazing way. Through fundraising and all the cards and letters and love that he received, Terry inspired our country, and Canada deserved to be a part of that, too.
>
> I think [about] it all the time. We know Terry as somebody who ran across Canada raising money for cancer research, but he's so much more than that today. So much more. We hear from people all [the time] who say that Terry's inspired them to do something else. Or maybe they weren't happy in their jobs and went and found something else. Terry inspired them to do that. I have a friend out of

Newfoundland, and Terry was running through his community one day in 1980. He happened to be in a bar — he's the same age as Terry would have been at the time. Life wasn't taking him in any direction at all, and he walked out of the bar, probably drunk or whatever, and saw Terry run, and that changed his life. And he's been a marathoner all his life since that.

May 30, 2008: Fred writes a note to the Willis family on the back of a wall Terry signed during his Marathon of Hope.

Courtesy of the Willis family

You meet people, you go to a school, people come up, they want to share their story, and it's awesome. And a lot of these people I'm meeting, they're in their fifties. So under ten, in many cases, when they saw Terry, and I've heard stories of, you know, "I was seven years old, and Mom and Dad dragged me at seven o'clock in the morning out on the highway so we could wait for two hours for Terry to run by, and I went shouting and screaming and kicking, and I didn't want to go, and it's the best thing that ever happened in my life" kind of thing. You hear those stories all the time.

Terry Fox inspired people in so many ways, not just in their cancer journeys. Fred has been visiting schools and communities for nearly thirty years, sharing Terry's legacy.

It was always about being the best you could be and doing better than you were the day before. We talk about that a lot [when] I'm doing media interviews for the Terry Fox Run. "What's your guys' goal for fundraising this year?" And I always refer back to Terry. Terry's attitude was he wanted to be better than he was the day before. And when it comes to our fundraising, we don't set a goal. We just want to make sure we raise more or "be better" than we were the year before. That was Terry's example.

April 12, 1980: Day 1 (12 ½ miles) Today is the day it all begins. I had a police escort out of the city and many people followed me in cars. The mayor ran a few steps with me. Along the way everyone was honking and waving.

April 15: Day 4 (23 ½ miles) We got up at 4:30 a.m. and drove back to the starting point. It was hard to get going when my feet, leg and stump are so sore. The only difference between today and Sunday was the wind was hitting my good leg and therefore not blowing me over. One man stopped and gave Doug $50 saying "I don't care if he makes it, he is making a lot of people feel good."

April 23: Day 12 (23 miles) Today we got up 45 minutes later because we were going to have to wait until 1:20 p.m. to arrive in Bishop Falls. With the RCMP and Fire Chief's support, we ran down to where there were all kinds of school kids and people waiting. It was a fantastic greeting and reception. With the kids behind me, we ran to the next school. Then, with Terry Hart, who had two brothers die of cancer, we drove to Grand Falls, and I met all kinds of people. During the day we collected over $2,000. It was a fantastic day!

April 26: Day 15 (25 miles) Today we got up at 4 a.m. We wanted to cover 14 miles right away because there was going to be a reception at South Brook Junction. I was feeling pretty good and the first 2 ¾ miles went quite nicely then all of a sudden, I was seeing 8 pictures of everything. I was dizzy and lightheaded, but I made it to the van. It was a frightening experience. Was it all over? Was everything finished? Would I let everybody down? I told myself it is too late to give up. I would keep going no matter what happened. If I died, I would die happy because I was doing what I wanted to do.

Terry and Doug smile from the Gilberts' kitchen with a number of teens who stopped by to meet them.

April 12, 1980: Terry collects water from the Atlantic Ocean before beginning his Marathon of Hope. He intended to run from sea to sea, raising awareness of cancer throughout the entire nation. The jug remains in the Fox family archives and will be dumped into the Pacific when cancer is cured.

Courtesy of the Terry Fox Centre Archives

A letter from Betty and George Gilbert. George was the mayor of Come by Chance, Newfoundland, and hosted Terry and Doug for a short visit. This letter, dated June 10, 1991, is written to Betty and Rolly Fox and describes their son's visit with the Gilberts: "We were the first ones to go after him to stay here. We flagged them down — him and Doug his pal. Brought him in our kitchen, had a chocolate cake made for him."

Courtesy of the Terry Fox Centre Archives

Brief ceremony

Terry Fox, a 21-year-old amputee who lost a leg to cancer in 1977, is running across Canada to raise funds to cancer research. He began his run in St. John's Saturday but before leaving the city he participated in a brief ceremony at city hall, during which he briefly donned Mayor Dorothy Wyatt's cloak and chain of office. Following the raising of the cancer society flag, Wyatt praised Fox for his endeavor and told him "our prayers and our thoughts are with you." Fox hopes to reach Victoria, B.C., by September or October.

May 3, 1980: Terry writes to his nurse, Judith Ray, updating her on his progress.

Courtesy of Judith Ray & Mission Community Archives [reference catalogue number: MCA-0183-PC19800503-001]

April 12, 1980: Terry stands with Dorothy Wyatt, mayor of St. John's, Newfoundland, at a brief ceremony at City Hall at the beginning of his Marathon of Hope. This article was published on April 16, 1980.

From Saltwire, The Telegram

HOPE
& POSITIVITY

"I will never forget the terrible days I had while in the cancer clinic and I am very happy to have the chance to help all those people with cancer but also all others who are experiencing emotional problems. You are right I do believe in climbing mountains. I would really like to thank you for all the help you have been to me. Now I have the chance to help others, just as you helped me."

— Terry Fox
Letter to Judith Ray, July 2, 1980

JUDITH RAY

Nurse at the Royal Columbian Hospital during Terry's amputation and stay in the pediatric unit

I sit with Judith and her husband, Fred — yes, the same names as Terry's siblings — in their living room in Mission, B.C. They sit on a grey couch in front of me and look like many retired couples: bright smiles and relaxed demeanours. They've worked hard their whole lives and now travel and enjoy their free time. They share that on their trips when people talk about Terry, they get excited hearing that Judith personally knew him. And she happily tells the story.

In 1977, Judith was the head nurse of the pediatric unit at Royal Columbian Hospital. One day, she received a call from Dr. Michael Piper, who was looking for a room for his patient Terry Fox. The adult ward was full, and he was looking for a bed as soon as possible; he was expecting the test results to reveal cancer of the leg, and they had to move quickly. Judith felt the pediatric ward would be better for Terry, as the adult ward was generally full of elderly patients. Luckily, they had a bed available in the boys' room that fit nine, but Terry's parents weren't happy. They asked for a private room because Terry was eighteen, and these were all young boys.

> I said, "He's going to have way more fun in this kind of a setting than he will going into a private room. So, trust us around this one, especially right now, while we're still dealing with what's really going on." He had a great time right from the get-go. And one of the first things he spotted was — I think at the time, we had two young boys who were probably around ten or eleven, hanging up from the ceiling in traction. In those days, if kids had a fractured femur, they didn't put pins and screws and things in. They hung them up and stretched it. So, these kids are hanging up with all these wires everywhere, and Terry's looking at them like, "Oh my God, they're in terrible shape." He's doing well compared to them. So, he was really, really interested. He went around and talked to kids; they had a great time.

Terry had to be taken to different areas of the hospital for his tests, mostly far from his ward, so Judith took it upon herself to porter him everywhere.

> That gave me a chance to chat and get to know him a little bit. It was interesting because one of the tests that he had done, the person who was doing it indicated to me this

definitely was osteosarcoma, but he, of course, didn't tell
Terry that. And so, as we were leaving Terry said, "Thank
you," just being the polite guy that he was, and the fellow
without thinking said, "Don't thank me." We're walking
back to the ward, and Terry said, "Why did he say that?"
And I said, "Oh, well, you know, we all are here doing
our job. It's not like we're doing it so that you'll thank us.
That's part of our work." I'm faking it a little bit till we
can get back to the room.

The whole family had assembled at the hospital, and Dr. Piper gave the
news. Terry was going to lose his leg and needed chemotherapy, and
it was serious but not necessarily fatal. Then Dr. Piper said that they
had just dealt with a similar case with someone who was also from
Port Coquitlam. Judith's heart sank because the girl had died, and she
knew the next question they would ask would be what had happened
in that case.

> That was, I think, the moment when he realized this was
> really, really serious. I know Terry's parents were some-
> what prepared for the news but still, of course, devastated.
> So, I'm there with the family going, "Oh my God." Terry
> started talking a little bit and I said, "You know what?
> This is a hell of a way to get out of all your exams this
> month. You've got a couple of choices. One is that you sit
> there and have this whole thing kind of roll right over you
> and take over, or you fight it with everything you've got,
> and you make a difference." And so that was the conver-
> sation we had that day.

From then on, that was Terry's attitude. It was a Friday, and Judith
told him he would be able to leave for the weekend and return for his
surgery on Monday.

> "These are the two days when you want to go to the
> places that are really important to you and do the things
> that are really important to you, to get your head around

getting ready for Monday." And so, they did. He left the hospital; I think both days, [he] went up to SFU [Simon Fraser University] and did a bunch of things that were important to him, so he could sort of be ready to move.

But then when he had the surgery, he was up like *snap*, still feeling sorry for these kids that are all hanging around in traction, because he's up on crutches already doing what he has to do. So, the rapport we developed between [us] in particular but also with the other staff was a really positive, "get at it" kind of stuff. He bonded with us in such a way that after he left the unit, it was not uncommon for him to come back every two or three months for a visit and just sort of check in. "Here's what's going on. Here's what I'm doing. Here's my wig that I'm wearing because I lost all my hair." He'd talk about trying to figure out what kind of prosthesis was going to work for what he wanted it to be able to do. And it was just really interesting. Not many patients or their families ever come back and visit afterwards.

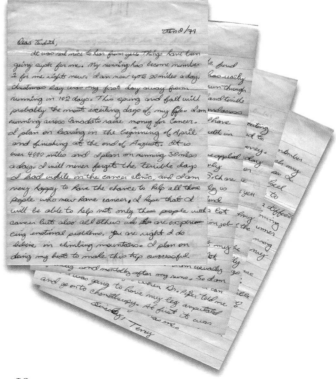

June 2, 1979: Terry writes a letter to Judith Ray, describing his training, asking about her time in Papua New Guinea, and thanking her for her care and friendship: "Since I won't see you again between now and my run I would really like to thank you for all the help you have been to me. I think you can remember how much I enjoyed my stay in the Royal Columbian. How many people can actually say that [they] didn't want to leave a hospital to go home. I give a lot of credit to you for my immediate strong attitude and drive."

Courtesy of Judith Ray & Mission Community Archives [reference catalogue number: MCA-0183-LTR-19790602-005]

Terry had left that ward after only a week to go to the cancer clinic. The treatment was very harsh. Back then, they threw everything at it, hoping something would stick. Terry always saw the upside, though. He could look at those around him and feel he didn't have it as bad. From those who were fighting cancer in the clinic to the kids around him tied up on wires while he hobbled around after his amputation, he felt he was better off despite what he was actually fighting.

Judith had a younger brother around Terry's age, eleven years younger than her. She missed out on some of their time growing up together because of the years between them. She had left home by the time she was twenty and feels this was part of what formed her instant connection with Terry. The two became very close. During one of his visits, Terry shared his dream of running across Canada; Judith was one of the first people he told.

> He sort of had an idea of when he was likely to catch me, so he counted on the fact that I'd probably be there and would just show up. He'd sit in my office; we'd chat away about what was going on and would cheerlead each other and on we'd go. It was almost like he wanted to maintain that contact because he got some support from us in terms of what was going on in his life. I'm pretty sure he knew that if he said to me he wanted to do something, I'd say, "How fast can you do it?" Not "Oh no, don't do that."
>
> I left the [Royal] Columbian in May of '79, and he'd been talking to me about it for probably six or eight months by that time, of how he would do it and the training that would be involved to be able to think about running. I don't think at that point he ever dreamed that it was going to be a marathon length every single day. But then I guess he started to figure out mathematically, this is what [he has] to do to be able to do it. As he was getting ready to do that, I was getting ready to go overseas to work in Papua New Guinea for three years. So, he was intrigued by what I was doing at the same time as I was intrigued with what he was getting ready to do. We were sort of talking each other through this process of getting excited about the next adventure.

1979: The Royal Columbian team says farewell to Judith before she heads to Papua New Guinea for three years. Judith stands in the second row, third in from the right.

Courtesy of Judith Ray

The first experiences he shared were the ones he was having at the cancer clinic with his distress at what he was seeing. Not about himself — he rarely talked about his own reactions other than the loss of his hair — but he would talk about seeing people who were so sick. He'd see them the next time and they looked even worse, or he'd go the next time and they weren't there at all. And that really, really upset him. That's why his focus, I think, right from the beginning was "Why aren't they making a difference? Why aren't they researching this?" Because he could see that what people were doing was fundraising for comfort, fundraising for the equipment you might need, or fundraising for the services that you're receiving in these specialized units, but they're not going to prevent you from getting sick. And that became his real interest: research and getting rid of this in the first place, instead of having to deal with it afterwards. Better treatment as well, of course, and not so harsh. I mean, he appreciated how harsh it was on him, but [felt] even worse about what he was seeing [for] other people. Because when you're looking out at the world, and you see somebody looking really, really sick, you don't think that's what you look like. That's what *they* look like.

1982: Judith with staff from the Highlands Region of Papua New Guinea.

Courtesy of Judith Ray

Snail mail took six weeks to arrive in Papua New Guinea, so she would get delayed updates. More touching was the letter Terry sent her in January 1980 before he left for his run. And at the end of each province, he would send her a postcard. Mostly, the postcards said the crew made it to their destination, and it was tough, but they kept going. In wanting to explain how Terry did it, I ask Judith if she, as a nurse, could explain the physiology, the intertwining of emotion, physics, mentality, and energy.

Now, from a physiological perspective, we know that people who run marathons even once in a while have the endorphin flow that gets everything working. It's a natural part of your body that gives you that kick to keep going. And there's no question [that] when you're running twenty-six miles a day, you're going to have lots of endorphins flowing along the way that will give you relief from what most of us would be feeling as pain and agony.

Terry mentioned pain often in his journal and that if he pushed through it, he'd get past it and be okay. He was also encouraged by the people who would cheer for him on the roads. Those positive interactions could have released endorphins as well, like the excitement you feel watching fireworks or enjoying a concert and getting caught up in the euphoria. It's endorphins being released, and it's a two-way exchange. People who saw Terry or spent a moment with him felt so euphoric that they were in tears, and then they gave this energy back to him as he passed.

> Can you imagine the euphoria when he walked into that City Hall area in Toronto? These amazing crowds practically lift you up and air-move you through the crowd, right? That would be very euphoric, I'm sure. Overwhelming at the same time because he'd be busy thinking, "I'm supposed to be back on the road. How am I going to do both of these things?" But it would have been amazingly reinforcing for him that he was on the right track, and it was the right thing to do.

Having such a packed schedule certainly exhausted him, and he didn't always sleep well, depending on their accommodations. At times, he preferred to sleep in the van on a quiet road because it was familiar, and he could get a deeper rest.

> All of that euphoria, what happens is you crash afterwards. Sleep, sometimes in exhaustion, isn't totally renewing because you're depleted, but necessary obviously. You can't run on adrenaline forever. You've got to start getting some reinforcement and replenishment along the way.

His heightened endorphins would accumulate so much that even if he slept poorly, he would still have some left with him in the morning. He was overflowing. He was able to wake up and get going. We some- times forget or underestimate what can happen when we are with others, this exchange of energy. Judith says it best:

> Looking back, you have no idea when you're encoun- tering somebody along the way in life, how that particular encounter at any given time will happen to be the right person in the right place at the right time. To either say the right thing or do the right thing gives people what it is they need at that moment to go forward. And often, we never know whether it made a difference or not.

Judith returned to Canada in the fall of 1982. She wasn't present to experience the effect of the Marathon, how it ended, and when the nation mourned. She hadn't seen him run at all.

> I was in Papua New Guinea the whole run. When he died, I was still away. I was doing health work, but I was visiting a school with some friends, and they were having a movie night. It's going to be about growing coffee. They take the movie out of the holder, set it up — it's a reel movie — and it starts to run. It's not about coffee at all. It was the wrong film in the container. It was a movie made about the International Year of Disabled Persons, and it featured Terry. It was so amazing because I'd seen no live pictures on TV of the run. I hadn't had any personal contact with him, and here I am in the middle of the highlands of Papua New Guinea watching him actually running as part of this movie. Well, I completely dissolved in tears. This whole group is sitting there, watching this woman watching this movie, wondering what on earth happened to me. So, then I had to try and explain to them why I was so impacted by this, and the fact that I knew this person who was being talked about in the movie. But it was one of the things that was absolutely critical in terms of dealing with my own closure around the whole thing because it had all been such a remote kind of experience for me after the whole front end of everything that went on was done. It was just mind-blowing.

In 1994, Judith became a regular member of the Mission Rotary Club. Over the years, she has supported community projects like the Terry Fox Run and would often find moments to share Terry's story, whether it was during Rotary meetings, at the beginning of Runs, or most recently on vacation with her tour group.

> He never ever portrayed himself as a victim in any way. He always was a survivor, right from the get-go. I think those are the two positions that people can have in any

TELEPHONE PLAZA 4-1234

CABLE ADDRESS UNICEF

UNICEF
UNITED NATIONS CHILDREN'S FUND · FONDS DES NATIONS UNIES POUR L'ENFANCE
UNITED NATIONS, NEW YORK

26 February 1981

Dear Terry,

I am the Executive Producer for UNICEF of the film IT'S THE SAME WORLD and I cabled you last week to announce you that the film has been nominated for an Academy Award and to thank you for your extraordinary contribution to this film.

The film is to be shown in Canada by Global TV on Thursday, 26 or Friday 27 and I do hope that you have a chance to see it. I am mailing you today a 16mm copy so that everybody can see it around you.

Last month I was in the Ivory Coast making a film on disabled children, and I told the story of our film IT'S THE SAME WORLD to an old Ivorian friend, who is an art collector. He was so moved by your story that he selected a statuette in his collection and gave it to me. It is an antique, from the North of the Ivory Coast and represents a woman with one leg. I made a picture of this statuette, and I am sending you attached a copy of this picture. We have decided to use it for the publicity of the film.

With my warmest regards and best wishes.

Yours sincerely,

Bernard Gerin
Chief
Radio-TV-Film Services

Mr. Terry Fox
Royal Columbia Hospital
New Westminster
British Columbia, Canada

February 26, 1981: A letter from UNICEF thanking Terry for his participation in their movie highlighting the International Year of Disabled Persons. The executive producer, Bernard Gerin, writes, "I cabled you last week to announce you [sic] that the film has been nominated for an Academy Award and to thank you for your extraordinary contribution to this film."
Courtesy of the Terry Fox Centre Archives

bad situation. You either see yourself as a survivor and figure out how to do that, or you see yourself as a victim, which means you don't have the capacity to change it or to be in control. A survivor is in control. A victim is not.

He wasn't a star individual in terms of academics or athletics; he was a regular person who did amazing things. And if he, as a regular person, could do amazing things, so can you. And that's the thing that I think is so important for people to hear. Because often, if they see somebody who's incredibly successful at some feat of some kind, they already were superlative. And so, of course, they would do well. Terry was Joe Average in every way in terms of his expertise, and he did things in spades. And so can everyone else. You are of value in terms of [being a] part of the world that you're involved in. You don't have to be doing it internationally; you can do it in your own little corner and make a real impact on one person even. And that's huge.

SHARON HELPARD
Mother of Greg Scott, a young amputee who bonded with Terry

Sharon invites me into her dining room, but she is cautious, reserved, and nervous. Although it has been forty-two years since her son, Greg Scott, passed away, the pain of that loss still gets stuck in her throat and sits in her chest. When she speaks, the words come out softly in strained whispers but with thoughtful intention.

Greg had the same bone cancer as Terry and had his leg amputated on June 6, 1980. He was ten years old. Terry had already begun his Marathon, and some of the staff at McMaster Children's Hospital, where Greg was receiving his treatments, suggested that maybe the two should meet.

Sharon cannot recall how the meeting came about, but Terry was coming to Hamilton, Ontario, and would be running by Dundurn Castle around mid-July. Greg was allowed out of the hospital, using crutches to get around until he could get used to his temporary leg. They drove an hour from their home in Welland to Hamilton but missed him because Terry hadn't stopped at the castle. However, they heard where Terry was headed, and when he stopped at a Sunoco gas station, they met him there. It was a short meeting as Terry didn't like to stop for long, but Terry told them that he would call them. Greg had to start his cancer treatments, so they returned home and continued their visits to the hospital.

July 14, 1980: Terry signs an autograph for Greg at a gas station in Hamilton, Ontario.

Courtesy of Sharon Helpard

So, we knew when he was going to call. I remember saying to Greg, "What are you going to talk about?" Greg answered, "I don't know, we'll just talk." So, Terry called, and they started chatting on the phone. We are sitting there, and they are just chatting away, chatting away, chatting away. It was like they were long-lost friends.

Terry called Greg a couple more times, and Terry's PR coordinator, Bill Vigars, arranged their next meeting. At the same time, the City of Welland offered to hold an All-Star baseball game with some hockey players who played baseball to help raise funds for Greg. Then another fundraiser was held, and they raised enough money to fly Greg and his family to meet Terry in Terrace Bay.

Greg couldn't fly in a pressurized chamber because he had spots on his lungs. They connected with a local pilot, Don Chabot, and we flew out of the airport just over here to Terrace Bay, and we saw Terry. Actually, we took him some peaches.

After landing, the family was driven to meet up with Terry, and on his break, he spent a little time with Greg. It was August 27, 1980, day 138 of Terry's run. When Terry continued his miles, Greg went with him.

August 27, 1980: Greg bikes behind Terry as he runs through Northern Ontario.

Photo by Charlotte Kneipp

It was my understanding that Terry didn't like a lot of people with him while he was running, especially bikes and things like that. But he did want Greg to be with him. And so, we did find a bike, and Greg learned how to ride in the basement at home. We put a bike up on blocks so that he could try it, and he kept slipping off. It was hard to keep his artificial leg on the pedal, but he mastered it.

Greg, like Terry, was a fast learner. He just had his amputation that June, and by late August, he was walking around and riding his bike as Terry ran. When Terry finished his run for the day, they went for a swim. Greg was an excellent swimmer, but Terry was not.

> Terry was a little hesitant to go in the lake, and Greg just kind of splashed in and said, "You better get in here!"

Photojournalist Boris Spremo captured this moment in the famous pictures of Greg and Terry in the water, splashing and having fun. Greg had taken off his hat, showing the baldness from his treatment, and he was still wearing his Marathon of Hope T-shirt. It's a very happy moment. Two boys laughing and carrying on.

> Greg wasn't in awe of him. It was like they were buddies — buddies and brothers or something. It was a strange,

very strange, and hard-to-understand relationship that the timing — everything just kind of fell into place. They were destined to meet, I believe.

After their swim, everyone went to dinner. They sat at a long table, and it was like a large family picnic. The boys were throwing sugar packets at each other, and there was an atmosphere of some normalcy, putting aside the weight of cancer, the worries, and for Greg, the horrible treatments.

Later that evening, they attended an outdoor reception in the area, and Terry spoke to the crowd that had gathered. In a short clip from CBC's archives, Terry can be seen standing at a mic, talking about his treatments, but he also gives a heartfelt shout-out to Greg.

> After the operation is when I started to go through my chemotherapy and drug treatment. And I'll tell you right now that a lot of people say I need courage and guts and stamina to run across Canada on one leg. But the courage I needed to get through that was way worse. It was unreal. I'll never forget it. And . . . [Terry's voice wavers] I'm crying now because there is somebody here right now who is going through the same thing that I went through. The exact same thing, and he's only ten years old. [Terry exhales and lets out a sob.] And I had the most inspirational day of my life today. [Terry wipes a tear as the crowd applauds in support.]

August 27, 1980: Terry speaks to a crowd in Terrace Bay, tearing up as he shares Greg's story.

Photo by Doug Vater

Terry could understand what kind of courage and strength Greg needed to get through the very harsh, painful treatments, and he knew that the next day, Greg would leave and return to those treatments.

August 26, 1980: Terry and Greg splash in the water of Terrace Bay.
Photo by Boris Spremo via Getty Images

It was good for Terry. It was inspirational for him and encouraging. And Greg [Sharon pauses, and her hands fan out incredulously] — it was like he knew him all his life. He wasn't nervous about meeting him or talking to him or anything like that. They were so comfortable with one another, whether it was on the phone or whether it was in person. And you gotta remember he was ten years old. He was beyond his years.

It was a bond formed through great adversity, innocence, and pure hearts. And they both understood the necessity of having hope and being positive and how essential they were in their fight to live. The desire to stop what Greg was suffering through was why Terry was running. And on that day with Greg, he probably knew that his own cancer was coming back. Six days later, Terry would be forced to end his Marathon.

Terry knew that Greg had spots on his lungs. He said, "If Greg needs me . . ." [She takes in a deep breath and exhales out the words in a whisper] "I'll come to him." It was a setback for Greg when Terry had to stop. It was a setback for everybody. [She wrings a napkin in her hands.] [Terry] tried some experimental drugs and stuff like that. And there was always hope. Always hope for everybody that deals with cancer.

They never talked again after their meeting in Terrace Bay, each going through treatments and Greg undergoing more surgery. Terry stopped running on September 1, 1980, and passed away on June 28, 1981. Greg passed away only six weeks later in August 1981. Forty-three years later, Terry's strength of spirit still lives on in Sharon's memory.

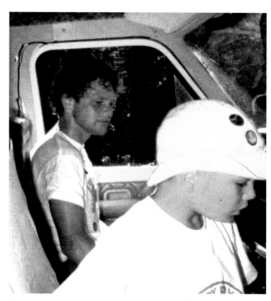

Terry and Greg sit together in the Marathon of Hope van.

Courtesy of Sharon Helpard

The sound that he made — [Sharon copies the sound, the skipping pattern of his steps] — yeah, it was actually chilling and very unforgettable. That sound, I can hear it in my sleep. It's just something that you never forget. I just think Terry couldn't understand why people had to go through it, young people. He just took it on himself to do something about this, [and that probably gave him] a stronger feeling than I've ever had in my life.

ALISON SINSON INCE
End-of-life nurse, Fox family liaison at the Royal Columbian Hospital

Alison's son brings me into her kitchen, and she is ready with a folder in front of her. She has spent years sharing Terry's story with interested groups at conferences and schools, and she's prepared copies of her speeches to give to me so I can be sure to have the details right. She

Alison stands proudly in her kitchen wearing the 2023 Terry Fox Run T-shirt.

Photo by Andre Sinson

has a warm grandmotherly air, one that takes no nonsense. A strong woman who has survived her own cancer, she has a fortitude that she garnered while holding back the press and managing the expectations of the world by giving them hope when Terry ended his run and returned to their care at the Royal Columbian Hospital for his second battle against cancer.

In 1977, because of the pain in his knee, Terry was admitted to a newly developed teen unit on Pediatrics. Alison was the nursing supervisor for Maternity and Pediatrics and had worked closely with Judith Ray, pediatric head nurse, to develop the teen program. Teenagers didn't really belong in a big general ward or with toddlers and younger children. However, they thought that Terry would benefit from being with young people nearer his age, and it would also allow them to more effectively evaluate the program. Part of that was the concept of having one nurse act as the contact for the family. Going through such a life-changing event was stressful enough, dealing with multiple people would make it worse. Families needed assurance — a central belief in hope and positivity.

Judith was the person who was assigned to talk to the family [about] what was going on with Terry and, consequently, to talk to Terry about what was happening with him. It's not the nicest thing in the world for a very athletic eighteen-year-old to be told "You've got to have your leg taken off," period. So, at that point, I stayed out of it. I said hello to him, and that was about it. I don't even know if he knew I was there. [Judith] would come to me and say, "Look, we need to get a hold of Simon Fraser University," because he'd just started his first year there. So, I would phone SFU and say, "We need this for him." And they would then send it to me, I would give it to her, and she would give it to him. So, I was kind of working in the background, but she was the voice that was speaking to him.

Terry wasn't in the ward for very long because they wanted to start the chemotherapy treatment quickly. Those treatments took him to the cancer clinic in downtown Vancouver, which was very different from his experience at the Royal Columbian. It was a dark, dismal place, but the treatment, though brutal, did work. Terry would return to visit them, to the ward that was bright, hopeful, and full of the positive energy of young children.

He came back one time to the hospital to talk to somebody needing an amputation, too. That boy died sometime later, but I remember that they phoned me and said, "Can Terry come back and talk to him?" And I said, "Yes, he can talk to him much better than any of us can because he's been through it." So, he did.

Terry started the Marathon of Hope, and the hospital staff followed along, believing that if anyone could do it, it would be him. When Terry had to stop in Thunder Bay, Dr. Piper called Alison and asked if he could be brought to the Royal Columbian because Terry did not want to go downtown. He wanted to be with them, those whom he knew would keep him upbeat and focused on the positive. The people who made him believe in hope from the very start. Alison went about making all the arrangements while Terry and his family were in the air returning to B.C. By this time, the press was starting to gather outside the hospital, and Alison and other administrators were there waiting with them at the main door. Then her beeper went off, and she was informed that they had taken him up directly from the garage to avoid the media.

We went upstairs then, we saw him, and his mother said, "Why the hell won't they just leave him alone? He's tired. He has to go to bed." And he's saying, "No, Mom, I need to do this. This is what I have been doing. This is why I have been doing it. I need to do it." So, we then said, "Well, we're not taking you anywhere else other than in this building." There was a little room downstairs, and we said, "Right, we'll take you down. Terry, sit in the chair." Terry, of course, refused to get in the wheelchair, and so there is a lovely picture of my rear end pushing an empty chair. Anyway, we went down. His mom was grumbling, and he didn't stay very long because we told them, "This will be very short because he is exhausted. And he needs to get some sleep."

September 3, 1980: Terry and his parents at a news conference at the Royal Columbian Hospital.

Material republished with the express permission of Vancouver's *Province*, a division of Postmedia Network Inc.

Alison was the one to receive from the Fox family the list of visitors who would be allowed to see him. It was mostly just family and a couple of close friends. She instructed Terry to get to bed and helped the family get settled. Then the phone started ringing. It was midnight, and people were bombarding the emergency lines, calling about Terry.

> One of the security guys told me the RCMP have a list of all the nighttime talk show hosts. I had to call the RCMP, and they gave me this entire list. I had to sit down then and call all of them. The next thing I knew I was on the line, saying, "He's fine, he's sleeping soundly. Let him get some rest. We have six hundred patients to look after, so please do not tie up our emergency lines." I also called Dr. Antonick [medical director of RCH] and I said, "Look, we got to do something about this." We knew that the public was interested, but we really had no idea of the depth of that interest. And so, from the next morning [onwards], we had to set up special lines that only answered things for him, and then all the ones that they couldn't answer came to me. So I got all the kooks, which was very interesting. Most of them came from Toronto. [Alison throws her head back in laughter, her hand touching her cheek.]

Many of the calls were from members of the public who genuinely cared and wanted to impart their advice as to what was going to help Terry the most. However, there were also many strange callers offering "cures."

> The switchboard operator called me, and she said, "Alison, you better take this one because I don't know how to answer this man." So, I said, "Alright, put him through." He says, "Do you have a garden?" I said, "Well, yeah, we have some grounds here." He said, "All right, I want you to take a flashlight and go out there right now. You dig up some earthworms. You crush them down, and you feed him the blood from the earthworms because that is the only thing that is going to cure him." So, I said, "Well,

do earthworms even have blood?" I mean, I really didn't know, and he got quite upset with me. He said I had to go and do that.

And then another one told me that we didn't know what the hell we were doing, except he used slightly more colourful language. He was on his way to look after [Terry], and until he got there, the only thing that he could eat was nuts, seeds, and something else — I can't remember. So, I said, "Well, could you tell me the flight you're coming on? We would love to meet you." He promptly put the phone down, and I think we discovered afterwards that he was calling from a psychiatric hospital.

Then there was the mail. Many were simply addressed to *Terry Fox, Canada*. They came from all over the world, and there were days when up to nine large mailbags were dropped off. The hospital had to give them to the family because Terry was concentrating on his treatment.

Alison only gave out the information the family and Terry allowed. There wasn't a lot more to be said as they were waiting to see if the

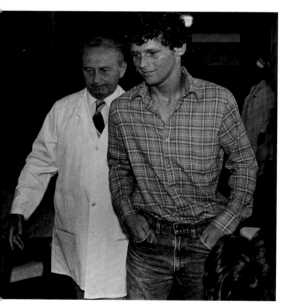

September 1980: Terry stands with Dr. Antonick, preparing to speak to the media.
Photo by Chuck Stoody, Canadian Press

new treatment was having any effect, and that took a while. The new treatment was their last hope because he could not be given any more of the drugs he had received the first time. His body would be incapable of surviving those again. The public's urgent desire for information was constant. Dr. Antonick would do the news conferences, and Alison would stand in the back. They set up bulletins every day, and she added in little bits of info she thought would be of interest. She learned to work with reporters who would tell her the kinds of questions they were getting from the public, and Alison would do her best to answer what she could.

Most of the reporters were absolutely super. They really were. And this one I remember, she said, "Dr. Antonick, we know that you can only give us a certain amount of information. People are really interested. And if you could just give us something." Like, are we getting a lot of mail, or what kind of mail are we getting? And who is it that is sending it? Is it all coming from Canada? He looked at her, and he said, "You see that lady hiding down there in the back? She's the one that can tell you all of this." And that was it. I did not wish to be involved in that at all. Nobody had ever trained me to do anything like that. So that was how I got involved in the first place.

Unfortunately, not all interactions with the media or the public were pleasant. When they realized Terry was not going to make it — which hadn't been said outright, just implied — all hell broke loose. The feeling from the public was "How dare they say that!" One girl asked, "Does that mean he won't be able to finish the run?" Medical journalists were up in arms. One reporter, whom Alison calls the Barracuda, was found looking over the shoulder of the person typing out the updates each day so she could see them first. One day, Alison found her in her office using the phone. Alison hung up the phone and told her to use the payphone as this was a private office with patients' personal information. The reporter argued back until Alison insisted that she leave. The hospital reported the incident to her media outlet, and she never returned. There was one call, however, that almost tipped Alison over the edge.

This guy who shall be nameless, quite a well-known radio person at that time, phoned and said, "What have you got today?" And I said, "Well, have you seen the press release? Just a minute, I will read it for you." And I started to read it and he stopped me dead. He said, "I don't want to know that. I want to know what his face looked like when you told him." And I took a deep breath and I thought, "Alison, do not open your mouth." I just put the phone down and cut him off. I sat there, and I seethed, and I cried. I was so angry.

Terry went home as much as possible, returning to the hospital whenever he needed specific care. He wanted to be home. His brother Fred
and Theresa were planning their wedding, hoping he would be present.
Alison joined the family on Christmas Eve that year, taking part in the
family tradition at the time of taking a swig from a large bottle of
alcohol. She became very close to the family, talking often with Betty
and becoming her shoulder to lean on and her confidante, giving her
hope and keeping her positive.

> She called me about nine o'clock one night and she said,
> "I'm really worried about him." And I said, "Why, what's
> the matter?" And she said, "Well, he's gone to the movies."
> And I said, "So?" She said, "Well, he's lost weight, and his
> prosthesis is not fitting that well now, and I'm afraid he's
> gonna fall and he's gone." I said, "Well, who has he gone
> with?" She said, "Well, that's the problem because he's
> gone with Rick Hansen and Peter Colistro." I just started to
> laugh, and she said, "Why are you laughing? It's not funny."
> I said, "Well, can you think of three more resourceful young
> men in the whole of British Columbia than those three? If
> he falls, they'll figure out something, I'm sure."

Terry didn't need coddling or handholding, just the comfort of having
someone sitting with him. One night at the hospital, after they knew he
wasn't going to make it, Alison sent an exhausted Betty and Rolly home.

> I said to them, "Look, go home. You need to get some rest. I
> will stay with him." That last week that he was there,
> I literally moved into the hospital and just lived there. I
> went in, and I told him, "I'm just going to sit here with
> you." And I did; I didn't say a word. He didn't say a word.
> Now and again, he would open his eyes, make sure I was
> still there and give me a little grin, and I would do the
> same thing back at him. I tell you, four hours went, it just
> went, and there was this incredible sense of peace and
> serenity in the room. I think he was a very spiritual kind
> of person. I think he thought very deeply. He was always

interested in other people. And that came through, even when he didn't necessarily say anything. And I remember that particular day, specifically, it was just a beautiful oasis in the middle of everything that was going on.

At this point, they kept the media in another building, away from the unit where Terry was. The family was sticking close together at this difficult time, and Alison was trying to gather her thoughts and write them down, knowing she'd need to speak to the press soon. She would have to change from giving the nation hope of his recovery to giving them the news that Terry's fight was coming to an end. She had just laid down for some rest when Judith Fox came to get her.

> She says, "Mom says you better come." And so, I got back up, and I went down. I was very grateful to them all that they wanted to include me when he went. And it was just beautiful. It really was. I stayed up for a little while and made sure that Judy and his parents got away. I got them out with security because I wanted them to be home before we made any official announcements. Darrell and Fred were with Hank Erickson, who was our chaplain and was really good with Terry. So, I knew that the guys were at least being looked after.

Alison had been a strong support for the Fox family. She was the only one brought in to be with them when he passed on. Because of her strength, they were able to carry on each day. Once the family was gone, she went over to a room where the doctors, people from the Canadian Cancer Society, and some friends had been waiting. Everybody was crying.

> It was "Well, what are we going to say? How are we going to say it?" And then Dr. Antonick said to me, "Well, I know you had written a few things." We were all trying to say how we were going to do it and couldn't. Finally, I said, "Look, just let me speak. I'll just talk from the heart." And that's what I did.

June 1981: Alison speaks to the media at the Royal Columbian Hospital.

Photo by Nick Didlick, Canadian Press

Alison shares that the only way she could get the words out was by looking at the clock in the room and nowhere else. Everyone was crying, and she felt she would break if she looked at anyone. The CBC cameraman told her the next day that he wasn't sure he got anything at all because everything was shaking while he was filming. He had been crying while trying to keep the camera steady. Alison broke the news with positivity, not speaking of the loss against cancer but of what Terry accomplished and the deep love for him. She said:

> Terry has completed the last kilometre of his Marathon a short while ago. At approximately twenty-five [minutes] to five [a.m.], B.C. time, he died. He died surrounded by love. The love of his family, all of whom were with him, and the love and prayers of the entire nation.

Dr. Antonick then added:

> There's a little Terry Fox in all of us. Royal Columbian Hospital deems it a great honour to have been called upon to serve to the best of our ability a great Son of Canada. May he rest in peace.

DR. ROSHNI DASGUPTA

Pediatric surgical oncologist, recipient of the Terry Fox Humanitarian Award

Roshni is so busy with her work that I am interviewing her on the phone while she is in her car between appointments. She is a no-nonsense, serious person, and I know I can ask her difficult questions regarding life and death and the struggle of maintaining hope because she deals with it so often.

Roshni was only eight years old when Terry ran. She was living in Calgary when her parents told her what he was doing. As the media coverage increased, so did the time her family spent following his Marathon. She remembers it being a sad day when he died. As a child, she doesn't think she fully understood the impact of what he did, but she remembers being impressed by his tenacity, endurance, and willingness to continue.

When applying to McGill University at seventeen, she also applied for and won the Terry Fox Humanitarian Award. Established in 1982 in honour of Terry, the TFHA is awarded to those who have overcome a challenge and displayed humanitarianism to help the world become a better place. From there, Roshni went on to medical school at the University of Toronto, where she was also a track and field star. Following graduation in 1996, she became a Rhodes Scholar and was happy to have two other Terry Fox Award — winners with her at Oxford University. Roshni felt the encouragement from this group of fellow recipients and like-minded thinkers whenever they met.

> We would have these meetings of Terry Fox Humanitarian Award recipients, and they were just amazing people, and you would see the great things that you could do. You come out of these conferences being super inspired to give back and think about cancer research. For me, because I knew at that point that I wanted to be a doctor, to think about what are the attributes that he embodied, and how to live your life in that way with that perseverance, diligence, and all those things. So, I think that was a really special award. I went on to have some other special awards, but that one was really formative. When you're young, you're looking for some guidance, and that sort of overall principle of giving back and perseverance and working hard to [achieve] a goal was really impactful when I was younger.

In medical school, Roshni became fascinated by surgery. Through surgery, she felt she could actually *cure* somebody. Take something out and fix the problem, hopefully for good. She got involved with cancer research, wanting to help patients, especially children, from a surgical perspective. She had also lost her father to cancer in 2000, so the cause is near to her heart.

February 6, 2024: Dr. Roshni Dasgupta stands in the OR of Cincinnati Children's Hospital.

Courtesy of Dr. Roshni Dasgupta

You want to help people who couldn't help themselves. I'm a pediatric surgical oncologist at Cincinnati Children's [Hospital] in the U.S. I went on to do my residency at Harvard. I went back and did a master's in public health to run clinical trials, particularly in cancer. And now, I've been a pediatric surgical oncologist for almost nineteen years. It's one of the greatest pleasures. I mean, I operate on patients with osteosarcoma probably once or twice a week. I run a national osteosarcoma trial, which looks at treating patients who have lung metastases and how we can help these kids. You sort of trail it all back to like, "Hey, that's what Terry had, and that's what happened." Can you draw a direct line? I don't know. But I definitely think that early influences really shape you.

Roshni often has to tell her young patients their diagnosis and prognosis. For patients with osteosarcoma or lung metastases, there's still only about a thirty to forty percent survival rate. Even still, she has hope and tries to pass it on to them as well. She's had patients who were football and baseball players, athletes who are sixteen or seventeen years old and at the prime of their lives. They have a sense of immortality, and it vanishes in an instant.

> They're looking for any strand of hope. They realize the calamity, but they are looking for any bit of hope. I have brought up Terry Fox a lot of times, like "this guy who has what you have, and he's doing this, and you can do this." [Many] Americans have not necessarily heard of him, but I make them go look him up. And you know, they come back and have been like, "This guy was amazing." Especially for kids that are in the doldrums, I would often use Terry as a sort of inspiration to be like, "Hey, you guys can do this. And we can get through this." We'll tell our amputees, our patients who've had limb salvage procedures, all of those things, to get out and walk and run and do stuff. They're like, "I can't do that. I don't have a leg anymore." We'd be like, "Look at this guy."

Some kids are doubtful they can do what he did, but she responds if they can even do a tenth of what Terry did, imagine what can be accomplished. With athletes, she enforces the thought that keeping in shape is important. The better shape they are in, the better they can tolerate surgery and chemotherapy.

I ask how she translates what Terry did to people who are not athletes when it's not something physical they are facing but a more spiritual or mental challenge. She pauses and considers her answer very carefully.

> That's a hard question. I think when you are faced with whatever personal tragedy or whatever has happened, you're all-encompassed by that, right? You feel like that is the end of the world. You can't really look outside yourself. When you see examples of true heroism, like what Terry did, you can *start* to back up a little bit. This seems overwhelming. The pandemic is overwhelming. All these things are happening. But look at this kid — like he's a kid. And look what he did. Look at the amazing

accomplishments that he had. He built on it; this was something that he started and continued, and he persevered and endured. And once you change yourself, you're also having that impact on others around you, too. So, it's not just you, it's your circle, and then that circle, and then it becomes exponential.

As a doctor, Roshni can understand what it would have been like for Terry and his family in his last days. She has been there, giving her support to the families and helping them find some acceptance and peace. But then again, she'll often use Terry as an example of how to stay positive, have hope, and keep going.

These kids have been through so much, and they know. Sometimes they're young, and you think they don't get it. They get it, no question. I had a twelve-year-old pass away a couple of months ago, and she [asked], "Did I do good?" I'm like, "Yeah, you did great." It's hard to have a child die. But when you have a disease like this that's relentless, that comes back, it's not fair. Those are incredibly difficult conversations because you're taking away that last hope. At the same time, you've hopefully built a relationship with the families that they understand we've tried everything we can, and I think they find solace in that. It's never good. But like Terry, he fought until the very last minute. You can continue to do that and then be like, "You know what? I fought a good fight. I'm good."

I feel kind of sad because I know that younger people today, even in Canada, maybe don't know or understand the enormity of what he did and what it meant. I think it's important to put that into people's psyche that this is a *kid* that did this. People have heard his name, and my nieces and nephews are like, "Oh yeah, we run the Terry Fox Run." But do you really *know* what that is? Do you really *know* what he *did*? Learning or understanding that would put a lot of people's despair into perspective, where you are like, "This isn't bad. Yes, I've lost my job, and it sucks. But this guy's life was threatened, and he was still getting up every day. He didn't have a leg, he ran, and he wanted to raise awareness. He did all this stuff, not for himself but for other people and to make an impact on a disease that he had." I think that if we had a little bit more positivity in our lives, it'd be easier for people to get out of those doldrums and be able to look outside of themselves, like, "Hey, you know what? My situation kind of sucks. But look what this guy did. I think it's going to be okay if I take a little bit of what he did."

May 7: Day 26 (3 miles) Last night we didn't sleep all that well because of the rolling ship. We got up at 6:30 a.m. Nova Scotia time. I watched as the captain docked the ship in the North Sydney harbour. I left the ship and met George Thom who did a marvelous job organizing the day. I ran with a group of kids to city hall where I met the Mayor. We drove back out to where we left off and I took off. CBC was filming me all the while. They were only going 5 miles an hour when I heard this huge freight truck barreling up and not slowing down. It hit the CBC vehicle at 50 miles an hour. One CBC crew member fell back onto the highway and into the ditch. I thought he was dead. It was terrible. If I was 5 yards further ahead, I would have been killed. I couldn't run anymore.

May 15: Day 34 (27 miles) Today I got up at 4:30 a.m. I felt better than yesterday. The cysts didn't hurt so much. After my break I ran until a lady from Sheet Harbour came to see me. They had a reception set up at the schools for 5 o'clock and they wanted me to run with the school kids. I found out that it was nearly positive that Darryl Sittler would be there to meet us in Toronto. Also found out that Darrell [Fox] would be coming out at the end of the month. I went out and ran 2 ½ miles with the kids. I really burned it just to show them how fast I could go. They were tired and puffing. Allright!

May 20: Day 39 (24 miles) Today I got up at 4:30 a.m. and we drove out to my starting point. I ran 10 miles that got me 1 mile passed Truro. After that we drove back to the Holiday Inn in Dartmouth. From here I drove to a point 3 miles away from Halifax City Hall and then ran back with a police escort. I met the Mayor in Halifax. We took the ferry across the bay met the Mayor of Dartmouth. Then I ran to the Vocational School with 50 students. They had raised $3,000. A great group of kids! Too bad not everybody was doing this. I did my speech and couldn't help but cry when I said Doug had to have the courage to put up with and understand me when I am tired and irritable.

Terry and Doug photographed on the East Coast early in the run. Terry says in his journal he "couldn't help but cry when I said Doug had to have courage to put up with and understand me when I am tired and irritable."

Courtesy of the Terry Fox Centre Archives

May 15, 1980: Terry runs with children in Sheet Harbour, Nova Scotia.

May 12, 1980: Terry writes to Judith Ray in Papua New Guinea, updating her on his progress.

May 11, 1980: Terry stands with the mayor of Port Hawkesbury, Nova Scotia, Billy Joe MacLean (left), and George Fox, no relation (right).

One-legged runner has brush with death

By Leslie Scrivener Toronto Star

Terry Fox had a brush with death this week when a transport truck plowed into a CBC television crew filming his cross-Canada run.

The CBC truck and crew from Sydney, N.S., were flung into a shallow ditch, narrowly missing Terry. Fox, 21, who lost his right leg to cancer three years ago, is running across Canada on a marathon of hope to raise pledges for the Canadian Cancer Society.

One CBC technician is still in hospital with back injuries after Wednesday's accident near North Sydney, N.S. A reporter was badly shaken up and a second technician was treated for facial cuts.

"It was very close," a Sydney reporter said yesterday in a telephone interview. "The CBC truck was beside Terry to get a parallel shot. Had he been a few feet forward, he might

Running with Terry

very well have been seriously hurt — God knows, even killed. It was a miraculous escape."

Even though he has completed 807 miles since he set out from St. John's, Nfld., April 12, Fox was in no mood for celebrating yesterday.

His mind was still on the accident, which he called "a tragic thing."

"I saw one man come flying out of the truck into the ditch and I thought he was dead," Fox said in an interview from Baddeck, on Cape Breton Island. "I couldn't run any more after that. I was so shaken up."

Fox and his companion, Doug Alward, who travels in a van with flashing lights and brightly lettered signs to warn motorists that Terry is ahead, visited the injured newsmen in hospital in Sydney.

"It was a great relief to find out they were going to be okay," Fox said.

Though he ran only three miles in his first day in Nova Scotia, he completed 28 miles yesterday and said he feels strong enough to run 30 today.

It was a disappointing setback for Fox after his jubilant send-off from Newfoundland Tuesday night.

He'd learned that the people of the coastal town of Port-aux-Basques opened their hearts and their pocketbooks and pledged $10,000 — a generous display of support since the population is only about 6,000.

According to Canadian Cancer Society estimates, Fox had raised between $20,000 and $25,000 in his 577-mile run across Newfoundland.

"I was very, happy to finish the number, one province," Fox said with a note of enthusiasm back in his voice. "I remember people in St. John's telling me if I make it across (Newfoundland) I've done very well. Now, I feel like I've gotten somewhere."

Fox is aiming to cross Canada from east to west, finishing in Vancouver, near his home, Port Coquitlam, sometime in October. He says he is living proof that cancer can be beaten and he has chosen this dramatic journey to prove that loss of a leg doesn't mean that he is disabled.

He is taking advantage of the run to share his message of hope with as many young people as possible. During his breaks he sometimes speaks to students in nearby schools, explaining what cancer is and how it affected him.

He uses himself as an example. "I didn't even know what cancer was, until I got it," he said.

Fox was an 18-year-old student of kinesiology at Simon Fraser University in Burnaby, B.C., when he learned the pain in his right leg was a cancerous tumor.

Fox passed another milestone this week — he wore out his first pair of running shoes. He was about to throw them in a garbage can when Alward reminded him they might make a good souvenir.

Pledges for Fox's run continue to come through the Canadian Cancer Society in Metro and the Four Seasons Hotel chain, which has challenged Canadian companies to sponsor Terry for $2 for every mile he runs.

The Four Seasons reports it has received 37 pledges totalling $1,973 — mostly from individuals and small clubs.

The Toronto Star is carrying weekly reports on Fox's progress every Friday in the Family Section.

Terry Fox: Cross-Canada marathoner was almost run over by truck in Nova Scotia.

May 9, 1980: *Toronto Star* reporter Leslie Scrivener reports on Terry's near-accident on the highway on May 7, 1980.

THE COMPANY YOU KEEP

"I'm just one member of the Marathon of Hope. I'm no different from anybody else. I'm no better, I'm no lower. I'm equal with all of you. And if I were to change that attitude [about] myself, then there's no use in continuing."

— Terry Fox
Speech in Scarborough, Ontario, July 10, 1980

CLAY GAMBLE
Childhood friend, retired Air Canada pilot

An early morning ferry takes me over to Vancouver Island for my interview with one of Terry's closest childhood friends, Clay. It is a crisp, cool morning as the ferry glides across deep blue waters with a slight fog on the horizon. Clay lives not far from the port in a beautiful cottage-like home on the side of the island. He had built most of it himself, with the help of a carpenter friend who helped guide him through the more complicated construction. The back deck oversees the bay, with steps that lead right down to the water. Clay built his little paradise once he retired as an Air Canada pilot. He is a tall man with a gentle face, wearing a khaki shirt with cargo shorts. His serene energy belies a quiet

Port Coquitlam Legion soccer team, 1971. In the back row, Terry stands second in from the left, and Clay stands second in from the right.
Courtesy of Greg Hart

intelligence. He is pleased to share stories about his good friend Terry, whom he admires and who has shown him much about life and living.

They first met on the soccer field when they were about eight years old, and although they didn't go to the same school until high school, they connected due to their similarities. They were into all kinds of sports. Terry and Clay both came from loving families of four children, each with three boys and one girl, where they were the second eldest and mediator.

> I don't know if this was the reason we met, but both Terry's parents, Rolly and Betty, and my parents were often the only people standing on the sidelines in the pouring rain. Their love for their children was unconditional. It definitely affected who we were and what we were, in morals and values.
>
> We just liked to play sports and play at a very high level. The only way you could do it was to train and run

and do all those kinds of things that build up your stamina and build your strength. He had more of a natural talent than I did, but it didn't come easy for him. To make these teams, he had to work hard because the competition was so high. And so, what he lacked in ability, he made up for in hard work. When he set himself a goal, he tried to meet and surpass that goal.

They were very competitive, even when it came to board games. It was a good-natured push between friends.

Terry always liked board games. When he played, he played to win. I guess that's why it was a healthy competition. We want to beat the guy during the game, but then afterwards we would go for coffee or something like that. And there was never any animosity. The goal wasn't to beat each other. It was just to be better at what we were doing. He liked to pick somebody who was slightly better, slightly faster, slightly taller, and then use those as his inspiration to get better for himself.

From grade eleven onwards, the two developed a very close relationship. They spent every day of their school breaks together. Terry and Clay joined a running club, and Terry kept careful track of his miles, setting goals for himself.

I never liked running and I just participated for the [sake of] running. And my recollection is he didn't really like *just* running. But you're running to chase a soccer ball or basketball, and so both of us joined the team just to develop our stamina and build up our strength and build up our ability. As you know in any sport, the fitter you are, the easier it is to beat the opponent.

Because of their families and the values instilled in them, they didn't swear, addressed parents as Mr. and Mrs., didn't get involved with drugs, didn't drink much, and weren't easily swayed. Terry stuck to his values and also put a lot of effort into getting better grades. When he and Clay were in grade eight, they were both C-students and saw others around them getting As and Bs.

> I decided that they aren't any smarter than me — they just, obviously, work harder, so I started working harder at school. We were both taking science courses: calculus, physics, and biology. He didn't take the easy courses, he took the harder courses, and I did, too. I think we were both trying to think, you know, "What are we gonna do after graduation?" It was important to get some kind of education past grade twelve and to do that you needed decent grades.

A counsellor had planted the seed of becoming a pilot into Clay's mind. After high school, he went to Trinity Western for their aviation program, while Terry went to Simon Fraser.

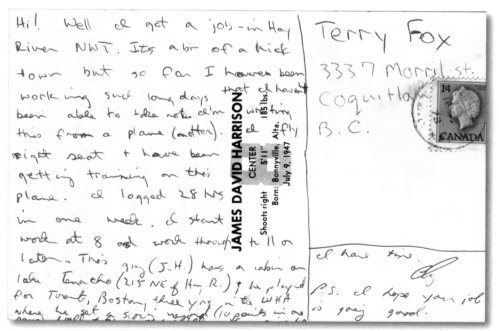

A postcard Clay sent to Terry while he was going through his pilot training, commenting, "I'm writing this from the plane."

Courtesy of the Terry Fox Centre Archives

We didn't see [each other] much between September and December. We were at different schools and had a very heavy course load. But Christmas break, basically two weeks, we would have seen each other every day. We did stuff together, we met up with other friends, we'd go to the odd party and stuff like that. And you kind of look out for each other when things get out of hand, so he always had my six and I had his.

It was after one of these Christmas breaks when Terry was diagnosed.

The way I found out was, like I said, we were together almost every day for two weeks straight. We didn't see each other for a couple of months, and I got a call from Mrs. Fox saying, "Things are happening pretty quick. Terry's not doing that good. He's got cancer, and they will be taking his leg off in the next couple of days." I just couldn't believe it was actually real. At first, he wasn't seeing a lot of people from what I understand, but I did see him and just basically tried to be upbeat and stuff like that. It was pretty heavy and intense, the first meeting — it was pretty much everybody in shock. But the second time I saw him, and the third time anyway, for sure, he was already starting to make jokes about it. I don't think he ever wanted to be a burden or to be the first to drag things down, kind of thing. I mean, he learned to deal with adversity quickly, as opposed to just dragging on and on and feeling sorry for himself.

Clay visited once before the surgery. Terry's former basketball coach, Terri Fleming, had brought him a *Runner's World* article about Dick Traum, the first runner to complete a marathon with a prosthetic leg. Terry showed it to Clay and asked, "Do you think it's crazy if I start running across Canada?" Clay answered, "Yes, it is crazy!"

But the idea of it had taken root. Terry started walking, then hopping, and then developed his stylized "Fox Trot." During one visit, Clay was able to join him in training, and Terry shared how he began tackling the miles.

He showed how individual his training was, like he ran along, and there was a telephone pole. He'd touch the pole, start his run, and then at the other end touch the pole, figure out and keep track of the distance. Then the next day when he came out, he didn't start somewhere out here, he started right back at that spot. [It was] very important to him to be making sure that he's not shirking or trying to take the easy way out.

He trained more miles than he ran in the [Marathon]. He had one hundred and forty-three days; he did more than one hundred and forty-three days of training, or to the point where I think I might have even suggested, "Don't train every day. Train every second or third day." It was important for him to do it every day and start-stop at the exact spot that he left off the day before.

He would get sores, and he showed me. I know he didn't like to show off his leg, but he showed me a couple of times. Essentially, as he ran, he got stronger and bigger. The prosthetic wouldn't fit; it would be rough, chafe, and stuff like that. But he managed to push through those times. That's why I would suggest [to him] taking it easy, don't push so hard. But he didn't listen to me. Nor should he [have].

Clay would also take Terry up in a plane when he was accumulating his training hours for flying. One time, they brought Clay's brother along, who was a very nervous flyer. As Clay kept turning around to talk to him in the back, his brother told him to keep his hand on the wheel. Clay explained that the plane was controlled more with his feet. And besides, Terry was the one flying. His brother exclaimed Terry didn't have a leg! It was okay, Clay responded. Terry did have something there — his

Terry smiles from the co-pilot seat of a plane, while Clay flies to accumulate training hours.

Courtesy of Clay Gamble

prosthetic. Clay chuckles at the memory as he looks at the picture I show him of Terry looking back at his brother.

During the Marathon, Terry had a day off in Montreal, where Clay was stationed as a pilot for Air Canada, and they got to spend the day together.

> He called and we went to "The Big O" to tour the stadium. It was still pretty new at the time. Exciting. And then I think the Canadian Open was being played somewhere in Montreal, and I couldn't go because I was going to work later that day. So in between, at the hotel, I'm getting ready to leave and he's going, "What else do we want to do?" He turned to me and said, "Clay, you hungry?" I said, "Yeah I could eat." So, he took the phone and called room service and he said, "I'll have two cheeseburgers, two fries, and two large drinks, and Clay, what do you want?" Uh, half of what he just ordered! [Clay laughs with a wide grin.]

At the Four Seasons Hotel in Montreal, Terry shared his experience of the Marathon with Clay.

June 2, 1980: Terry shares his experiences on the Marathon with Clay during a moment of rest at the Four Seasons Hotel, Montreal.

Photo by Michael Flomen

He could be very high some days, and some days you wouldn't see a person the whole day or they're trying to run him off the road. The police actually stopped him and told him he couldn't run on certain roads. And so, I think he was frustrated with the fact that he couldn't seem to win over the hearts of the people going through Quebec. But he was upbeat, as upbeat as you could be, but there definitely was frustration with some of the days. Like, he would run and run and run all day and then have a quick shower and go to a school or a club, and he has to sit there and talk for a while, and then he'd stay and sign autographs. He must have been exhausted a lot of the time.

And you noticed a big change, too, in his build. When he was training, he was also weight training, and he was getting pretty buff. But when I saw him in Montreal, his leg — his good leg — looked twice the size, and his upper body was not the same build. As a runner, you don't want too much extra weight because you have to carry that extra weight with you. He talked about how it was a lot harder than training. Training all day, you go home and sleep in your own bed. You didn't have all those extra demands on your time. I think that was the biggest thing that he just ran out of time. And he got tired and frustrated and maybe lashed out the odd time at Doug [Alward]. I think it was just because he was mentally and physically exhausted, running on fumes. Yeah, so, there were some frustrating days. But then he always talked about the good days, too, meeting young kids dealing with cancer themselves, and he felt sorry for them and empathized with them and tried to be upbeat for them.

Clay kept up with the run on the news as everyone else did. He saw Terry have a lot more confidence when speaking in front of people and still feels Terry understood the necessity of it, the importance of speaking to people to gain their support.

The more he spoke with other people, the more important it was that he'd do it because it was having a positive effect [on him, too]. It wasn't bragging about what you're doing and not doing anything; it was really heartfelt. It was a good, positive change. Just watching him mature, I was very proud of him. It was a really nice thing to see the maturity and his dedication to the cause.

I think [the crew] were just floored that people were actually running up to them and throwing money in a container or whatever. There's a little bit of surprise just how giving people can be, supporting a good cause. He never wanted to ever let people down, not himself, not his parents, not Doug. He felt a big responsibility that people were behind him and supporting him, and he felt he couldn't let them down.

Clay learned that the run had ended when he saw it on CBC.

It was hard to watch that. Being carried away, he's saying, "If there's any way possible, I'm going to continue to run." It was quite an emotional time for everybody. I think deep down he knew it was pretty serious. But it was always "When I'm better, I'll continue." I hoped for the best. Plan for the worst; hope for the best. I mean if you don't have hope, what do you have?

You never know what kind of lasting effect you have when you meet somebody new or experience something together with somebody else and they all bring in their own biases and expectations. I'd say maybe [it was] fortunate that Terry and I had loving and supportive family and friends. You can succeed when you don't have those, but it's just a bit more of a challenge. It's important to be a positive influence on all the people around you, just by setting a good example.

It was Betty who called Clay to tell him Terry had passed and asked him to be a pallbearer. He was very proud to have been asked but was still in Montreal.

It was summer, which is the busiest time for flying, and I had to talk to my supervisor to get permission to get the time off. At first, they said no. I can't remember who the actual person was, but it might have gone over that immediate supervisor's head and further up the food chain. In the end, they gave me a confirmed seat both ways, so that I could get back to work but also so I could be there.

He saw some friends he hadn't seen in years, and all of them were very sombre. It was an emotional time and a whirlwind. He doesn't remember much but remembers how inspired everyone was by Terry — and still is.

Clay has also participated in the Run internationally, in Hong Kong, China, and London. Every year, the Run is a very special and rewarding time for his grandkids. Clay's wife, Tami, comments that the kids have asked Clay a lot of questions over the years, but their questions stray more into the "how." How did his leg work? How did he develop his running technique?

> Tami: They asked some really surprising questions. It wasn't just the general "Well, isn't that great that he ran?" They wanted to know *how*, and I think that's inspiring in itself that young kids realize it is okay to set these goals and try to achieve them. And you might have to pivot along the way and readjust your goal.

Clay adds proudly, "It is the fact that this is a guy from Port Coquitlam, from where he started and where he ended up — this phenomenal story — and it's real."

RIKA SCHELL
Girlfriend, children's ministry director

I meet Rika at her church in Vancouver, B.C. She has a very calm demeanour, slightly reserved but pleasant and welcoming. She describes

Terry smiles with the Vancouver Cable Cars.
Photo by Rika Schell

herself as a perpetual volunteer, always wanting to help others. She doesn't give interviews about Terry anymore but has made an exception and agreed to share a few of her experiences from that time.

Rika met Terry through the wheelchair sports community when she was a coach for the wheelchair volleyball team with renowned coach Tim Frick, a friend of hers. Their relationship developed over the time they spent together at practices and games.

Terry was at a different level as far as determination, aggressiveness, and stubbornness, and Rika learned to be a very patient person. It was how their relationship worked. She says she doesn't like putting Terry up on a pedestal because he was a human being like us. He also had his flaws and could be difficult and self-centred like a lot of youths. Still, there was his extraordinary gift to her of one of two gold medals he won at the National Wheelchair Games. Because there was not enough money to send all the coaches, he thought Rika should have one. That was Terry, too.

Terry shared his plans of running across the country with her very early on. She knew when he got something in his mind, there was no stopping him, so she was not surprised. She joined him a few times when he trained, either in her car or biking behind him, but he mainly went by himself. Betty would not have been in favour of Terry training to run across the country, so preparation for the run was done in secret. His family was told that he was training to run in the Boston Marathon.

> At the beginning when he told me [about his plans to run], he's like, "You're coming." No "Would you like to?" or "Would you think about it?" It was more along the lines of "By the way, you're coming." My immediate thoughts were woah, woah, woah, because I had stuff on the go, too, and how long would I have to put my life on hold? A year? More? Then I thought, "Oh, it's going to be a nightmare." Closer to leaving time, they still didn't even have a van; they were not ready. When I finally saw the van on display in Victoria [years later], I looked in and thought, "Where did those two idiots think I was going to sleep?" [She laughs.] You know, female! Guys don't normally think of stuff like that. Just [fly by the] seat of their pants. I heard Terry brought an extra change of shorts and socks so that was good planning. I knew I would be doing all of the dirty laundry and all the cooking. I was actually a pretty good cook, so they would have been well-fed, but if I had gone, Darrell would not have gone because we would have [had] our three. So, it was good that I pulled out.

Having to tell Terry she wasn't going to join him on his run was a big fight. He assumed she would because it was the most important thing in the world to him, so why wouldn't it have been for her? Darrell ended up joining later, and to this day Rika contends he was the glue that kept the whole thing together because Doug and Terry would have killed each other. She was getting letters from them both, and she would see

Darrell and Doug goof off near Toronto, Ontario, bringing levity to the Marathon of Hope.
Photo by Glemena Bettencourt

59

the frustration, but the letter after Darrell arrived was full of jokes — they were now the three musketeers!

> I remember thinking, "Once Darrell's there, it will settle down." It was divine providence that he went and not me.

As Bill Vigars was arranging events for Terry every day, she doesn't think they understood how tired Terry was.

> He called me the day he had to stop. They took him to the hospital and did all those tests and stuff. He was crying. It was a hard day for him because he is not a quitter. He never stopped fighting. I think he fully intended to complete it once it was all resolved. I mean he beat it once. He could beat it again.
>
> I tried to be encouraging, trying to keep my composure because I don't want him to be upset that I'm upset. He's looking to me for strength. I'm trying to give him some wisdom and some perspective. I mean what do you say? I'm his age. We were just kids, right? Don't have a lot of wisdom. [Rika laughs at herself, shrugging her shoulders.]
>
> But I think the pressure on his lungs, running every day, that much stress brought it back to him. If he had to die on the road, he was happy to make that exchange. It was worth his life as long as Darrell and Doug were there, and people were supporting him.
>
> He did ask me when he got back — we went out to a movie, and we were sitting in the car talking about life. He said, "Do you think I'm gonna die?" Me: "I don't know. It's up to God. Maybe I'll go before you. Fifty-fifty [chance], you know? Maybe or maybe not." It's not like the weatherman, ten percent. It's either raining or it's not raining. There was always hope for a sunny day.

The deeper questions about life were always looming. It's hard not to think of it while you're going through the treatment, which wasn't as advanced as it is now.

Rika and I talk about the hospital and some of the kids Terry saw there. She isn't sure if, at the beginning, his motivation was compassion or just outright anger. A rage that this could happen, especially to a child. And then his compassion grew. He was more personable on the road, meeting all these people and listening to their stories.

> He learned how to be a human being. I think he became less about him and more about others. Just the tone in the letters changed, still very naive, but he was beginning to be a little more understanding of people. I remember he called me near the beginning, and he was so surprised. "People are being so nice to us. They're inviting us for dinner," kind of like, "Wow!" They were probably thrilled to have him for dinner. But he never thought of himself like that. He didn't catch on to that. "Yeah, Terry. People want to be around you."

The letter sent out to companies, such as Ford and Adidas, asking for support was written by Rika. She still has the rough copy somewhere. Up on a hill, she and Terry sat on two folding chairs with a pen and paper. They knew they had to write some kind of letter to get sponsorship. Terry handed her the pen and paper: "Here, write it." It was Terry's personal experiences, but Rika had, of course, heard a lot about it. All the things he had told her, she wrote down. Then she gave it back to show him.

> That's why I was just able to write it in one pass. I wrote it, gave it to him, and he was happy with it. He was not a writer, but I knew him well enough that [I knew] this was what he wanted to say.
>
> "Okay, so I think we could say it like this." "Yep." "And I think we could put this in." "Yep." Signed it. Done! I was so young and so not a polished writer. I think I'm much better now. When I look back at it today, it seems like it was written by a child.

Still, the letters were effective. Adidas gave him shoes, Ford lent them a van that could hold extra gas, and different airlines contributed flights to get him to the East Coast. There is a famous line in Terry's letter that was actually written by Rika: "Somewhere the hurting must stop, and I am determined to take myself to the limit for this cause."

For Terry's birthday that year, on July 28, Rika wrote him a poem. She's not sure how long it took to get to him and if he did get it on his birthday. The poem was titled "Dragon's Quest."

Dragon Quest

For Terry. On your birthday.
They say the dragon never sleeps
He stalks his prey in silence cold
And when he strikes, what evil fire
Within his venom,
One day the snake in careless greed
Dared seize a knight born of the sun.
The bite burned deep, right to the soul
The snake held fast, the damage done...
Or so he thought, but did not know
That he had inspired his greatest foe.
For though the fire had pierced him through
The knight of the sun held strong and true...
Fierce was the battle, bitter the cries
But death could now win, the fever broke
The serpent fled, one limb his prize...
The knight rose up, these words he spoke:
You have broken my body, but not my spirit.
I will not mourn, nor will I fear it.
Beware, dread beast, you have not won this battle.
My quest has just begun.

LOVE RIKA

Rika wrote a poem for Terry for his birthday, July 28, 1980.
Courtesy of Rika Schell

It was his present to keep him going. Terry loved *The Lord of the Rings*. I read him *The Hobbit* kind of like a bedtime story. He loved it, so he went out and got the whole set. Not only did he read those, he also read *The Silmarillion*, which no one reads, but he read that, too, because he needed to know the backstory. Even I had not read it, and I'm a fan. But he loved that kind of imagery, the power of it, good and evil, and just very straightforward, uncomplicated, "get a ring to the mountain," that kind of thing. So that's why I wrote [the poem]. He was on his own quest, so I connected it to *The Lord of the Rings*.

He was definitely a reader and a bit of a philosopher because he also read the entire Bible. He finished it not too long before he left for the Marathon. He began attending the church that Rika and I were sitting in. Terry wasn't religious before Rika; it was part of their journey together. He didn't have a lot of time to study the Bible before he left, but he did bring it with him on the run. He referenced some verses in the journal and in his training journal.

When he became a Christian, he decided to be serious, and he read the whole Bible and came to church and had a lot of questions. It was just before they left. A lot of the imagery in the Bible is similar [to *The Lord of the Rings*]. It's always powerful, passionate, very clear what's good and evil. He liked that clarity. He didn't like complicated stuff; he wanted it to be straightforward.

Rika was on Vancouver Island on tour with a youth choir when she received the phone call. A photographer was taking pictures of the trip. On the other end of the line was a newsperson.

I felt bad because [this] guy's taking a picture of me, and the person on the line said something about Terry passing. And I said, "What? He *died*?" Because I was fully expecting him to recover. I mean, he's so stubborn. He's just going to beat everyone. So, the poor photographer quietly slipped away. But yeah, I have a picture of me on the phone with this look of concern on my face.

In the present, Rika is the children's ministry director at her church. Most of the time, if people ask about him, she'll remind them how he was like everyone else and how he put others before himself.

> He came up with things like, "This happens to everyone. It's not just me." So, [he] just kind of got his head straight about reality. "Nothing special about me. Happens to a lot of people."
>
> Sometimes, I talk to groups of kids, and my thing is we don't want to turn him into a god or some kind of idol. He had human flaws. He had angry days and good days. Kids mostly want to know about *him*. Maybe not so much about the run, the technical part of it. What kind of ice cream did he like? Stuff like that. They want to connect to a human being. He didn't have a cape. Just a person. Your dad's a person, you're a person, you can do good things, too. I don't want them to think that it's so out of reach, that only a superhuman person could do this. I always put a faith message in there, too, because this is a story about hope. Because at the end of the road, what else is there?

MITCH FIDDICK
Neighbour, friend, and training partner; retired RCMP officer

I meet Mitch and the Fiddick family at their home in Vancouver, B.C. His wife, Alicia, and their two boys, Wes and Jack, are there. His parents join us a couple of hours later. Everyone is excited and eager to recall their days with Terry Fox and what the experience had meant to them. Mitch, a retired RCMP officer and his wife have set up the kitchen table with scrapbooks and photos they have of Terry.

Mitch begins by saying he has been thinking a lot about the time he spent with Terry, as it's been forty-three years, and memories begin rolling out of him. Mitch first saw Terry at a wheelchair basketball tournament in Burnaby at the British Columbia Institute of Technology.

> My uncle, Gary Manson, was involved with amputee sports at that time. My mom loved basketball, and Gary said, "You should come out and watch this, this is awesome."

Mitch loved sports but, unfortunately, wasn't allowed to play many.

> In 1976, when I was eight, I broke my hip. I had a cyst on my hip bone, which we didn't know about, and one February afternoon we were playing in the front yard and the kids were playing rough. I fell down, and another kid fell on me and broke my hip. I was in traction at Royal Columbian Hospital for, like, six weeks, and then I was in a cast, and I went through this long rehab, and the bone was still very weak. And so, I wasn't allowed to play a lot of sports. And all I did was play sports back then. But my mom *would* let me run.

On a walk with their dog, Mitch's dad stumbled across Terry running at the Hastings Junior Secondary track. He told Terry that they had just seen him at wheelchair basketball and that he had a son who was into running. Terry said he'd love to have a running buddy if Mitch wanted to join him.

> I was like, "Oh, that'd be fun!" So I went over the next night, I walked over, and Terry was sitting at the start, stretching, and I sat down, introduced myself to him, and he started asking all about me, and he said, "Well, do you want to go for a run?" And so, we ran two laps.

It was the spring of 1979, and Mitch wasn't sure he could run as far as Terry could. He was running a mile at the time, and he told Mitch he was going to increase it by two laps — half a mile — every Sunday. After running for a week, Mitch realized he could do it and adjusted to

Spring 1979: Mitch and Terry training on the Hastings track.
Courtesy of the Fiddick family

Terry's pace. After running, they would sit and talk, often for longer than they had been running.

Although he was just a kid, eleven years old by then, Mitch didn't ask Terry about his prosthetic at first.

But it came up right away when we started running because there would be pain. The way that the stump fit into the leg was always an issue. It just never was comfortable. At first when he was running, he had the foam around it, so it looked like a leg, almost like what women wear on their legs, a double nylon thing. The problem with that was that it had this release valve in it, and as we were running, sweat would build up and then blood would build up from all the sores that were occurring. So, then he took that off, and then we'd be running, and some people would be grossed out because the blood would be running out of this vent. So, we sat, and we talked about that, we talked about being in the hospital and how it all happened, and when he lost his leg.

They often talked about shoes because the miles they were putting on them were wearing them down, and they couldn't afford to keep buying new shoes. Instead, they kept tubes of Shoe Goo on hand.

I remember us sitting there putting new Shoe Goo on at the end of the day and changing our shoes, so the next day it was dry and we could run again. Some days if we didn't get it clean enough, it would peel off and a piece would go flying off while we were running. We'd be like, "Ah you blew a tire!"

Eventually, the two discovered they had the same doctor at Royal Columbian Hospital. When Mitch started to feel pain in his hip from running and training with Terry, his mother took him to see Dr. Michael Piper, and he shared that he had also taken care of Terry when he was in hospital. He told Mitch that he would just have to judge by how much it hurt. When Mitch told Terry this, Terry said, "Well, then let's keep going, but we'll kind of watch each other and make sure we're not overdoing it." But Terry didn't know the meaning of not overdoing it.

> Training and running go together with pain and discomfort attacks. There are the euphoric portions and all the physiological factors that go along with it, but there's always pain, and there's pains that you didn't have yesterday. All of a sudden, your ankle hurts and now your hip hurts. The amount of time and training we did, we always knew it would go away. In my mind, I always went, "Well, sooner or later this will go away, so just suck it up." As for words of encouragement to each other, Terry was very much like that. He's like, "Well, let's just work through it. Let's just work through it." Always work through it. There was no stopping; the focus was just too great.

By keeping up with Terry and running many more miles than a boy his age normally would, Mitch developed Osgood-Schlatter disease in both his knees. Overuse of the knee causes a painful bump and swelling on the shinbone. Children who are heavily into sports too young can develop it, and it causes pain to shoot through their legs.

> But I didn't really think anything of it as I got older in life. Then my kids made fun of me and said, "Dad's got four knees." But that was a direct result of running way too early, training way too far.

They started their training with three miles on the track, then completed additional miles off the track, then returned to finish at the track, cool down, and stretch. By mid-July, they'd run twice a day, a few miles early in the morning, running up hills, and then again later in the day, totalling five to six miles. One day, they even hit twelve miles. Then it was August, and Terry decided it was time to hit the Simon Fraser University hill.

He came over and he talked to my mom — Terry and my mom would chat a lot — and he said, "Well, is it okay if me and Mitch go up to SFU?" He had to deliver a term paper that day, and he goes, "Well then, let's go run SFU hill. We'll run it up and down, and then I've got to go up and I'll show you the university." And so, he took me to the university, and I remember us walking through and he went to the prof's door, and he couldn't get in. He's like, "I gotta deliver this paper; it's due." We went around the outside and he's looking through the windows. I'm like, "What are you doing?" And he goes, "Seeing if this window's open."

Mitch completes the Prince George race in 1979.
Courtesy of the Fiddick family

He's just prying this window open. He climbs in, his leg gets stuck, and I'm trying to push his leg to get him in there, and he says, "This is okay. I'm not taking anything. I'm just gonna deliver this paper. It's got to be done." I think we went for a Slurpee [after] and went home.

He treated me like I was a teenage brother of his. I don't remember this big difference. The way he treated me, I think he understood, I think he had a lot of respect for me, like, we have this mutual respect.

The two had been training for the Prince George race, which is seventeen miles — the test to see if Terry was able to complete that distance, almost a full marathon. He finished last but was thrilled to have completed it, and Mitch, who was in the youth group, finished fourth. Many others participated, including Terry's brother Darrell and friends Doug Alward, Rick Hansen, and Peter Colistro. Along with the Fiddick family, they waited for him at the finish line to celebrate.

Mitch and his parents were some of the first to hear about Terry's plan to run across Canada. This didn't surprise Mitch at all — he knew Terry could do it. Mitch's mom even helped Terry reach out to companies for fundraising.

> The only thing I do remember is talking about "Okay, well, how are you going to run that far every day?" And he's [like], "Well, I'll run all day long." And I'm like, "Yeah, I suppose if you just run all day long, and you're able to take in some nutrition, some hydration." I mean, to me, it still seemed feasible for him to do it. Very feasible. So, "Okay, that's the plan."

He was already training ten miles a day, and even when something broke on his prosthetic leg, he didn't stop.

> He was doing [it in] the winter and his leg had broken, and he stopped by to see if my dad was home. Because my dad was a plumber, he knew we'd have these clamps. I said, "Well, Dad's not here." So, [we] started going through the carport where Dad's tools were, and it was one of the only times I ever saw his leg off. He quite often didn't take his leg off when we were together. And so, we're looking for clamps; he says, "Well, we got to get this somehow together. I've got to finish the run this morning." [No luck.] So anyways, [my family] left that day for like five days for the Christmas break, and when we came back, he had left this card on the front door. It said, "Well, I found three clamps. I went to the welder on Saturday, but he couldn't weld it because it's aluminum. So, I bought six clamps, and I clamped it together. I was able to walk, and I went out and tried running. It lasted for five miles."

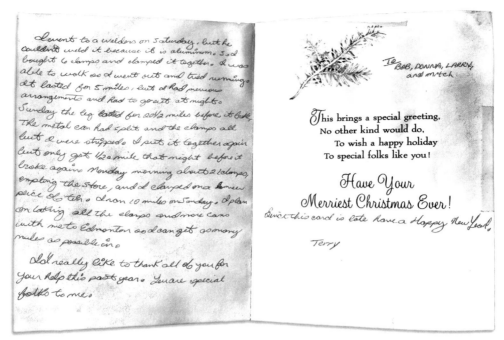

Terry's Christmas card to the Fiddick family, 1979.
Courtesy of the Fiddick family

Terry sent only a few people postcards during the Marathon of Hope, and the Fiddick family received four of them. Most were updates from the East Coast, as things got very busy once he hit Toronto. The last postcard they received was from London, Ontario. Mitch's mother remembers Terry calling from the run, giving updates, asking her to send messages to his girlfriend, Rika, and having some words with Mitch. They felt very lucky to have that contact with him.

> I would watch the footage in the evenings, and I would have a different take on it than someone else looking at [it]. I'd be like, "No, he's actually doing fine. I can tell by his [gait]." His gait was his gait, but you could also tell on a certain day if he is having a good day or not having a good day. Sometimes you didn't know. But yeah, I could tell if he was smiling and laughing. I mean, generally, if he was focused, he was quiet. And I watched him run through some towns and in the video footage, he would put [out] his hand. Everybody wanted to, you know, touch

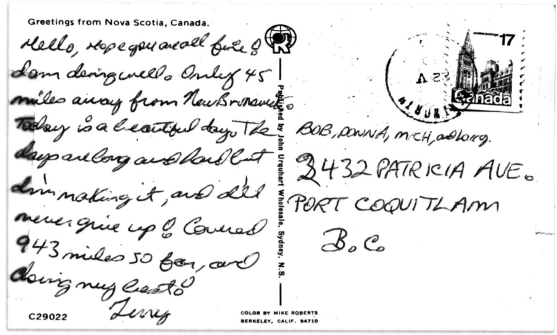

A postcard from Terry to the Fiddick family during the Marathon of Hope.
Courtesy of the Fiddick family

his hand, that sort of thing, and he would shake people's hands. He didn't like stopping, and I can only imagine what it'd been like. He knew it was important. I think that was part of it early on, where he was starting to be told, "You have to interact, too. Yeah, I get it, you have to be focused and run, but you're out here to raise funds and awareness." And I could see that would have been a hard transition for him.

Mitch has carried his time with Terry throughout his life, especially when he was getting into the RCMP.

I always drew on that. I had to train when I went into the RCMP. Six months in Regina, some very, very tough times where I couldn't even believe I was contemplating quitting because it was my goal. By the time I was sixteen or seventeen, I made the decision and I waited. I went through five or six years of trying to get in, and I thought, well, six

months here is no big deal. So, when it came to the physicals there, even the physicals were harder than I thought.
The running was no big deal, but the strength training
and the fighting and the injuries . . . What I learned in
1979–1980 was never quit. And that's the inspiration, I
think, that a lot of Canadians have from him showing
that level of commitment, and people trying to put themselves in his shoes and say, "How does this guy do this?"

I ask Mitch about how so many people connected with Terry and
almost looked for solace in him. Was it his authenticity, his purity —
because he really was just a kid — that made people believe in what
he was doing? At this point, Mitch becomes quiet and excuses himself
from the table. His wife, Alicia, speaks up.

I don't know if you know, but I'm battling sarcoma right
now myself. And for me, I draw on this, too, because I
can't feel sorry for myself. I don't want to feel sorry for
myself. But again, you say people are regaling [you with]
Terry stories, and it's amazing. As soon as someone knows
you've got cancer, they want to start telling you.

Alicia's birthday is the next day, and Terry's birthday would have been
the day before. She will be forty-three, and it has been forty-three years
since the run — an amazing connection and intertwining of lives.

I didn't experience what Mitch did. And I hate running. Like
I *hate* running. So, I listen to these [stories], and I don't get
it. But I'm sure if I dug deep, there's other things in my life
where I can parallel that, certain things I don't give up on.

You pose good questions. In this day and age, with
eighteen-, nineteen-, twenty-year-olds trying to be influ-
encers, it's all self-serving. And so I think the difference
with Terry is that you're trying to figure out how, what,
why. You can answer a lot of those questions, but really
you have to take a moment and go, "That is pretty unique."
Especially given his age and circumstance.

Mitch returns to the table, and I assure him that getting emotional is very understandable, especially considering what he and his family are going through and the stories he's sharing.

> I think I know the question you're asking, and I'm struggling to find the answer. My view on who he was, at the time I knew him, and why he was the way he was, it's still a bit of a mystery. But we can all say the same thing. Was there authenticity there? Absolutely. He was authentic. There was no putting on airs with him. He just was who he was. He was a massive factor in my life and many other people's. All I can do is tell you that, number one, you have to be thankful.

Alicia nods in agreement and adds "gratitude," as Mitch blinks away tears and continues.

> I'll tell you a story. The first time, when I talked about running at his pace after we had trained for, I don't know, two, three months, I remember, he had a kick at the end. He'd be like, "Okay, we're a mile out, let's make sure we save a little bit," and he would really crank up his pace. And I remember me going, "Okay. Let's pick it up. Yeah, I'm with you." We had a mile to go, and I took off. I finished and I waited, and he wasn't happy. He was not happy at all. He wasn't mad at me, but he's like, "I thought we were doing this together?" Never again did I take off. I realized, yeah, we're a team, like we're training together. And you have to remember, I didn't know what he was doing at that time. I didn't know what he wanted to achieve with it. He knew it. He knew by then, and he told me after.
>
> I think we all — I've always — wondered why. Like, I didn't think I was just his running partner. He didn't just come every day because he wanted someone to be there with him.

Terry had never shared with Mitch that in those first couple of days after his amputation, he had gotten up, hobbled around on his crutches, and went around to the boys laid up in traction and entertained them. Judith Ray, his first nurse, told me this in our interview. He'd make them laugh and play games with them to keep their spirits up. The children he bonded with in that ward touched him so deeply, their suffering motivating him to do something. The very ward where Mitch had also been a boy stuck immobile in traction for six weeks. And I was happy to inform him of this connection in the days after our interview.

Their parallel and shared experiences are what bonded them together. Serendipity also had a hand when Terry's two best friends were unavailable to train with him. Clay Gamble was training to be a pilot, and Doug Alward was studying at a different university. Mitch became his training buddy, someone who inspired Terry every day to make it through training and reach his dream of running across Canada. Mitch was indeed much more than just his running partner. He personified Terry's purpose.

Mitch, again, tries to answer what made Terry who he was:

> When you go through the time that we spent together, did I just inherently have some of the traits that he also maybe had inherently that weren't learned, and [we] just jived together? Watching what he accomplished solidified in my mind what you can gain and what you can achieve if you just put your mind to it, and you don't have that "Well, I'll try another day" attitude. As for what made him tick, I mean, I think back to some conversations [we had] about when he was in the hospital. We were both in Royal Columbian, we both had the same doctor, we were both going through a similar thing, albeit his [was] extremely serious, and the trauma that he went through, and what he had to do to fight on that ward every night from the time he was told to the time he had to recover and start training again. The only thing I can think in my mind is, during that time, he drew on whatever was inherent in his own mindset and psyche, and he developed it a thousand-fold to a new level that a lot of people haven't seen. I believe other people have that type of ability and that

inner strength and fire to do it. He just happened to be one who took it to the next level and made it a worldwide exhibition.

A letter the Fiddick family sent to the Fox family after Terry's passing in 1981, in which they say, "Even at the very beginning of our association with him, we were well aware of how special and unique a person Terry was. . . . if even a little of your son's qualities have rubbed off on ours, how very fortunate we are."

Courtesy of the Fiddick family

JUDITH FOX
Sister, legacy giving manager at the Terry Fox Foundation

Judith joins me on Zoom from B.C. Wearing a multi-coloured toque and a mustard fleece coat, her eyes are framed by black-rimmed glasses, and dimples appear when she smiles. She has a fiery grit to her energy. Being the youngest child and the only daughter of the fiercely competitive Fox family, she had to be as loud as the rest of them.

> We're a family of sports. A family of play, I guess. And a family [that's] loud. We're a loud family. Nobody was singled out on that one.

After going through traumatic events, most people block them out in their memories to protect themselves. For Judith, she had to live through not just her brother's cancer but also through everything he did, the legacy it created, and her recollection wavers. She was twelve when Terry was diagnosed with cancer.

> I didn't know what was going on, and I was really protected by my parents. But also, Terry protected all of us. Like Dad would take him to his chemotherapy treatments in downtown Vancouver, and he would just make my dad leave. My dad was not allowed to walk in with him. Or he said, "I'll call you when I'm done." I think he was eighteen. How remarkable is that, to have the wherewithal to protect his family that way? Goes by himself. Very private with regard to his stump and his hair. He lost his hair and gained that beautiful mop.

Her mom, Betty, was very strong, and Judith believes it's because she had gone through grief before.

> A lot of people don't know that she had a sister. I don't know how young she was, maybe thirteen years younger than my mom. She had come from Manitoba to live with us, and she was a paralegal or something like that. She

was here for two years, I think. She was driving into work one day, hit black ice, and went straight into a semi-truck and died. And I know that [Mom] would feel blame for that, like take the blame for that. She brought her little sister here. And then five years later, Terry was diagnosed. She was a tough cookie. She just did what she knew she had to do. That was her duty, to be by his side and protect him, and to be the matriarch that she was.

Terry said himself that he was very selfish, and I kind of remember bits of that, like, "Leave me alone." As a big

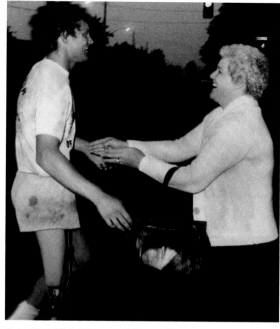

July 10, 1980: Terry and Betty Fox reunite near Whitby, Ontario.
Photo by Keith Beaty via Getty Images

brother, you know: "Don't bother me." But then after his cancer — well, you know what happened — his heart just opened, and he just wanted to help in any way he could. I'd seen my mom saying to him, "Why don't you just run across our province? Why do you have to do the whole country?" But you know, go big or go home, I think [was what] Terry's attitude would have been, right? "No, I'm gonna do it. People right across Canada get cancer and around the world."

Judith was in grade nine while Terry was running the Marathon of Hope. Her entire tenth year of high school was marked by their family going through Terry's second fight against cancer. From September 1, 1980, when Terry ended the run and returned home for treatment, to June 28, 1981, when he passed away.

He really was just my brother. He wasn't this icon, hero, whatever you want to call him. He was my brother. I had no choice in that, although I would never change that for anything, except for maybe a cure for cancer. In grade ten, when he was sick, I remember that year being really hard. And I don't have real details of what went on, but I did everything I could not to remember what was going on.

She remembers people lined up outside the house trying to get a glimpse of Terry through their windows, as well as the large grey duffle-style mailbags full of letters. With help from friends, the whole family sat and went through every piece of mail, each with their own letter openers.

Her parents used to be very strict with her, and she would fight with them because her brothers didn't have the same rules, such as being in by midnight. If out a minute late, she'd be grounded the next weekend. It wasn't until her kids had grown that she understood that her mom didn't want to lose another kid.

When I went into grade eleven, it was after Terry died. September — a new school. And there I have vivid memories of walking through and people just talking about me. I had to just ignore it. Actually, my counsellor from then, Bruce Moore, was also a coach of Terry's. He was a soccer coach, and he's huge in our life. He was the emcee for the hometown [Terry Fox Run] for years and years and years. He's a cancer survivor. Anyway, he saved my life absolutely. We see each other quite often, actually, at least once a month. Almost every time, I tell him, "I'm serious. I'm here because of you." I was doing things I shouldn't have done, like any teenager rebelling, and I went into the bathroom one day and happened to go into a specific stall that said "Judy Fox is a disgrace to her brother." And that changed my world and changed me going forward, realizing, "Okay, Terry Fox is my brother. I have to be the best that I can be." If I could find that person [who wrote that], I would thank them. Because if that had not happened, who knows where I'd be, or how I'd be, or the person I would become.

Judith allows other people's memories to be hers. When she chats with people, she'll ask if they saw her brother on his Marathon back in 1980. It means a lot to her when people share not only their memories but how they were inspired. She heard many stories when she was working at the Terry Fox Foundation, looking after the monthly donations and calling donors. She particularly remembers one man from Ontario.

> I think he's a three-time cancer survivor. He is just such a great guy and a huge Terry Foxer, like he just loved Terry so much. And he said that he has his life because of Terry. I've heard that often. People believe that it's because of Terry [that] they're still alive. And that's pretty special. Like, that's really something else, and I'm so proud of that. I'm so proud to be a part of that. Somebody that can make such a difference in one person's life, even just one person, it's huge.

Tom Cochrane, the Canadian musician, is another example that she mentions to me. He was on his tour bus in Northern Ontario in 1980, not having successful shows and ready to give up his career. Then his bus and the other tour vehicles slowed to a snail's pace on the highway. He went to see what the hold-up was and saw Terry running in the road. Seeing Terry so dedicated to what he believed in, fighting through adversity, inspired Tom not to give up.

July 10, 1980: Terry stands with his family near Whitby, Ontario. They flew out to surprise him, meeting him on the highway.
Photo by Keith Beaty via Getty Images

> It's a funny thing we joke about — there's a little Terry in all of us. But there is. We all have that, and we just have to look for Terry. When you [talk to] to a group of kids, they are excited to know that they can be Terry, they can be

a part of or like Terry. And it's daunting. That's why I have trouble because I think that I have to *be* Terry almost.

Judith remembers the time they went out to surprise Terry on the run near Toronto. It had been her first time on a plane, and she was so excited to see her brother.

Breeda McClew and Judith Fox attend the fifteenth annual Abu Dhabi Terry Fox Run in 2011.

Courtesy of Martha McClew, Terry Fox Foundation

Going out to see him, I do remember being anxious. I probably was the first one to go out [of the car] — because I was, you know, the little sister — and meet him. Mum was running towards him. I remember him kind of laughing like, "What are you doing here?!" and being excited to see us. Then [he said], "Okay, that's enough time. I gotta keep running. See ya later." Yeah, he had his job to do.

If only he could see now what he started then and how it has grown. Judith became the international director of the Terry Fox Foundation and has seen the Terry Fox Run happen in many countries and the wider global impact of her brother.

The UAE, for example, the lead scientist at the Terry Fox Lab, said to me, "Judith, I would not have a career if it weren't for Terry. And everybody else here knows that they would never have been a scientist. They would not be doing the work they are today if it wasn't for Terry." It was Terry's raising of money in that country that started the research in UAE.

I went with Mom to Cuba, because basically the whole country would do their Terry Fox Run — I'm sure it's still going on. We've never known a proper total of people. I was there with Mom and Dad, and I was running, and people are coming out of their homes or their stores or whatever. "Oh, Terry Fox Run!" And they would start running in Havana. It was amazing.

Another memory that touches her deeply is about another run that she helped start in India. She received an inquiry from the mother of a teenage boy and ended up forming a relationship with him to make his dream of a Terry Fox Run happen.

I received a call from a woman named Sujatha from Chennai, India. She wrote me because her son had cancer. The husband worked in the UAE, so they knew about the Terry Fox Run. When their son [Akash] had cancer, he was like, "I wish I could do the Terry Fox Run," because he was sick, and he goes, "We should do a Terry Fox Run, Mom." So, his mom phones me and says, "How do we do a Terry Fox Run?" I think he was fifteen or sixteen years old. I worked with him and [his] mom, but mostly him, on what he thought and where it should be, and all that stuff. And he was very smart and very kind. He was like Terry in the fact that he was going through this but thinking about people behind him and before him, and he wanted to do this Run. It ended up becoming a nineteen-thousand-person Run. I was there. I can vouch. Amazing to witness, and that's what happened in Chennai, India. It was incredible. I was just so blessed and fortunate that I was able to go and participate

February 8, 2004: School children in India participate in the Terry Fox Run in Mumbai, India.

Photo by Aijaz Rahi, AP Photo / Canadian Press

and learn about that. Sadly, I was keeping in touch with them all the time, and [then] they weren't returning my calls or emails. Finally, Sujatha did, and Akash had died. It had come back, and he had died.

Terry knew more about his condition than everyone thought — at least, Judith believes he knew. He knew his fate, and he just wanted to get to it and do what he felt needed to be done while he was here on Earth.

It's just still mind-boggling for me, you know? It's been a hard road, but it's been a blessed road, too. You get on the phone with somebody that's donating or participating with the Terry Fox Foundation. It's a world of amazing people. Every single one. Amazing, wonderful, beautiful, lovely people.

KERRY ANNE HOLLOWAY
Daughter of Bill Vigars and young volunteer on the Marathon of Hope

Kerry Anne arranges our meeting at an open-air shopping district in Burnaby, B.C. It is a beautiful day, a strong warming sun, and early enough that the shops are still closed. There are people sitting in the square, coffee and breakfast in hand, and some men are unloading a truck nearby to set up for an afternoon of entertainment. Kerry Anne arrives in shorts and a loose cotton blouse, and we sit on a stone bench in the sunshine, talking about her once-in-a-lifetime experience as a child meeting Terry Fox on summer break.

Young Kerry Anne sits with her father, Bill Vigars, at one of the crew dinners during the Marathon of Hope.
Photo by Glemena Bettencourt

She remembers her dad, Bill Vigars, taking her and her brother out of school. Her parents were separated, and the kids were spending summer vacation with him. Sounds standard, except that their dad happened to be the guy organizing and promoting Terry's Marathon of Hope. Kerry Anne was nine years old, and her brother, Patrick, was eight. "Irish twins," she laughs. They joined the run in Montreal.

> We were at the Four Seasons Hotel. I remember being in the pool, and my brother and I were just swimming. I knew that my dad was gonna go get [Terry] and bring him down. So, the first time I met him, I was swimming in the Four Seasons pool, and he walked onto the deck. First of all, I was already nervous to meet him because I'd heard so much about him and what he was doing. He hadn't really gained a lot of momentum yet, but it still felt larger than life to me. And then I had never seen anyone with an artificial leg, so that was the other part of it. I was really shy as a kid. I remember meeting him, but I kept going back down under the water. But right from the get-go, he

was just so open and warm and friendly to us. I think that I really did see another side of him, because there's that other part of him that's very determined and driven and strong. But [we] definitely saw a gentler side of him.

July 2, 1980: Terry, Doug Alward, Darrell Fox, Kerry Anne Vigars, and Patrick Vigars stand with Prime Minister Pierre Elliott Trudeau.

Photo by Bill Vigars

She doesn't remember him getting in the water or removing his leg, but he was being friendly and trying to engage them in conversation. Kerry Anne cautions me that her memory is that of a nine-year-old. She remembers the kickoff at the football game, which would have been the Ottawa Rough Riders. She thinks that's the first public part of the Marathon that she saw. They also ran with Terry in Ottawa, possibly to Rideau Hall, and met Prime Minister Pierre Trudeau.

The kids joined Terry's crew for two months, except for the festivities in Toronto when they had gone home to nearby Welland to be with their mother. There was too much happening in Toronto with the huge crowds, and Bill was busy organizing for the Marathon of Hope. Kerry Anne was bummed about missing Toronto, but then they joined the run again after and nearly all the way to the end in Thunder Bay. She remembers the crowds and the impact Terry was having. People were cheering their admiration and support all the time from the road, and she had seen it grow in her time with the crew.

The kids got used to the routine. Sometimes they'd be left alone in the motel room when the boys left in the early morning hours to do Terry's first miles. Then someone would return and get them. Some of the time, like the rest of the team, they were given duties.

I remember giving him oranges and water. We weren't doing that all the time, but there were times that we were doing that. So, we were in the van, but as time went forward, we gathered more vehicles. There were motorhomes and stuff, maybe two. I don't know if it was one or two donated by Ford or something like that. I remember being in those a lot as well. I think sometimes I was in, probably, the back

From left to right: Jack Lambert, Kerry Anne, Bill, and Patrick Vigars count the day's donations.
Photo by Gail Harvey

of a police car. I think we were just kind of passed around a little bit but also not having any hard feelings about that. It just felt like an adventure. One time, being in one of the vehicles, there was this guy named Cam. My brother and I were in the motorhome looking out the window, but we were also fighting and bickering as we did. I remember Cam said to us, basically, "Shut up and look out the window and watch Terry because you're never gonna see anything like this again." And I think that was a really pivotal moment for me on the run. That made a huge impression.

He truly was, I think, like a kid around us and really playful. Something that really stands out to me is when Greg Scott joined the run for a little bit — the three of us hanging out with Terry and how inspired Terry felt by Greg as well, just how he was interacting with him. I don't remember anything specifically that he said about that. I would say when he was there Terry focused his attention on Greg. It was nice to have another kid on the run for a little.

At those times, Kerry Anne could feel the difference in Terry. She describes it as a lightness that not a lot of people got to see. Most of the time it was all adults, business, planning, and sometimes conflict.

Terry's reason for doing the Marathon came through in his speeches. Most clearly, she remembers the speech he gave in Gravenhurst outside of a motel.

> I feel like this is where I learned his reasons for doing it. Knowing that I was a part of something special, watching everybody else watch him, seeing the impression that he was making on everyone. It made me sit up and listen to what he was saying. I could see how he touched people as well. I think he gave a voice to, I don't know, maybe grief or something that a lot of people didn't have the words for, like the collective experience of people being touched by cancer or their families being touched by cancer. I just remember this general thing that would happen where people would approach him and tell him their own personal stories or thank him for what he was doing because they've been affected by it somehow.

The magnitude of Terry running a marathon a day wasn't understood by Kerry Anne and Patrick as kids. When she did see him run, she could tell he was very focused in his zone, more serious. But when he was with them, he was kind. At mealtimes, especially, is when they would have fun.

> Terry would just order everything on one side of the menu, which I understand [now] how many carbs he would have to eat to be doing what he was doing. A lot of the time, I just think decorum flew out the window, and someone would throw something. There were a few restaurants where we definitely did have food fights. I don't remember [the restaurateurs] minding either. I don't remember us ever getting in trouble for anything. And honestly, I think that the [Marathon] crew would have been respectful enough to help clean things up as well.

Terry was a normal guy to them. They would play and joke around outside before or after dinner; they would rough-house, and he would tease and play with them like a kid. Because he *was* a kid, fresh in his twenties. With them, he could let the day go, and they provided him with some relief, joy, and purity. They were kids on a carefree summer vacation. But eventually, they had to say goodbye.

Terry was sitting in one of the motorhomes. My dad gave my brother and me these posters. One I have framed here.

Kerry Anne's poster signed by Terry.
Courtesy of Kerry Anne Holloway

He said, "Go say goodbye to Terry and have him autograph this poster," which I was resistant to because I was like, I know him. I feel so stupid asking him for that. I was still shy, and I thought it was a dumb idea. I'm so glad, obviously, that I did. But I also remember Terry crying when he said goodbye to us. I thought that he was just sad to see us go, which I believe to be true. I also wonder if he knew that he was sick. I wonder if it was sort of two-fold, and I didn't recognize that until I was older. I always had this narrative as I was growing up that Terry was crying because my brother and I left. Now, I think it's both.

Kerry Anne and Patrick did see Terry again. It was after the run had ended, and he was back at home in Port Coquitlam. Her dad had brought them out to B.C. to see Terry at the hospital, and she remembers a bit of meeting the family, having not met them when they joined him in Toronto.

I remember I was uncomfortable [as] a kid and you see an adult show emotion. So, I probably ducked out of there sooner than I would have liked to. And I think the same thing when we came to [the Royal Columbian] before he died — which I now work at. Again, I wish I had known. As a kid, I never believed that he would die. I wish I had said a better goodbye to him. I think I just gave him a shy hug or something. That would have been the final goodbye, but the one that really sticks with me is being in the trailer. Terry was an emotional guy, so it's not unusual he wore his heart on his sleeve. His emotions were close to the surface a lot of the time, but that was the first time that it was ever directed toward us.

After they returned home to Ontario, she later learned of Terry's passing.

I believe that we were at [my dad's] sister's — so my Aunt Beth and Uncle Vince, who lived in St. Thomas. Everyone was sitting in the kitchen, and they told me that Terry died. I saw how emotional my dad was, and then I think he drove me back to Welland, so it was about a two-hour drive. I don't remember if Patrick was in the car or not. Probably. But I just remember my dad crying all the way and having to be in the car with him, just the enormity of this moment and me sitting there with all of this emotion with him. I was ten. It was the first time, too, that I'd ever experienced the death of someone close to me. And certainly, it was the first time that I'd ever witnessed such profound grief. I think that was my reaction. My sadness came later because I felt like in that moment I had to be strong for him or protect him or something.

I remember having a big reaction when I was in grade five, like just having this big cry at school one time. We were doing some sort of school run. I don't know if it was the Terry Fox Run, but it was a run. I think I just got really tired trying to push myself, and then it all just clicked. I remember being super embarrassed about it. My grade five teacher was so kind to me. I think she saw that I needed some support. She did that thing where she didn't talk to me personally, but she showed the class a movie on grief, which was very sweet of her. I would see her around the neighbourhood, and she would always talk to me one on one, not about Terry or anything, but I think she was trying to emotionally support me. I think she knew I was going through some things.

Kerry Anne has since gone to elementary and high schools to talk about Terry and her experience. She's also gone on to work with kids with developmental or physical disabilities. She believes her experience helped shape who she became, her determination, and how she remains present in the world.

It can be a small thing, like being at a spin class and being too tired, and then just thinking that's nothing. Or bigger things, like going back to grad school when I had a kid, that sort of thing. It's hard to not do things when this has been a formative experience in my life. That also comes into my counselling sessions. I don't self-disclose a lot, and I try not to make it about me. But if I think that it can be helpful to someone that I'm working with, and inspire them in some way, then I will bring it up. And that's a lot of what counselling is — it's instilling hope and feeling hope for other people when they don't feel it themselves and being able to express that to them. I try to help people find it and believe it's there when they don't. They can't see it for themselves, so for a little while I see it for them.

It's funny how life just unfolds, and you don't really see how it's unfolding in a particular pattern. But it has. I've created this wonderful life for myself. And a lot of it I owe to that experience.

PATRICK VIGARS
Son of Bill Vigars and young volunteer on the Marathon of Hope

I speak with Patrick over Skype as he is in China and has been teaching English there for the past seventeen years. He lives a simple life and has remained focused on his work. Recalling pockets of memories from the summer spent with his father and sister on the Marathon, he speaks in a slow, steady rhythm and with the childlike levity and nostalgia of just being a boy.

Patrick remembers when he first saw Terry Fox. He was swimming in the pool at the Four Seasons in Montreal, jumping in and swimming the length, then coming back. Reaching the end, he looked up through the water at the edge of the pool and saw a blue Adidas running shoe. Then, an artificial leg.

> Then I did pull up. All of a sudden, I was just at the bottom of his legs. Shock and awe kind of thing, like I was surprised because I wasn't expecting it. And back then, I was some-what shy. I was embarrassed, I guess. I remember getting out of the pool, and I don't remember the conversation

Patrick smiles excitedly with his fishing rod as the crew leaves a small store in Northern Ontario, heading to the lake to fish and rest. The store proudly displays a Marathon of Hope poster.
Photo by Gail Harvey

or anything after that, just introducing ourselves and then walking away. From there, it's just a blur to me.

He was only eight years old. A kid out of school on summer break, spending it with his father, who was travelling across the country with Terry. To Patrick, it was an adventure.

I do remember the feeling of always being embarrassed because he would grab my nose like a lobster claw. He would pinch it a little hard, I do remember that. I just let him do it. I guess I felt grateful, shy, and embarrassed all at once. I can remember it being a good time when we were playing around with him.

They would wrestle around a lot. There is a famous picture of Patrick, Kerry Anne, and Terry outside a motel. Patrick on one side and his sister on the other, each with their fists outstretched and Terry in the middle, fending them both off. They never won.

Terry tries to "steal" Patrick's nose during a moment of levity on a break from the Marathon.
Photo by Gail Harvey

He was too strong! He wouldn't let us win whatsoever. Even when you see us playing outside . . . [Patrick pauses] I didn't think about it. No, he never let us win. That's hilarious actually! He was *strong*, like easily strong. He would have had a tree trunk for a leg, but I'm just talking his upper body strength — it was phenomenal. He had no problems holding up my sister and me. He would be able to hold up one person like this [Patrick raises an arm with his fist forward] and just play with the other one with no trouble. You think of an eight- and a nine-year-old kid, just full of energy, and you think we'd be able to break free. Not a chance!

Patrick laughs heartily at the memory. He and his sister really enjoyed playing with him and can see now how it must've been a relief for Terry. They would get yelled at sometimes by their father to stop bothering

Terry fends off both Patrick and Kerry Anne (successfully) during a rest stop on the Marathon.
Photo by Gail Harvey

him because it was so frequent. They'd always be seeking Terry out to play with him. But the van was another story.

> That's one thing I can specifically remember, the first time walking up to it, it just stank! *Staaank!* I think I was at the side door and it was just — oh my God! I can remember how the bedroom was right here and the toilet was towards the back. If I didn't have to go in there, I pretty much didn't want to. It was horrid. It was just foul.

In the evenings, when it was Terry's alone time, no one was allowed to disturb him in his room. It would be his time to unwind. But one night, Patrick knocked on the door, and Terry let him in.

> I remember sitting on the edge of his bed and he was lying there. There was a knock at the door, and I can remember

starting to panic, and I was running back and forth. He was like, "Hold on." Then he put me underneath the bed, and I'm just lying there while they came and talked to him. And then they left, and he was like, "Okay, come out." So then I sat back, and we started talking again.

I wasn't supposed to be in there, but I don't think he really cared. One could say that we distracted him because we were so young at that time. He probably just enjoyed being around us because we were so young and playful. And then he could revert to being childlike also. He didn't have to be as serious all the time like he was on the run.

And they were indeed kids, getting into mischief. When John Simpson and Scott Hamilton were filming a documentary about the Marathon, Patrick was often in trouble.

The cameraman [Scott] would always be yelling at my father because I would always run into the shots. Not that I'd ham it up, but if the camera was on me or if I saw a camera, I'd just walk up to it and start staring into the lens. I was famous for ruining shots. There's even one in the telethon where the balloons fall at the end. I got into that shot, too, because I just ran up to the stage. This is live TV, and I started grabbing all the balloons.

Like Kerry Anne, Patrick also remembers the team dinners being relaxed and playful with lots of jokes going around. The dinner table was another place where Terry could unwind. What they ate for dinner Patrick doesn't remember, but he knew it took up a lot of space. The plates of food just kept coming, so even if they were sitting beside Terry, they'd still be a bit away because of all the plates.

Like most memories, the specifics are blurry, but Patrick can still feel the emotions those moments brought out of him. When he was told Terry was running across Canada on one leg, his reaction was simply "Okay, cool." When he first saw the artificial leg, he thought it was strange, but he also found it interesting because he had never seen anything like it before. Quickly, it just became normal, like it was nothing. To him, it was just a part of Terry. Patrick didn't understand the weight of what was happening — going around with Terry was just a fun adventure.

Patrick's father, Bill, had joked with me during his interview that, now and then, he'd look around and not know where his kids were. But he knew they were in the crowds somewhere. Patrick agrees that his father probably didn't know

Clockwise around the table: Patrick, Doug Alward, Marlene Lott, Terry, Kerry Anne, and Bill at a restaurant during the Marathon.

Photo by Gail Harvey

where his kids were most of the time. That's why they had *Patrick* and *Kerry Anne* written on the back of their shirts in bright blue so that they would stand out in a crowd. But everyone looked out for them. He and his sister were free to roam and could do anything they wanted. He would even sit on the hood of the car, as they were following Terry. Parenting in the '80s!

When they had to return home, Patrick wanted to stay. He didn't know why they had to leave. There was no rush — school wasn't the next day. Like Kerry Anne, he was also embarrassed to ask Terry to sign the poster that his father had given them. He has no memories of the end of the run or when Terry passed. He thinks, eventually, he knew what happened but just went into denial and carried on with his life.

Patrick first spoke about Terry at a primary school in Hong Kong, and it was better than he could have imagined. Many of the teachers were Canadian. He talked about his time with Terry, and all the kids from five to twelve years old knew everything about him.

> I feel very privileged and lucky. It's made me the person I am today. He's instilled things in me that I believe to this day. Integrity, hope, will, honesty, having a moral compass. Not giving up and not quitting, trying to do your best every day, just helping others really. That's one of the reasons I came to China. The reason I've been here so long is to try and bring out the best in people and help as many people as I can.

May 24: Day 43 (28 miles) Today, I slowly got out of bed. I was still tired from running into the wind. We took our break and then left again. I had 11¾ miles to go to the ferry, and I made it perfectly for the 2:30 pm ferry. We met the captain on board, and he spent the 1 hour with us. Then I took off and ran 4¼ miles into Borden [PEI]. We came back to the motel where we met people in Charlottetown who were doing a fabulous job. Then I had a great shower and watched part of the 6th game of the Stanley Cup Championship playoffs between Philly and the NY Islanders. Then I drove to Summerside. It is beautiful country!

May 25: Day 44 (28 miles) Today, I made it out of bed again at 4:30. Boy, was it a beautiful morning. PEI is beautiful! A guy from the local radio station was actually there at 5 am when we took off. He covered us all day. What tremendous support. There were tons of people out to cheer me on and support me. We collected over $600 on the road today, our best. We also learned that in Newfoundland they now have $40,000. I was very sore and tired now. It is hard to even walk. When I came out of the van after my rest, I was weary. There was a long line-up of cars and people to cheer me on. So, I made it. I had another dizzy spell [⅕ of the way].

May 26: Day 45 (18 miles) Today, I was scheduled to run into Charlottetown at 9 a.m. Therefore, I got a chance to sleep in. It was great! We got up at 7 a.m. I went and ran 3 miles into town. Along the way 2 schools greeted me and cheered me on. Many people are congratulating me here, and I can't figure out what for. It was an outstanding reception by a great town and province. We busted our butts out to the ferry! From Cape Tormentine I ran 15 miles along highway 955. Highway 955 is very rough — this is part of the reason my runners are wearing so fast, and I am getting blisters + chafing.

Amputee On Island As Part Of Run

oss country runner Terry Fox of itlam, B.C., was welcomed rd a CN ferry on Saturday noon as he made his way to d. as part of his run to raise s for the Canadian Cancer ty. The young man had one of egs amputated due to cancer years ago. He was welcomed rd the ferry by Captain Steve ang and given a tour of the e, as well as being treated to a . Terry began his run in oundland and hopes to be back C. by November. The Simon er University student left Nfld. ril 12 and has so far logged 1060 s of his run, averaging 28-30 a day. Over $100,000 for cancer arch has been donated or ed in support of the run

already and Terry is hopeful the total will exceed one million. He was scheduled to speak to students at Elliot River this morning and will also visit City Hall in Charlottetown, with plans to leave the Island on Tuesday. He is shown here shortly after leaving the ferry in Borden, accompanied by a number of children from the area. Travelling with Terry in a van across the country is his close friend Doug Alward who carries two extra artificial legs in the van in case of problems. Terry's only comment as he began his run across the Island on Saturday was that he hoped the wind would be at his back. Complimented on his sun tan he said actually it was "windburn."

May 26, 1980: Terry sends a postcard to Judith Ray in Papua New Guinea, updating her on his progress.

Courtesy of Judith Ray & Mission Community Archives [reference catalogue number: MCA-0183-PC19800526-003]

Terry poses with the ship captain, sailing from Nova Scotia to PEI.

Courtesy of the Terry Fox Centre Archives

A postcard Doug Alward wrote to Yvonne and George Fox (no relation) to update them on their progress.

Courtesy of Yvonne Fox

CANADIAN CANCER SOCIETY

P.E.I. DIVISION
P.O. Box 115,
Charlottetown, P.E.I.
C1A 7K2
Telephone 894-9673

May 28th., 1980

Dear Rolly and Betty

I have just experienced a very pleasant and heart warming weekend with Terry. He restored my almost forgotten belief in humanity, he sure is a great young man and you must be proud.

Terry arrived in Prince Edward Island on Saturday May 24th., 1980 and left us on Monday May the 26th. I am enclosing clipping from our local papers for your information. The people on P.E.I. loved him and are showing this in form of the many donations that he has generated. It will be some time before we will know the exact total.

I will be in B.C. in October and plan to give you a call at that time.

My steno is out and I am picking at this letter myself so please don't be a critic.

Warm and fondess regards

Jim Fox
(Exec. Director (PEI)

May 28, 1980: Canadian Cancer Society executive director Jim Cox updates Rolly and Betty Fox on Terry's Marathon, saying, "I have just experienced a very pleasant and heartwarming weekend with Terry. He restored my almost forgotten belief in humanity."

Courtesy of the Terry Fox Centre Archives

COACHES
& MENTORS

"That night [before my amputation] was an awful night for me because I didn't know what lay ahead. But the following day, all my old friends and relatives, basketball coaches, teammates came into my room, and [in] the days after, my [hospital] room was covered in letters and cards from other people, and I decided right away that I wanted to show other people what I could do. Show myself what I could do."

— Terry Fox
Speech in Wawa, Ontario, August 18, 1980

BOB McGILL
High school teacher and basketball coach

Bob welcomes me into his home in Port Moody, B.C., for our interview. It's a condo high in the sky with a beautiful view of nearby parks and gardens. He has a bright face, positive energy, and a booming voice. He is retired from teaching but still speaks to kids at schools, motivating them like the natural coach he is and reinforcing his advice with stories of Terry. From elementary schools to high schools to universities, whether a hundred or 2,500 kids, when he does his speeches, there's silence in the room. Teachers may share public stories with their kids about Terry Fox, but Bob has stories they have likely never heard before. He was there in the beginning.

Bob first met Terry in 1971 at Mary Hill Junior Secondary School, when he became Terry's science and phys. ed. teacher. Terry was a very quiet, almost introverted grade eight student. So small that in science class, at his desk, his feet didn't even touch the floor. Bob remembers one time that a girl turned to say something to Terry, and he turned beet red — just about died of embarrassment. But in phys. ed., Bob began noticing the amount of effort Terry put in and recognized his quietness as resolve.

> I can remember in the PE class when he came in, he was without a doubt the smallest, the shortest, probably the slowest. We're going for a run, and I can remember this little guy at the end. For the first week or two, always last. One thing I noticed after about three or four periods, though, was that he wasn't last because he was goofing off. He simply was slow.

Suddenly, Terry wasn't running in last anymore. He wasn't first either, but he was moving up. Bob wouldn't hear a peep out of him, but he had a smile on his face and kept pushing himself. At the beginning of basketball season, Bob put out a call for players.

> I just happened to get a group of kids that came in that were big and fast. And then I had Terry. I can remember after about three or four practices, I pulled him aside and suggested, "You know, Terry, there's these kids that are so much bigger than you are, stronger than you, and they've played. And you haven't to the same extent. You might be better off going out for wrestling because we need somebody in your weight division." And I guess that's when I started getting a different feeling for him as well because all of a sudden there were a couple of tears, and it was kind of like, "Well, Coach, are you cutting me?" And I

said, "I don't cut anybody. But understand something. Only the best can play."

The team played twenty-six games and practised during the week. Terry never missed a practice, never missed a game, and at the end of the season, he played all of twelve minutes.

> I can remember Terry coming in; it was the end of February when the season was over, and he said, "Coach, how come I didn't play more?" I said to him, "Terry, you didn't play because I told you only the best are gonna play. It's only fair to them. This wasn't intramurals." And he said, "Yeah, but I came to every practice." I said, "Yeah, you did, Terry, but you just went through the motions. [It's] one thing coming in and putting in time, and another thing putting in quality." So, I said, "Look, you're still dribbling with your right hand. If you're going to be a guard, you've got to learn to dribble with both of them, and that's what I've been saying all season. Your passes are very weak, and you've got to learn to pass with one hand or two, okay?"

Terry was getting ready for the track season but wanted to improve his basketball skills at the same time. Bob told him he could practise in the gym when he arrived in the mornings, and Terry beat him there every morning. He had paid attention. He was doing the drills Bob told him to, thinking of his form, and developing his game.

> He showed me in a very quiet way. If somebody was in the gym that was a little bit better than him, then he would challenge them to a one-on-one. He never won. Doug [Alward] probably played him a thousand times and Terry didn't beat him. And that starts to show you something about what the young man is made of.

But that was Terry. He may not be big, tall, or strong, but he was going to work those guys. He knew he had to improve.

One day, they faced a team who were much bigger and stronger. A few even went on to play at the professional level; they were that good. They took playing Terry's team as a joke. One opposing player had the ball and was driving down the floor. Everyone could see he was going to drive right through Terry, who had taken his position and was holding firm. Terry was hit so hard that he went flying back against the concrete wall, hit his head, and was dazed. Bob ran out to the floor before the whistle, and there were tears and a bit of blood running from Terry's nose. The room was silent.

> I just said, "Come on, Terry, let's go back." Then he looked at me, and he was hurt. I know it. Through tears, he just said, "Hey, Coach, I worked too hard to get out here. Don't drag me off, I want to stay." I was never a very smart coach, so I left him on. [For the] next sixty minutes, those kids played the game of their life. I just sat, shut up. I couldn't believe what they were doing. But it's not a fairy tale. When the game was over, we hadn't won. We'd lost and by only a few points — not by even thirty. But at the end of the game, not one kid on that other team was laughing. When they shook hands, there was respect. There's Terry, quiet, no BS, just showing and demonstrating and making other people around him that much better. That's the kind of kid he was.

Off the court, Terry was having trouble with school. He had received his grade eight report card, and Bob saw him by his locker, clearly unhappy. He had a lot of disappointing grades. Bob took him into his office.

> I said, "Well, is it the teacher's fault?" And he looked at me and he said, "No, Coach, like you say, you got to be responsible for yourself. So, it's my fault." I said, "Well, I've got a classroom before and after practice that's open if you want to come in and study." I remember him after a few months saying to me he was so frustrated because he said, "Doug just looks at the page, and he knows. And I have to read it and read it and read it." And I said to him,

"Terry, you're not dumb. You're not stupid. Okay, Doug is a smart boy, but so are you. Here's the difference. You just haven't learned a strategy yet to learn. And it'll come. Believe me. Because I walked in your shoes. It took me a long time to grow up and to develop a strategy."

Subsequently, Terry made the honour roll. After he graduated and went on to Simon Fraser University (SFU), the two kept in touch, and one day, years later, Bob received a phone call from Terry.

He thought he had done something to his knee in a practice, and then when I heard a few days later about the cancer, I was devastated. I still remember racing up to the hospital, and him looking at me as I walk in. I mean, I'm beside myself, and I can still remember walking through there and Terry's looking right at me, and his words to me were "Coach, you heard what I've got?" I said, "Yep." He said, "Are you with me?" I said, "You bet." Now, doesn't that say something about the kid? Once again, not thinking about himself. Just "Okay, I got a challenge. I'm gonna need support. Are you with me, Coach?" Yep. Let's go.

Bob went to visit him a few days after the operation, and when Bob tried to talk about his leg, Terry didn't want to. There were bigger things on his mind.

He said, "Coach, I can't believe all these kids that are giving up." And I said, "What are you talking about?" "Coach, I always thought it was just old people that got cancer. There's all these young kids and they're giving up. What can I do?" He just had his leg removed. All the emotions that people get: depressed, frustrated, upset. A lot of people go inward. Not Terry. He wasn't even thinking about himself. And my comment to him at the time, which was kind of corny, but I said, "Terry, I can't tell you. You've got to look in your own heart because I can't tell you. It's got to come from you."

Now and then, Bob would get a call from Terry. One phone call, he told Bob he had gotten his prosthesis, but it was really just a peg leg. He had put it on, and the doctor had told him to try it out in the foyer, and then they'll make adjustments. Terry went out and fell flat. The two or three adults milling about the foyer laughed at him. Terry was emotional over the phone.

> It's probably one of the few times I barked at him other than being at practice. I said, "Don't you ever phone me again and feel sorry for yourself. Because if you do, I'm gonna kick your butt. If I was in that room, I'd have taken care of those three idiots, okay? Don't lower your-self to their level. You're too good."

When Terry was starting to train again, he asked Bob if he would coach him. Not sure how to coach someone on a pros-thesis, Bob joined him at a track on a Saturday. Terry tried running, and he fell and fell and fell. That same day, a soccer game was being played on the grass inside the track.

> This lady came racing across and pointing her finger at me. "You! You!" And she pointed her finger at Terry. "You get that freak out of here. He's upsetting the kids playing soccer." Like what the hell? Once again, what do you say? I was speechless. The young girl that

March 1980: Terry trains on a running track in his hometown, Port Coquitlam, B.C.

Courtesy of Port Coquitlam Heritage Museum Archives

was beside me wasn't. She just turned around and said, "Lady, the only freak here is you." So once again, when Terry started doing this, if anything it was the adults that were putting clamps on him. It was always kids his own age, always kids, who were saying, "Hey, it's just Terry. He wants to do it."

Bob can still remember when Terry told him he was going to run across Canada. At first, Bob said it was crazy and stupid, but then he stopped himself. He had been saying to his students all the time that if they wanted something, reach for the moon. How could he just push Terry down? He asked Terry why he wanted to do it, and Bob still shares Terry's response when he speaks at schools.

> His first thing was "Look, I want to get the people who've got cancer and/or this challenge some hope. And if I can get out there, if I can run, that gives them hope. Secondly, maybe I can make people who are much more fortunate, that don't have cancer, stop for just a moment and think of those that are less fortunate." When you start putting that together, what does it say once again about Terry? You take a look at so-called heroes — the sports heroes and all that kind of stuff right now — and so many of them are jaded. And then you take a look at a person like Terry, who was *doing* it. "I'm gonna do it. Not for me. And it's not about me." And I think that's what started connecting [with the public].

At the beginning of the run, Bob would get calls from Terry saying that he didn't know if anyone was paying attention. He said there were some young people out in the mornings, some teenagers out on the roads, waiting to see him. Bob laid it out for him during one call.

> "You know what, Terry? That's the future of this country. Forget the old people like me, okay? We're gonna die anyway, all right? The young people are what it's all about, and you are connecting with them."

It was the kids. They believed, they dreamed, and they saw Terry making his dream happen. It was kids who wanted to run with him. It was kids who affected him the most. When Bob visited Terry in the hospital after he returned to B.C., Terry told him a few stories from the run.

> Apparently, on this one day, he was exhausted at the end, and then there's a knock at the door of the van, a mother basically saying, "Look, if you can find it in your heart, can you come with me? Because my son's dying of cancer." Off he goes, and he's there. Talked to the young kid for twenty minutes, and then before he leaves, the young kid just pulls his mask off, and Terry bends over, and Terry said [to me], "I'll never forget [it]. He said, 'Run, please run. You're the only hope I've got.'" Stop and think of that. And he said, "Hey, Coach, if I can make a difference for one person, it's all worth it."

On one of his last days on the run outside of Thunder Bay, Terry had had to stop a few times. But suddenly, some kids arrived outside the van and wanted to run with him. Terry got out and ran right past them. Bob shared this story when he was giving a talk at the University of British Columbia.

> There was a lady, a mature student, who afterwards came up to me and said, "I just wanted to let you know, I was one of those students outside of Thunder Bay. I've never seen somebody in so much agony or pain. But boy, the determination. No matter how bad a day I'm having, man, I just think of what Terry was going through. [And it's] a piece of cake."

A few days before Terry passed away, Bob was visiting him again at the hospital. Terry's parents weren't in the room at the time, and Bob tears up as he remembers this moment:

> He was, you know, in pain, and I remember him turning over, and the sun was coming through a lot — this will stay

with me till I die — the sun came through the window, and it was kind of shining in on him and I said, "Here, I'll get the blinds." And he said, "No, Coach. Just leave it. I like that." He said, "Coach, do you think people will remember? Will people remember?" Those are the last words [I heard].

FRED TINCK
Junior high cross country and track and field coach

Fred picks me up at the SkyTrain station in his light blue Subaru Crosstrek to take me to his home in Coquitlam for the interview. Wearing his Terry T-shirt, he is excited to speak to me and describes the articles and pictures he has gathered as we walk along the side of his beautifully manicured home. The yard is filled with flowers in full bloom and plenty of bird feeders. His wife brings out some snacks to the back porch as we flip through all the material he has collected over the years that features Terry.

Fred had been one of Terry's junior high coaches. Bob McGill coached basketball, and Fred coached cross country and track and field. Bob had arrived at the school a year ahead of Fred, so in 1972, Fred asked him if there were any students to look out for as possible cross country runners. Bob said a few names, including Terry and Doug Alward. Terry and Doug were fourteen, and Terry was extremely shy, but he did get out and run.

Some people have the impression that Terry just was a superstar, that he was just an incredible runner and everything else — that is so wrong. He was not a great runner. He was not a superstar. He had an incredible, incredible work ethic that is really hard to describe. I mean, he gained motivation for minimal success, really, at the beginning. In those early years, I can remember one race that he ran — I used this when I did talks in schools — an eight-hundred-metre race, there were nine runners in the race. And Terry was running in this race, and after the first lap of the track, first four hundred metres, he's in ninth place. And everybody thinks that I'm going to lead up to this incredible story that Terry is going to win this race and come from nowhere to win this race. And then he gave everything he had. You know where he finished? Eighth. And that describes Terry.

Fred pauses and apologizes for getting emotional. I reassure him that everyone gets emotional talking about Terry, every single person I've interviewed. It's July 28, Terry's birthday, and he would have been sixty-five. If he only knew how deeply he touched people and that people still have so much love for him.

I just admired him so much in those early years. And if he was alive today . . . I still see Doug on a social basis once in a while, and I would still connect with Terry. He was just that kind of kid you never forget; he was an amazing young man.

If you look at statistics on what the world's best runners do with two legs, two *good* legs, they will run six to eight, and maybe even if they're really stretching themselves, twelve marathons a year. A year! Those are the very, very best in the world. Terry did that in a little over a week — on one leg. It's absolutely astronomical. Up until that point, this would have been classified as an impossibility for a human being to do.

April 12, 1980: Before Terry set off on the Marathon of Hope, Doug Alward sent a photo of him and Terry at the Atlantic Ocean to Fred Tinck with a note on the back.

Courtesy of Fred Tinck

I had some really incredible athletes in track and cross country who worked extremely hard. But he was just the kind of kid that gave it all. And if you said he couldn't do it, "Terry, you're not good enough for this" or whatever else — big mistake. *Big* mistake! Because that was a huge challenge for him; he was just going to take off and do it. And people told him before the run, "Big mistake. Can't be done." Big mistake on their part.

When Fred first heard that Terry was going to run across Canada, he didn't have any doubts.

Fred has coached kids who became professional athletes, some who went on to the Olympics. He believed in motivating them. If they finished first or fiftieth, it didn't matter to him as long as they tried their very best. It was most important to him, and he worked the kids very hard. One thing he would do with these fourteen-year-old boys was refer to them as "men."

Doug told me how much Terry liked that and just felt so grown up as a result of something as simple as that. And he was more of a man than a lot of men that I've met, too. Terry had a vocabulary, but there's a few words he didn't know. Like one he didn't know was the definition of the word "impossible." He didn't understand the definition of the word "quit." He didn't understand the words "can't do it." Those just got him going. That's just the kind of kid he was.

When Terry was in hospital after his cancer diagnosis and surgery, Fred didn't get to see him. His own mother was also sick with cancer, and he was very close to her. Tending to her and seeing Terry going through it would have been more than he could have handled at the time.

Fred had heard people doubt Terry at the beginning of his run. It was something impossible, especially for a disabled person. Back then, people with disabilities weren't as visible or out and about in a way that enabled others to see that they were the same as everybody else.

But Terry and his friend and teammate, Rick Hansen, were going to change that.

> I think they proved — those two men proved — that a wheelchair or an artificial leg doesn't hold you back from doing incredible things. They have proved that beyond question.
>
> I can't imagine the stress that he would have in his spine. When you think about that artificial leg and the joint action that he would have when he put that artificial leg down, all of that force has been absorbed by the stump and generated into the spine and to his hips. That's a tremendous amount of pressure coming up there when you're running. And when you run, you're putting a tremendous amount of pressure on your legs.

It's difficult to answer the question "How does someone do what isn't really possible?"

> It's an excellent question, but what did he have inside him? He had a tremendous drive. I know that if he saw a challenge, it was something to be overcome. If he saw the impossible, he was the one who was going to make it possible. That was, I think, probably a fair description of Terry. "If it can't be done, get out of my way — I'm doing it."
>
> I don't think he ever saw a problem as something that we need to accept. I think he saw things as a challenge that we need to overcome. And I think that can apply to all of us in some way. Today, when we think of the pandemic and things like that, yes, there's been some terrible things that have happened. People have died and people have lost their homes and things like that. But we also need to go through challenges in life to make us grow stronger. Nobody ever became a stronger person by being given everything on a platter their entire life. The one way that we all become stronger is through adversity,

through the pains, through the failures, the things we've gone through that have brought us down a notch. We've got two choices: we need to get up and work and fight our way back from the adversity, or we can accept it's only going to get worse. Terry always would choose the first one. Always! He would never, ever accept the fact that he was beaten.

When Terry's run ended, Fred cried watching it on TV.

> I heard it live, all the details, and I remember Terry on the gurney with Rolly there right beside him, and Terry describing how the cancer had got into his lungs. "If there's any way I can go out there again, I will." He knew he wouldn't.

Fred, like many Canadians, felt that Terry wouldn't be able to return to his Marathon of Hope. When he speaks about Terry in schools, he tells them that this is why they must run.

> "We're all going to go for a run now. And the reason why we're going for a run is because we're going to finish this run together. Terry never was able to finish his run across Canada, and that's why we have a run every year until this cancer is beaten."

The Terry Fox Run also goes on around the world with over twenty-five cities participating internationally. His message is still very much alive, but even more so here in Canada.

> A very important message that we all need to understand because this young man, as I said, unified our nation in a way that I've never seen in my life before or since that point in time. He also did so much to raise awareness of disabilities, raise awareness of the disease that he had. And the fact that this is still going on, I think it's just an incredible legacy to this young man.

Fred believes that most people have a desire to help and do something good for others, even if there is negativity in society. Giving to someone else when you're not feeling your best is not always easy, but it is rewarding.

> I think most people inherently have a desire to want to be good people in our society and want to do things to help others. And so, I think we've all got a little bit of that inside us, which was what Terry certainly had. I think Terry was probably a product of who he is; I think he's also a product of who surrounded him.
>
> I've had the pleasure of coaching some incredibly great athletes who have made it to the Olympics and some incredibly great athletes who couldn't run a hundred metres in twenty seconds but were wonderful human beings. And that's the important thing. If anything I, or anybody else, has ever done in their lives to make them feel a little bit better, then consider the work done. Because that's what we're all — in my view — here for. To try and make the world a little bit better of a place than what we came into. And Terry didn't make it a little bit better — he made it a whole lot better.

July 28, 2023: Fred wears a Terry Fox Foundation shirt that is specially gifted to cancer survivors.
Photo by Barbara Adhiya

TERRI FLEMING
High school teacher and basketball coach

When I arrive at Terri's home in Port Coquitlam for our interview, he is power washing his back deck dressed in a kilt. He has a toothy grin, and I could tell by his energy that he found joy in living against convention. As a teacher, Terri gladly took on all the misfits; he connected better with

Terry's high school basketball team goofs off in a yearbook photo. Terry is top left, balancing over the hoop, and Clay Gamble poses at the top right.

them. By the end of his career, he was teaching children who had been thrown out of other schools. He's a rebel with a cause, even in retirement.

He begins by talking about the Fox family — he knew them all quite well — and how the entire family has this incredible drive and an inherent stubbornness that they were born with. Terri had coached both Terry and Darrell Fox, and the family's reputation for being tough and determined was well-known. He once had a chat with Alex Devlin, coach of the junior varsity basketball team at SFU and said that it was great that Terry had made the JV team, but he was a little surprised about it. Alex looked at him seriously and said, "Everyone needs a player like Terry," and they both started laughing. Terri knew exactly what he meant. If you were a star player but a slacker, Terry was going to take your spot. No question. It didn't matter how much bigger you were.

For grade twelve community recreation students, Terri would get the kids involved in activities they could continue after graduation. One of those was hiking. In the first week of school, they'd get set up with equipment and learn how to pitch a tent in the classroom. They would purchase freeze-dried food, go up the Black Tusk in the Garibaldi Provincial Park, and stay for four days. On the return, Terri would hike down last behind all the kids.

> Terry and Doug Alward and I were coming down last to make sure there were no stragglers from the class well ahead of us. It's a pretty good trail, but it's steep. So, we started running and got this long stride, and it was magical. All of a sudden, we are in this zone, and it's like we are the best runners in the world. I'll never forget that. It was the

love of movement. We didn't talk to each other, we just sped up more and more and more until we were running, then just running stupidly. Took us about half an hour to get down, certainly cut the time in half. But that's what really sticks out, the joy of it. And that was really our bond.

Terri taught many students, but Terry was one of a kind. He was a solid kid, who loved basketball and deserved to be on the team because he put in the work.

The Ravens basketball team with Coach Terri Fleming (left) and player Terry (second on the left). Terri signed this photo for Terry saying, "To Terry, with enormous respect and affection. Terri Fleming."

Credit to the Terry Fox Secondary School and Terri Fleming

There's nobody like him. There were lots of amazing students. It's hard to separate the man from the myth. He was just going to beat you. But he beat you fair and square. He was popular, a pleasant kid, and he had a sense of humour. And he enjoyed life. He had that determination and integrity for the game. He played it properly, played it well. He really wanted to win, but he had no cheat in him. [He just did] it the right way. I never had to worry about foul trouble because he worked at skills and balance and footwork to be the right distance from people, so he didn't get dumb fouls.

One of the stories I heard about Terry's run across the country was that they used to put a rock or something on the road, so they knew where they finished and then drive back [to start from the same spot]. And they couldn't find it [one day], so Terry made them drive back to the previous rock. [Terri waves his hands up in disbelief.]

At SFU, whenever he got on the floor, Terry always powered through the games. After one SFU basketball game, Terri, who was attending the game, saw him limping but thought it was the special surface of the floor, as players' knees often hurt because of it. A few weeks later, Betty Fox, Terry's mother, phoned him at the school, telling him that Terry was in the hospital and had to have his leg amputated the next day.

When Betty phoned, it's like your own kid. It's like *Boom!* She asked me to go and see him. I said, "Of course, I'll go to the hospital." I'm feeling it now. [Terri pauses and takes a deep breath, tearing up at the memory of hearing that news.] But what am I gonna do? He's lying in bed. I'm good at being up; not good at being down. What am I going to do, stand there with my dog face hanging out? And in my despair, I remembered that there was a *Runner's World* magazine in the Port Coquitlam Senior Secondary library. I just grabbed it because there was an article on Dick Traum. I thought this is perfect. I went to Terry, we talked for a while, and I said, "Look, I'm just saying, I'm not trying to tell you what to do. I want you to read this article. Dick Traum is a one-legged marathon runner, and there's a message there, I think, for you."

Betty said later that same night, the night before the operation, Terry had a dream about running across Canada.

I think there's a pretty healthy dose of stoicism. The next thing I know he showed up in the gym, trying to learn how to run, and he said, "How did the guy do it? How did Traum run?" I said, "Well, I can't remember exactly. But it was like he took an extra step." So, we played around in the gym and Terry kind of lifted one leg and tried to run, and it's pretty natural after a while, doing the hop, because the prosthetic needs more time to get through. So, the hop gives it time to get through. And he worked on it, but we were both just brainstorming. But again, that's his style. He was willing to put in the time to succeed.

The 1977 *Runner's World* magazine Terri gifted to Terry, featuring Dick Traum running the New York City Marathon.

From *Runner's World*, Hearst Magazines, Inc.

He knew Terry was training at a running track near his home. One day, Terry met him at the Port Coquitlam Senior Secondary school gym and told him about his plan to run across Canada to raise money for cancer. Terri was as gobsmacked as when Betty informed him of the amputation.

> He thought big! But ordinary people can do extraordinary things with enough determination and effort. Most extraordinary things are done by some ordinary person going to extraordinary effort. That's nothing new, right? Not everybody's a genius who doesn't work at it.
>
> CBC Montreal, in the twenty-fifth year [of the Run], interviewed me, and I think they asked me what Terry meant to me. Thank God they warned me. I was never able to answer that question very well, but I think I came up with something that works. I don't know if I can remember it exactly, but I said, "Terry is basically a validation of

what every teacher does. Every teacher. We never know the individuals that we teach. This unassuming little grade ten, how he's going to become Canada's greatest hero? And so, to me, that is a validation of what we do."

ALEX DEVLIN

JV basketball coach at SFU, former Team Canada basketball player at the 1976 Summer Olympics

Alex comes to the Terry Fox Library in Port Coquitlam for his interview. He is thin and very tall, an imposing figure and what you'd expect from a former university basketball coach. He sits back in a chair with his arms crossed, just as he might in a discussion with his assistant coaches on who to keep and who to let go on the SFU team.

As part of their fitness training, all the players trying out for the junior and senior varsity basketball teams at SFU would go after class and run around the trails next to Burnaby Mountain. Then they'd return to the gym and play, and the coaches would observe. This went on for six weeks from September to mid-October 1976, and over those six weeks, Terry won every race.

> He won every single race, every single day. It became that everybody tried every day to beat him because somebody's gotta be able to beat this guy.

Alex had not heard of Terry before he came to SFU. In grade twelve, Terry was Athlete of the Year, but he didn't have a lot of basketball skills. Still, he tried out for the junior varsity team and was winning the races during training. If Coach Stan Stewardson and Alex were picking the team based only on basketball skills, Terry wouldn't have made it.

> But Stan said, "It's embarrassing to our program if we don't honour a kid that accomplishes what he does." And Terry earned respect, even from the senior players — but that's the way it went. Extraordinary, looking back. It's so easy

Terry takes a shot during an SFU basketball practice with another player.
Courtesy of Simon Fraser University Archives

to see that incredible, I would say, stubbornness. He's got
a drive in him that we were only beginning to learn about.
So, he made the team.

Alex feels it was a compliment to Terry's previous coaches that he
came out with so much desire and drive. No one worked harder or
improved more within one season than Terry did. He started as elev-
enth or twelfth man, and because of his drive, he made it to sixth man
by the end of the season. If he returned, he could have been a starter.
Alex says it was possible he would have had a shot at being on the
senior team, even though he wasn't six-foot-six and didn't have the
comparative talent. It's hard to cut a guy who outworks everyone.

There were stories about Terry and how he competed in everything
and anything. He was quiet at practice but competitive. It wasn't until
the last weeks of the season that he told some players that his knee was
bothering him. Then the season ended in early February, and Alex got
a call from Stan Stewardson saying that Terry was at the hospital and
having an operation the next day to remove his leg. Alex was stunned.

> [Terry] said he wants us to go up and see him, that he'd like
> to see some of the guys. So, we went up to Royal Columbian

that night, and it was one of those surreal [moments]. Like, yesterday in practice, a week ago in practice, two weeks ago in practice, it was all effort. And he's sitting up in the bed, and you look under the covers and there's his feet, and you can't process it. [Alex shakes his head, still in amazement.]

Visiting him the night before his surgery, Alex says Terry he wasn't depressed or down. He was accommodating and glad to see them. Alex doesn't know if it was naivety, as if Terry didn't know what was going to happen. Of course, he did. He knew very well the life-changing magnitude of it, but he was Terry.

It was coming to the end of the semester, and Terry asked for extensions in all his classes. Alex was impressed that Terry didn't drop his courses entirely. And he passed them all. When he returned in September, Terry became team manager of the JV basketball team. He wanted to be involved, and Alex never saw bitterness or resentment. Terry continued to laugh and have fun in practices.

When he was a manager, he'd come to practice, and you could smell the medicine on him. Whatever they put on his leg, it had a smell to it. But he never complained, nothing. When I heard about the article that Terri Fleming gave him, I think it was an instant [snaps his fingers], like "No, I'm doing this. I got a dream now. I used to have this dream, and now I can't do that, but I can do *this* dream." I think it was that quick. I think he just flipped a switch. That's rare. At that level, like I said, he's in a class of his own, I don't know anybody else that I would put in that category of being able to do and suffer what he went through. He flipped the switch, seemingly — I couldn't compare anybody [to him].

Alex heard stories of Terry's time in early practices with the Vancouver Cable Cars wheelchair basketball team. It didn't surprise Alex one bit that when the ball bounced off the backboard, and everyone's chair would get jammed up in the scramble, Terry would just get up from the chair and grab the rebound, the team laughing. Of course, standing up out of your

SIMON FRASER UNIVERSITY
BASKETBALL NEWSLETTER

APRIL

Terry Fox is not your average Simon Fraser athlete. Oh, he is tough alright, and a great competitor, but he was just a walk-on last Fall (not recruited). A quiet, unassuming 5'10" guard who wanted to keep playing basketball after high school. Terry graduated from Port Coquitlam Secondary School in June of 1976. He was named the basketball teams outstanding player, in a school where basketball is not really big. He also played soccer and rugby for the Ravens. He was named the school's outstanding male athlete.

As a coach, you had to be impressed with Terry. Not possessing refined fundamentals on the court, he made his presence known by always giving 100% effort. He consistently finished near the front of the pre-season distance runs and performed with intense aggressiveness in the games which followed the strenuous conditioning work-outs. He was so coachable, and though his friend and fellow team-mate was cut, Terry was named to the Junior Varsity team this year. Alex Devlin, J.V. coach, describes him — "Terry was not a big scorer, but he is the type of player every team requires. He always played great defense, came up with loose balls, and never quit working. Terry was a real team player, totally unselfish and disciplined."

His mother mentioned to me he occasionally complained of a sore right knee, though Terry never told Coach Devlin about it, and played as fiercely right through the final game.

On Monday, March 1st he twisted it and could hardly walk it was so sore. On Tuesday, Terry could not get out of bed. The doctor was called and Terry went to the hospital for examinations. On Friday he was told he had a malignant tumor — a rare form of cancer.

On Wednesday, March 9th Terry had his right leg removed above the knee.

A friend once told me in answer to the question why? — that a grain of sand in the oyster begins as an irritation, but ends up a pearl. It is what we do after an affliction occurs that determines our make-up.

Well, I'm betting Terry makes it. He is already determined to pass the courses he is taking this semester and we expect him to take a major role as a manager next year.

I don't know of a better testimonial as to the value of athletics — than learning and knowing how to come back when you are down.

I would like to thank the basketball players from both teams as practically every player has gone to see Terry.

A benefit game was played for Terry on April 6th at 8:00 p.m. at Port Coquitlam Secondary School. The basketball game featured this year's Port Coquitlam Ravens with a few additions against the Simon Fraser Junior Varsity Clansmen.

* * * * * * * * * *

The N.A.I.A. National Championship was won by Texas Southern University of Houston, Texas. They defeated Campbell College of North Carolina in the final at Kansas City. Central Washington which represented our District lost in the third round. They defeated New Hampshire State 72-56 and previously unbeaten and tournament favorite, Newberry, South Carolina (whose five starters averaged 6'7") 58-57 before losing to Grand Valley, Michigan 75-71.

* * * * * * * * * * *

The N.C.A.A. championships were exciting. It was great to see Marquette win. I'm sure all the coaches who were in Hope last year for our Coaches Clinic were pulling for Al McGuire, our guest clinician. Next year it is Jerry Tarkanian's turn. His Nevada, Las Vegas Runnin' Rebels certainly are crowd pleasing. Jerry's team finished third this year. He is our guest coach in Hope this year. One of his topics is "developing the fast break." Certainly we couldn't have anyone more qualified.

* * * * * * * * * * * *

"HOME OF THE CLANSMEN"

April 1980: SFU newsletter alerting the SFU basketball community of Terry's amputation, saying, "I don't know of a better testimonial as to the value of athletics — than learning and knowing how to come back when you are down. I would like to thank the basketball players from both teams as practically every player has gone to see Terry [at the hospital]."

Used with permission of Simon Fraser University, located within the Terry Fox Centre Archives chair wasn't permitted, but to him, it's a rebound. Why not get up and get it? Then one day, Alex saw Terry jogging in the street for the first time.

I pulled over and we started talking, and he told me that he was training. He was going to run his first half marathon in Prince George that weekend. I was stunned, like, "What did you say?" [Then] he says, "I want to run a full marathon," and he gets telling his plans. And all you can say is "Good for you," but of course, I had met his mom, Betty, through the process somewhere along the line, and I knew she'd be worried. So [I asked], "What does your mom think about this?" And he said, "I don't care what she says." He's very forthright. Terry doesn't play games. If you asked him something, he'll tell you, just honest and almost naive. He's so innocent but so honest in his moral makeup.

His doctors and cardiologist were worried because the chemo drugs had affected his heart. But he was going to run. He was stubborn. If he was going to do something, that was it. He could still be a competitor, even if different now. He was going to compete. At the time, we didn't recognize [his drive] for what it was until later on, the magnitude of it. I mean, you see him running a marathon [a day] for three months straight or whatever, missing only two or three or four days along the way. How do you grasp that? It's beyond.

Somebody said they asked him one time, "How do you run a marathon a day?" and he says, "I don't. I just run one telephone pole to the next telephone pole." I mean, what an object lesson in motivation, to break the whole down into "I'm not gonna run that. If I ran [to do] the whole marathon, it'd drive me crazy to think I've got that far to go." Terry had a different engine going. Most people get tired, get fatigued, and then the fuel starts to burn out. But he had something different. Some kind of internal combustor. He could regulate it from his brain and drive himself.

Every coach, if you have one player on the team and he really wants it, that's enough. You can deal with the

March 1980: Terry training on Simon Fraser University's track.
Courtesy of SFU Archives, UNS-79234

rest of the guys. "Oh I can't make practice today, Coach."
Yeah, yeah, yeah, we've heard it. If you've got a player or
players who have a dream and want to find out, "How
good can I be?" — that's what coaches live for.

When Terry had to end the Marathon and was being carried on the
stretcher on TV, it was the first time Alex saw Terry look like he was
rocked. Like he didn't understand why it was happening, why he was,
again, back at the start.

It never came across that [the Marathon] was about him.
That's why I think it was such a beloved story, that it was
never about him. He couldn't even grasp that it would be
about him. He thought, "Oh this is good! They're starting
to give money." But he didn't realize why they were giving
the money; it's [him]. His belief, his hope, transfers through
and people say, "Well, maybe I can do better, maybe I can
do more, maybe I can fight harder."

There's a fate to Terry. A destiny that he was the one,
like somehow, some way, fate entered into this, because I
don't know how many people in the world could do what
he did and keep it going for as long as he kept it going.
Some destinies, maybe, are preordained, pre-written, for
some reason.

May 28: Day 47 (28 miles) Today we crept out of bed again at 4:30 a.m. We drove 15 miles to our starting point on the now divided #15 highway. My knee joint wasn't working for me today. The springs were worn away. I struggled and pounded out the 12 miles. Stan Barker took my leg to Fredericton to get repaired. I put on the other leg again and it was worse. I couldn't keep my balance on it and I was struggling to make ground. I didn't think I would make my 28 miles, but I struggled out the 28 miles. I couldn't believe I was looking at the back of the van for the last time that day. We ran right through the City of Moncton down Main Street. We collected a lot of money. We found out we are going to meet the Prime Minister, Darryl Sittler and Bobby Orr! Fabulous!

May 31: Day 50 (29 miles) Today I got up and slowly went again. I had a strong wind in my face all day. The first 12 miles were awful especially the last 3 during which I was dead tired. The next 10 were better. Darrell arrived and it was heartwarming to see him. Brought a few tears as we embraced. Got me moving a bit faster. We finished right in the middle of Saint John. My last 7 miles took me out of the city where, on my last 200 yards, a group track people [school kids] from Fredericton finished with me. That was great! We drove back to the Admiral Beatty where we ate and slept! Today, I waved goodbye to the Atlantic Ocean at the Bay of Fundy.

June 6: Day 56 (30 miles) Today it was a beautiful morning. No wind. We ran by Hartland and then got on the 105 on the east side of the Saint John River. After 12 miles I found out we had to drive back to Hartland and meet the mayor. The mayor wasn't there so I went to a school and spoke to a large group of kids. Then, exhausted, I slept. Today I had tremendous support. Everybody honked and waved. After 8 miles we drove back to Bristol for a dinner, autographs, and my speech. Here there was a young man who was in Saint John taking treatment for the same thing I had. I have been there, and I said some words of encouragement to him.

May 23, 1980: Terry arrives at the New Brunswick border.

Courtesy of the Terry Fox Centre Archives

June 6, 1980: *Toronto Star* article by Leslie Scrivener reporting on Terry's progress.

Marathon Runner Arrives In N.B.

A 21-year-old Port Coquitlam, B.C., amputee who is running across Canada to publicize the fight against cancer is due in Saint John Saturday.

Terry Fox, a university student whose right leg was amputated above the knee three years ago because of bone cancer, began his run across Canada May 12, in St. John's, Nfld.

He plans to run across Canada to Vancouver this summer. A major hotel chain, the Four Seasons Hotels, has pledged $2 a mile for every mile Fox completes and has called on other companies to do the same.

If Fox completes the 5,000 coast-to-coast run and other businesses responded to the hotel chain's challenge, Canada's annual cancer research fund of $15 million would be nearly doubled, says Canadian Cancer Society executive vice-president Dr. Robert Macbeth.

Ford Motor Company has provided the young runner and his companion, his childhood friend Doug Alward, with a camper van to use as a support vehicle. Imperial Oil Ltd. is supplying needed petroleum products and Addidas is providing running shoes and track outfits. In New Brunswick, Wandlyn Inns is providing accommodation for Fox who is to stay at the Admiral Beatty Hotel in Saint John.

Fox's run through New Brunswick is taking him from Cape Tormentine to Shediac, Moncton, Saint John, Fredericton and Edmundston. He is scheduled to leave the province around June 10.

During his run across Canada, he's begun his day at 5 a.m. and has averaged almost 30 miles a day. His run ends at 5:30 p.m. each day and he hits the sack no later than 8 p.m.

Fox got the idea of running across Canada when he read an article the night before his leg was amputated about an amputee who ran in the New York Marathon.

Those who wish to help financially support Fox's run are invited to contact the Canadian Cancer Society.

Terry's one-quarter of the way home in run for cancer

By Leslie Scrivener Toronto Star

In New Brunswick they call it the Fox Trot.

It's a double hop with the left foot and swing through with the right, but it's not as easy as it sounds.

To do it you need one leg and all the determination in the world like Terry Fox.

The 21-year-old British Columbian lost his right leg to cancer three years ago and he's running 5,200 miles across Canada on an artificial limb, raising funds for the Canadian Cancer Society.

Donated $5,000

Yesterday at mile 1,346, near Woodstock, N.B. — one-quarter of the total distance — the Fox Trot team learned that an anonymous Toronto woman donated $5,000 toward Fox's fight against cancer.

Although Fox wasn't available to hear the good news himself last night, his companion, Doug Alward, 21, said, "That's just fantastic. That's just what Terry needs to hear.

"Today (Thursday) was his hardest day. It was partly exhaustion, partly the blisters on his left foot, and partly the terrible wind. It was really blowing fast."

The artificial limb is still not fitting Fox properly, causing chafing and cyst-like growths, Alward said.

"He felt just terrible. The only reason he made it was because all kinds of people were out on the streets (in Woodstock) cheering him on."

Although Fox may be pushing himself too hard (his goal is to run 30 miles one day, 26 the next), "he's got to push to the limit as an example to cancer people — they can't give up when they're fighting it," Alward said.

"He needs the extra hour or so every second day to make phone

Running with Terry

calls and get publicity and just relax. The stress is just incredible — running all day, making phone calls, people wanting him to do things."

Terry's brother, Darrell, 17, who's fond of cracking jokes, joined the team in Saint John last week to help with the chores en route. He does the laundry, arranges meals, lays out fresh clothing and is water boy, rushing out to the road every 15 minutes with juice, water or cookies for the runner.

"It's fun," said the younger Fox. "There's always something to do. I'm not bored and I don't think I'm going to be."

By conservative estimates, Terry has pledges of at least $100,000 — $40,000 from Newfoundland, $50,000 from B.C. including a $30,000 donation from the provincial government, and $10,000 from Nova Scotia.

Small cities better

"But the money keeps coming in after we've left," Alward said. "In big cities we don't seem to do so well and we often go out of our way to go there. But in the smaller cities it's 'way better, maybe because the communities are closer."

Pledges can be made in Toronto through the Canadian Cancer Society or through Fox's biggest backer, the Four Seasons hotels, which have challenged Canadian companies to sponsor Terry $2 for every mile he completes. In Toronto phone 445-5031 or the toll-free number, 1-800-268-6282.

The Star is carrying a report on Terry's progress every Friday in the Family section.

May 28, 1980: The *Evening Times Globe* reports that Terry has arrived in the maritime province of New Brunswick.

June 3, 1980: Jeff Child for the *Daily Gleaner* reports on Terry's progress as he arrives in Fredericton, New Brunswick.

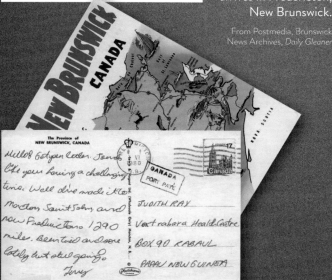

A postcard from Terry to Judith Ray, updating her on his progress.

Fox Reaches Fredericton

—He's On Cross-Canada Run

By JEFF CHILDS
Staff Writer

Running across Canada in the space of less than a year is something most of us could never hope to do, but a Port Coquitlam, B.C. man is doing it. No big deal perhaps, except for the fact that 21-year-old Terry Fox is doing it with only one of his own legs.

With his right leg amputated because of cancer in 1977, Terry decided to embark on a "Marathon of Hope," a run across Canada in order to raise money for the Canadian Cancer Society.

"After what I went through with my therapy, and watching some of my friends die because of cancer, I had to do it." While raising $1-million for cancer research is important to him, doing the cross-country run is just as important. "It's not giving up and doing the best I can. A lot of people want me to make it."

Terry's run began in St. John's, Nfld., on April 12 and he's covered just over a thousand miles at this point. He gets up every day at 4 a.m. and is running by 5 a.m. He usually goes 12 miles before eating breakfast. "You can't run on a full stomach." Most of what he eats are high carbohydrate foods, such as cookies and sweets. He said he tries to have one good meal per day.

He runs most of each day, pausing only for a couple of breaks, and then goes to bed at 8:30 p.m. Along with the constant running, there are fund-raising appearances in each town or city he passes through.

"It (fund raising) takes a lot of time, and between that and the running, he said he is starting to get worn out. "I'm not getting enough sleep, and when you run you need your rest."

COMMUNITY

"I had a strong attitude from the beginning, I never ever got depressed, and I took it as a challenge. In fact, the night before my amputation, a man from New York who is an above-knee amputee like I am now, I saw an article on him, and he was running on one leg . . . And I told myself right then that I would try and run one day, too, because he could run."

— Terry Fox
Speech in Wawa, Ontario, August 18, 1980

DICK TRAUM
First runner with a prosthetic leg to complete a marathon; founder of Achilles International

I interview Dick over Zoom. He is an energetic man and a spirited grandfather, happy to share what he knew of Terry and what Terry had done for him. Their lives intertwined in a crucial way, yet they never actually met.

Dick Traum was featured in a *Runner's World* article in 1977 for running in the New York City Marathon as an amputee. It was this

October 24, 1976: Dick Traum runs the New York City Marathon. A note on the photo from fellow runner Bill Rodgers says, "Richard, You have a slight edge on me in this photo; however we both had good runs at New York. Good luck, Bill Rodgers."

Courtesy of Achilles International

article that showed Terry he could still be active without one leg and sparked the idea of running a marathon. Dick first heard about Terry when a radio station called to tell him about Terry's Marathon of Hope and that he had been his inspiration. Dick thought that was nice but didn't think much more of it.

It wasn't until Terry passed away that Dick realized how special his story was and how it had affected so many people. Dick had inspired Terry, but as fate would have it, Terry returned the favour and inspired Dick to create Achilles International, an athletic community for disabled athletes. In 1981, during the first year of the Terry Fox Run, Dick was invited to Vancouver to participate.

> What had happened — this is very, very important — is
> that I was in Canada. He'd passed away, and they had these
> Terry Fox Runs [all around the country]. I think the first

One-legged Richard Traum and his friend Jonathan Rosen join the Terry Fox Run in Toronto.

Fox's mentor runs 20 kilometres in marathon to commemorate hero

By DOUGLAS KELLY
and BRIAN LAGHI

Richard Traum, the man who inspired Terry Fox's cross-Canada marathon, ran two 10-kilometre courses yesterday to commemorate the Marathon of Hope runner in the first annual Terry Fox Run.

Wearing anything but their Sunday best, 300 members of Scarborough's Knob Hill United Church listened to Rev. C. Gordon Ross give an inspired sermon on Mr. Fox and then ran their own marathons.

Mark Brennan, 77, ran 10 kilometres in 45 minutes, and 75 minutes later ran another 10 kilometres "just to get out and meet all the good people in Toronto."

Carol Hibbard, Shirley Constantine and Kathy Prue wheelchaired through Cabbagetown in honor of Mr. Fox.

These were only a few of the more than 6,000 people who ran, cycled, roller-skated, swam, wheelchaired and walked in Metro Toronto's 20 10-kilometre runs in honor of the Coquitlam native and his crusade for cancer research.

Ontario organizers expected the province would raise more than $1-million, $250,000 of which would come from Metro.

"It was just a lovely day and it's really hard for me to believe it all . . . It's mindboggling," said Mr. Traum, the one-legged New York native who helped influence Mr. Fox's decision to run across the country.

Mr. Traum participated in two runs in Toronto, once in the morning and once in the afternoon. He warmed up with a 14-mile run at Varsity Stadium in the morning.

Mr. Traum said Americans are among Mr. Fox's biggest fans. "As an event, Terry's run was on a par with the time we (United States) beat the Russians in Olympic hockey last year."

"It was not a normal Sunday for the congregation of Knob Hill United Church. The usual Sunday suits and hats were in evidence, but running shoes, shorts and even T-shirts were prominent.

In his sermon, Mr. Ross noted that Mr. Fox did not spend a lot of time saying, "Why me?" but went on to ask what he could do, and did it.

Albert Ash, the organizer of the Knob Hill run, said that when he traced the course on Thursday to check its distance, he found one of the bridges on the route had been removed without his knowledge.

It took only one phone call to Scarborough's public works department to have a new bridge in place by the next day.

Mr. Ross said he is "proud and delighted" with his church's response to the Terry Fox Run. "(Mr.) Fox provides an inspiration for us all. He mastered suffering, rather than being mastered by it."

He walked the route with his congregation and his 5-year-old son, Michael, who saw Mr. Fox as his run outside Gravenhurst.

William Eickersley, Ontario chairman for the run, concluded the day was a success.

"One little girl — she was only 4 — came up to me and said she was sorry she couldn't participate, but brought in a shopping bag full of pennies. She said to me, 'It took me a long time to save these.'"

Metro's largest run, which took place in Cabbagetown and boasted cyclists and roller-skaters, attracted more than 3,000 runners, including the group of three women in wheelchairs.

"We're working as a team together and that's the way we wish it to be. We'll all make it," said Mrs. Constantine, who suffers from two forms of palsy, a heart murmur and is blind.

"Last year, he (Mr. Fox) worked his way into my heart. Just to hear his voice, see his smile is happiness to me."

Mrs. Constantine said she went blind only four days ago, "but I don't feel brave about this. I just want to be helpful."

Fehim Kamali, whose leg was amputated at the thigh 15 years ago, said he participated in the run because "Terry did it for nothing and I think I can as well . . . He is dead but he is in all our hearts."

Mr. Kamali said he trained for the run by jogging three miles on Thursday and two miles on Friday. Mr. Kamali later shook hands with Mr. Traum and the two talked about their artificial limbs.

One participant, Donald Graham, who suffered cancer in the leg as did Mr. Fox, said he was happy so many people showed up for the event.

"I'm sure Mr. Fox would be awfully proud that we're keeping the flame burning. It's going to take all sorts of money to one day find a cure for this disease."

September 13, 1981: Dick runs in the first Toronto Terry Fox Run.

From the Canadian Press, *Globe and Mail*

one was in September of 1981, and I was invited. I was honoured to be invited to do some of the runs and to help them raise money. I thought what he had done was a good thing, and Canadians were probably a generation ahead of the Americans in terms of the comfort level that they had with disability. When I was there, people would ask me, "How did you lose your leg? Does it hurt?" Very, very normal, natural things. And then when I started running, it wasn't like, "Oh, I don't wanna get too close to him. Maybe it's contagious." They were the most comfortable, and I had never seen anything like that before in my life. And I felt very good about it.

After seeing the difference in how disabled people were treated in Canada, Dick felt it could be done in the U.S. He was inspired by Terry's ability to bring people together, to take on a challenge, to create a community of like-minded individuals.

In 1982, Dick started an eight-week course to encourage people with disabilities to run. Terry's older brother, Fred, attended the first meeting. Being supportive, Fred said to him that if just three people show, it would be a success. Two people showed up. Undeterred, Dick kept at it, talking to anyone he could find.

[People] would go to a place called Bryant Park and buy marijuana. Here's a kid, probably eighteen years old, selling marijuana and was an amputee on crutches. I went over to him and said, "Hey, you should join this group."

So, he joins the group, and I would pay for his subway fare to get there. I would find people one at a time, and by the end of the eight-week program, we had about half a dozen people who were participating.

Their first run was a five-mile run in Central Park, and they slowly built their mileage. Dick decided to change the course into a running club, and someone suggested the name Achilles.

The beauty of Achilles was he was an athlete but also a person with a disability. And we called it the Achilles Track Club, and we ran, and we held workouts twice a week. By November — this is in January — we had six people who were successful enough to enter the marathon. So, we had six people doing the 1983 New York City Marathon, and myself. I was very, very proud of that. And then in 1983 we exploded — we doubled to thirteen people. And then the following year, we had twenty-five people.

And the club continued to grow. Brian Froggatt, an above-knee amputee in New Zealand, had seen him on TV, and Dick coached him by phone.

Dick stands with his early Achilles Track Club marathoners in 1983.
Courtesy of Dick Traum and Achilles International

While Dick was proud to have run the New York City Marathon in six hours and forty-four minutes, Brian came and did it in four hours and fifty-four minutes in 1985. Brian then helped set up a chapter in New Zealand. Dick would provide support to anyone who needed it, whether that be a handshake, a T-shirt, or a hug. Now, Achilles International has members and chapters in over seven countries, including Canada.

> When you achieve something, you go ahead and you set a new goal, and I call this addiction to achievement. And what I've been doing over many, many years is I have been addicting people to achievement.

Through their remarkable achievements, Dick and Terry spread the message that the impossible can be made possible, but it's easier with a community. It starts with belief, and the more you accomplish something that wasn't thought possible, the greater that joy can be.

> We're dogmatic [at times]. So, I tell this story: I lost the leg and see a psychologist and the psychologist says, "Well, it's a shame, but it really isn't that big a deal. There's basically nothing that you will not be able to do because you lost a leg." I said, "Not correct." He said, "Give me an example. I'll turn it around. I'll show you it's the truth." So, I said, "I'll never beat Frank Shorter in the marathon."
> So, in 1977, I'm running and Frank Shorter's running [the] New York [Marathon], and he drops out at sixteen miles. And I finish. So, I beat Frank Shorter in a marathon. The Road Runners have this hall of fame, and I was honoured, and they asked me to speak. I tell this story, and Frank Shorter is in the audience, and everybody's looking at him. What's he gonna say? But the important point here, and Terry would have loved this, is that it's fun to do the impossible.

Terry had a team of people who not only gave him the insight and tools needed to overcome his obstacles but also made it fun for him,

PERSONNELMETHICS, INC.
522 FIFTH AVENUE
NEW YORK, NEW YORK 10036

RICHARD TRAUM, Ph.D.
President

(212) 764-3795

Mr. Terry Fox
Page 2
October 16, 1980

Enclosed is a picture
large volume of mail
identify me for you.

Cordially,

Richard Traum, Ph

RT:kg
Enclosure

October 16, 1980

SPECIAL DELIVERY   PLEASE FORWARD

Mr. Terry Fox
c/o Simon Fraser University
Vancouver
British Columbia
CANADA

Dear Terry,

Like everyone in the United States, I saw you recently
on television and read about you in the papers. I was
quite impressed. When I read that you had been motivated
by "some guy in N.Y. with one leg who runs," I was very
moved — that "guy" is me!

When you remember losing your leg, and when you remember
some of the more difficult running days — think of these
periods as "bad patches." That's what you're going through
right now. It's only by living through these situations,
the difficult days, that one appreciates and better understands those good times. It's better to have the ups and
downs than to have an ordinary, boring existence.

If I can ever be of help to you, please telephone me
(collect!). Also, would you be interested in coming to
New York City next week (as my guest) and helping our
company with the N.Y.C. Marathon October 26th? If this
is not realistic, perhaps you could plan to come at some
future date. In any event, please call me — I know it
would be difficult reaching you — I would love to share
notes and stories. When you run the second half of
Canada, I would be honored to run a few miles of it with
you.

...continued

October 16, 1980: A letter from Dick Traum to Terry, their first interaction, in which he says, "When I read you had been motivated by 'some guy in N.Y. with one leg who runs,' I was very moved — that 'guy' is me!"
Courtesy of the Terry Fox Centre Archives

sometimes running or biking alongside him. Dick recalls doing the same for a newer member of the running club.

Someone who had a stroke came out, a young little lady. She really didn't look like she could do very much. There are lampposts in Central Park, and I said, "Look, let's run, let's move from one lamppost to the next." And she did it. And I said, "You want to try another lamppost?" And she did. And she was smiling. I said, "Should we go for three?" and she said, "Yeah." And she went three lampposts and I said, "Turn around." So, she did it, she looked and said, "My goodness gracious," looking at how far she had gone. Three lampposts [there and back] is probably a hundred yards, and she'd never done that much distance in her life. And she was able to do that, taking her time, but she had achieved. We call it lamppost running, and the idea is that you start somewhere, and if you could do three lampposts, maybe next time you can do five lampposts. So she built [on it and went] from doing three lampposts to running twenty-two marathons. I say "running"; you know, it was very slow. She used a cane, but she completed twenty marathons. Along the way, she says, "What else can I do? What can I do next?" Somehow, she got involved with fencing, and she became a good fencer, and she was in the Paralympics as a fencer representing Brazil, her native country.

Dick is a strong believer in community because he knows the power of motivation when you're in a group. Groups can inspire, but they also give you a boost of positivity. When you're with like-minded people in the same situation as you, you can believe in what's possible because you are seeing that belief in others, and the fear and the feeling of impossibility diminish. Negativity from others can also become an incentivized challenge — from "you can't do that" to "watch me!"

The trick on this is, very honestly, the group. In other words, if you go ahead and run a hundred miles, there's nobody there to notice it. It doesn't really do much. The feedback from others is very, very important. This is what helped Terry because [when] he was out there, he was getting raves from the crowd. He was getting energy from the group.

It's very normal for people to have stressful situations. Everybody goes through this, [like the] loss of a job: what *do* you do? Ideally, you try this, you try that, you send out some resumes, you see people. And the trick is can you get to be with other people, in a situation where [you] can talk, bond, [and] help each other?

I inspired [Terry], but then he inspired me, and this would have never happened without that — thousands of marathoners a year with disabilities. There are all kinds of stories, thousands of stories, and had I not helped Terry, [they] would have never, ever happened.

BEN SPEICHER
Prosthetist

Ben begrudgingly agrees to be interviewed. He's been retired for a while and feels that everything about Terry has already been said. He joins me at the Terry Fox Library in Terry's hometown of Port Coquitlam and dresses like most retirees: casual slacks and a shirt, wearing glasses. He has a tranquil energy and not a lot of patience for commonly asked questions.

After his amputation, Terry was referred to Ben for his prosthesis. Like in most cases, Terry started on a temporary leg, which he wore for about a month. As he healed and underwent rehabilitation and stump conditioning, he progressed to getting his permanent leg. He was already walking by then, so it didn't take long to get used to. On a ride home with Ben, Terry shared that he wanted to do a run.

> You know what I did? I told him not to. [Ben laughs.] He went the other way. That's all you have to do, just tell him you can't do it, and he did it.

Terry started running around Port Coquitlam and on the school track at Hastings Junior Secondary. He was testing his endurance, his strength, his balance, and the leg itself to see if it would hold up and how far he could go with it.

> He ran a marathon almost every night. Then the knee would seize up, the artificial knee. He'd come to my house at night, sometimes at nine o'clock, knocking on the door, "Ben, the knee doesn't work." And we fixed it, and the next day he ran again.

At the time, the technology for a prosthetic was very basic. It was made for walking, not running. Terry didn't let that limitation stop him; he just had to make adjustments and think outside the box.

Ben had his own ideas of how to help Terry when fitting his leg. Ben was inventive, and he had a willing and imaginative patient in Terry. Together, they would break new ground and push what anyone thought was possible. Prosthetic legs were very basic at the time. Amputees all received the same leg that Terry did. But it was Ben's modifications that allowed it to hold up under the duress Terry intended to put on it. At times, it was only part of the leg that needed an adjustment or a quick fix. These were much easier to solve because the components were easy to find. His leg had springs, straps, and a hinge.

> It was nothing special. It was an average type of leg. The components were all just basic, nothing fancy; it's just the fit inside. Anybody can look at it — they won't know what I put inside the socket. I looked at Terry's muscular stump, and I gave him the fit that I thought he could run on. And he did. And I had phone calls from Europe, "What kind of leg did you make?" From France, from everywhere.

But it is not the tool or the prosthetic leg alone that allowed Terry to run. For the long distances and hard surfaces that Terry faced, he had to have the body, the strength, the muscle. It was something he built up.

> It was all muscle, his stump. When I measure somebody, I put tape around it, and I hold the tape and ask him to contract his muscles. And, usually, people open up to about an inch when they contract their muscles. Terry, he yanked that tape right out of my hand. In other words, the inch was way beyond him. If you don't have the muscle, you're not gonna run. Because every time you land, it jabs you up in the groin and [pain shoots] up on the bone in the back. You're not going to make one step. That hurts. He ran with his muscles.

The other essential component was the strap. Terry's stride and speed required the leg to snap forward in step with his speed. A regular prosthesis had straps, but they were not enough to keep up with him.

> The straps are actually the key to his running. Without the straps, he couldn't run. The first leg didn't have the straps, and he tried to run on it. He comes back to the shop and says, "This is too slow. It's lagging behind me." So, the

straps were the answer; the strap comes around the hip, and I attached the strap to the lower shin. And with the hip, when you start running, it kicks that leg to there [gestures forward]. It's almost there. So, when he is in his run, if the leg isn't there to land, he'll fall. If the leg is back here [gestures behind], and he wants to be there [forward], he'll fall. So that strap got him putting the leg to there [forward]. There's the elastic, and they're double elastic, actually. So, if he goes like this [forward], the elastic is attached to the bottom and [he] kicks this leg to there. Without that his stump has to do it. Too slow. So, the key was two straps.

Terry preferred to have Ben help him with the leg whenever problems came up along his Marathon of Hope. He trusted and knew that Ben would create a solution if one didn't already exist. He called Ben from London, Ontario.

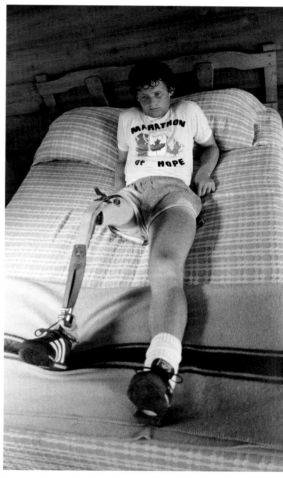

"Ben, I gotta get another fit." He's sinking too deep into the leg, into the socket, so everything goes up and it hurts. I flew there on a Friday night and got him off the highway and did a cast with him. We worked late at night, and then after I measured him and all that, he took off again. He was gonna carry on running, and I stayed at a local prosthetic shop. The prosthetic manager there says, "Ben, here's the key. I'm going on holiday. You take over." It was nice of him. I worked through the night Friday; I never slept till the morning. I had it ready, and then somebody from the cancer clinic

Terry rests on his hotel bed.
Photo by Gail Harvey

drove me and caught up with him on the highway because he already took off early morning running. We stopped him and I said, "You've got to give me five minutes to fit it." We fitted it on the highway, we aligned it on the highway, and I said, "Now you can run." I went back home here to Vancouver. We made the leg, fitted it, and then we sent it up — the War Amps picked it up and delivered it to him.

Everything was free of charge because of the War Amps. Terry had the community of amputees supporting him, and he was in turn supporting and promoting their work, creating change for amputees who would come after him.

Although Ben had made another leg for Terry, he didn't feel as comfortable using it. They had originally thought he would go through a few legs by the time he reached the West Coast again, but Terry kept running on that first leg. It was his favourite. It still felt good, and it was functioning as he wanted. They didn't have time to try out anything else because he was always on the run each day — he had to make his distance, that was the most important thing to him.

His pants were always full of sweat because there's a valve in the socket, that's how the leg stays on. If you remove the valve, the leg comes off, right? It's like a suction. It's actually a bleeder valve — some air comes out so when you sweat inside the socket, the sweat blows through the valve and his pants are all soaking wet.

Terry moved the evolution of the prosthesis forward. Most people had never seen an amputee, or if they had, they didn't even know it because the amputation was hidden under clothes. No one walked around showing the mechanics as openly as Terry did. And he didn't just show it by walking; he *ran* on it every single day. It opened a new lens of possibility for amputees, removing some of the stigma.

In September 1980, Terry was going to receive his Order of Canada, the country's second highest honour for merit. He went to Ben one last time. He had been battling cancer again and had lost a lot of weight, so his leg didn't fit anymore.

Terry is presented a shirt in Nova Scotia that says, "WE BACK YOU ALL THE WAY TO B.C."
Terry wore his shorts even when it was cold because it was important to him that everyone
see his leg.

After Terry had finished his run, when he came home here
to his house, he called me again and said, "I can't wear my
leg anymore, and I want to stand up." He was gonna get
an award, and he said, "I don't want to just stay on one
leg. I'm on two legs." I don't blame him. He wanted to be
proud and accept it on two legs. What did I do? I took his
old leg, and I filled it full of foam — Styrofoam, urethane
foam — and I took the measurements on him, whittled it
all out with the machine and fitted them in so he could
stand up. I knew Terry was getting smaller. And it wasn't
just because of the run; it was because of his sickness.
My first wife passed away also from cancer. I saw [her]
go from one hundred and forty pounds to just about a
hundred . . . And it was the same with Terry. He just went
downhill, and he was just skin and bone at the end.

Terry was very fortunate in finding Ben, and fate probably had a hand in
having their paths cross. Working with and belonging to a community

of amputees, they both had minds that were strong and not bound by limitations. To them, impossibility was just a temporary thing. Something to get through, something to solve.

People can do the impossible in life. You don't have to have big arms or anything. If you have the mind that you can do it, you will do it. You'll find a way. I always say, "Never give up." That's my favourite saying: never give up.

I always find a way of talking to [my clients] to give them hope. Say, "Don't give up. Carry on. Life goes on." Scott Patterson. Dan Wesley. They're all into sports. They brought gold medals home, and I made their legs. I made [Scott Patterson and Dan Wesley] the bucket. [Dan] went from one school to the other telling the kids, "Don't give up." He wore his artificial legs and showed it to them, which was a good thing. And that inspires kids: "Oh my God, he's got no legs, and he can do it and all this stuff. I've got my own legs and I'm giving up."

Everyone that loses a leg or a shoulder, not many of them come and are jolly. They're a little depressed. So, they need a bit of inspiration. "Oh, don't worry, I'll make you a leg and you will be walking again." And that's all I could do.

A young amputee supports Terry during the Marathon of Hope.

Courtesy of the Terry Fox Centre Archives

Ben has helped many people who have lost limbs visualize a way forward. He has seen many at the crux of their lives unable to process and handle what they had lost. With a community on your side, being with others who understand you, who can listen and support you and help find solutions, that can give you the final push to get up and try. Having hope and belief is just the beginning. With the right community around you, you can take that hope and *run* with it.

RICK HANSEN

Vancouver Cable Cars teammate, founder of the Rick Hansen Foundation

I meet Rick at his office on a Sunday afternoon, and he welcomes me warmly with a smile, a confident handshake, and a jovial demeanour. He is happy to share his experiences with Terry and how it has affected his life. The time they spent together was very special to him, a unique convergence of people. He feels strongly that fate had a hand in making everything come together the way it did.

Rick had been out with some friends, two of whom were at SFU, and they were discussing how to build their wheelchair basketball team, the Vancouver Cable Cars. Someone mentioned that there was a guy at SFU who had just lost his leg to cancer. He used to play basketball, so maybe Rick should call him. So, he did. Terry was excited about the idea and enthusiastically said yes before asking some questions about a wheelchair because he had never used one. Terry joined their practice within a week.

It was a dream team. Terry must've been blown away by this group made up of Rick, Peter Colistro, Murray Brown, Bill Inkster, and Eugene Reimer, who was the first person with a disability to be included in a Canadian sports award when he was named Canada's Outstanding Male Athlete of the Year in 1972. They had a strong team culture and inspired each other; if one thought they had problems, they could just look to a teammate, who had more problems. They didn't see disability. There was no pity party. They focused on improving their abilities and had fun together like any other team, trash-talking each other and doing crazy things on the court.

Terry and Rick clicked right away. At the time, Rick was in the phys. ed. program at UBC, and Terry was in human

Terry learns how to manoeuvre his wheelchair at a Vancouver Cable Cars practice.
Photo by Rika Schell

kinetics at SFU. They were both immersed in the athletic culture and loved playing sports. Terry arrived, hopping on crutches into the gym. They brought the chair out, and he dove right in.

Terry hadn't spent any time in a wheelchair and didn't know how it moved. He was slow and struggling at first, but Rick could see how focused he was, working up a sweat and giving it his all. He already had knowledge of the game and good ball-handling skills. Still, it's an adjustment to go from playing on your feet to playing in a wheelchair. There is so much strength needed in the arms, manoeuvring the chair while still trying to touch the ball. Terry was committed to learning and becoming a force for the team. Even while undergoing chemo, Terry was the first one in and the last one out. It was inspiring to see, and Rick thought this attitude could really help the team.

> We would drive my little green Honda, he would drive his beat-up piece of junk, and we'd park at the bottom of Lougheed Highway. Then we'd wheel all the way up this hill to the top of the mountain where SFU is. And then we would do a little weightlifting, and then we would do our practice. Unfortunately, because we were stupid enough to just leave both cars down there, we'd have to glide all the way down in the pissin' rain, totally frozen, and then drive all the way home and do it again [another day].

One of the few photos of Terry wearing a wig during his cancer treatment.

Courtesy of Clay Gamble

Terry set an example of not only strength but of perseverance. They couldn't believe how thin he was when they first saw him. He was still undergoing chemotherapy, and although Terry had lost his leg, he was more self-conscious about losing his hair. He wore a wig to cover up his baldness and never let anyone see him without it. Rick thinks it affected him more because if someone sees you with a missing leg and a bald head, then they know it's cancer. There is a stigma around that, and Terry wanted to look like he was cured as if the cancer was behind him. Ironically, Terry ended up with an even better, fuller head of beautiful curls.

> So, he comes in with a wig on, and we didn't know him before. We just thought that was normal hair. And the funny part, too, is that when we were playing, every once in a while, he would just have this little funny thing. I'm going, "Well, that's an odd twitch." I guess he was readjusting his wig, but I didn't know that! And then in the shower he'd never get fully wet showering. I'd be like, "Oh man, maybe it's the gel or something?" But it all came down to the time when we were playing against that big Spokane team, big bunch of dudes. And he goes driving to the key, gets the ball, and then *smack*. I, from a distance, see this puff of brown coming out of the scrum of guys. Then Terry jumps up out of his chair, hops over a couple of guys, grabs the thing, and goes like this [smacks the wig onto his head]. Then he looks around and gets back in his chair. The next thing you know, the wig is over on the bench and he's just out there saying, "What the hell," and he never turned back. I think it was a really interesting milestone. We all go through phases of adjustment when we have trauma, loss, and at some point, you get to a place where you accept who you are and shed some of those stigmas and perceptions that are your biggest handicaps. From there he just seemed to relax and flow into it. Everybody on that team came together and then went off and did whatever they did as a result of that experience. It was a moment in time. I know for a fact if the [Vancouver] Cable Cars team wasn't there, I never would have gone off and done my thing.

Rick's "thing" is a very modest way of describing his famous Man in Motion World Tour that was inspired by Terry. From March 1985 to May 1987, Rick wheeled over forty thousand kilometres through thirty-four countries, all to raise awareness about the potential of those with disabilities, as well as encourage the creation of inclusive, accessible communities. Rick has personally overcome what most would think is impossible.

Trauma hits, and cancer was Terry's trauma. But there's so many other traumas out there that everyone has. Like [actor and Parkinson's advocate] Michael J. Fox would say, "Everybody has their own bag of hammers, and some are visible and obvious, and many are not." And so that's where the magic is with Terry. He set goals, he found purpose, he constantly tried to improve, he was surrounded by family and friends. He inspired them; they inspired him. He was always looking for inspiration and growth. When trauma hit — his trauma, his hammer — he had to do more work and find out where his pain was coming from, which really wasn't from the fact that he couldn't use this leg. It's gone. It was here [Rick points to his heart]. It was in his attitude about his wholeness. And so, if that's the essence of Terry's direct legacy, the indirect legacy is: if we all do that in our own way, [figure out] what calls us, what's our strength, what's our role and how do we get involved to really pay it forward and express our gratitude, little acts, big acts, leading, following, it doesn't matter. I would say that's the real magic.

Because I think my biggest takeaway in life, from my friendship and the inspiration from Terry to me, has been some of the most important dreams in life can be killed by fear of failure, and the self-limiting beliefs that we have.

1979: Rick greets Terry in his wheelchair after the Prince George race.

Courtesy of the Fiddick family

Our attitudes and our stigmas can be our biggest handicaps. If we keep checking those, like Terry did, then we can find [them] out because sometimes those negative thoughts are really good safety valves, and we *should* pay attention to them; they're real. Like, "I want to jump off a building and see if I can fly." I'm sorry, that's not gonna work. Terry wouldn't want you to try that!

While Terry was running across Canada, Rick had started his Paralympic Games journey in Arnhem, Holland, but he got news updates regularly from their friends. When Terry had to end his run and return home for treatment, he had Rick and the rest of his community there to support him, and after all the Marathon craze, Terry hadn't changed at all.

5 September 1980

Dear Terry:

On behalf of Bill Lynes, myself and all your team mates of the Vancouver Cablecars, wheelchair basketball team and national champions 1979 - 1980, I wish to say how extremely sorry we were to hear of the return of your previous illness. We often wondered when we met how you could keep going as you did, day in and day out in your run across Canada to raise funds for cancer research.

All I can say on their behalf is that you were great and we are proud to be associated with you through sport and are pulling for you and a good recovery. We do hope you won't rush your recovery and that you'll think of yourself and get a good rest before you return to do your "thing". All I can say in closing is advice my doctor gave me back in 1940 - if anyone is going to beat it, it is you. When things settle down a bit, I'll be out to see you.

Sincerely yours,

Stan

Stan Stronge

Stan Stronge of the BC Paraplegic Association sends Terry well wishes on behalf of himself, Bill Lynes, and the Vancouver Cable Car team upon the return of Terry's cancer, saying, "We often wondered when we met how you could keep going as you did, day in and day out in your run across Canada to raise funds for cancer research."

Courtesy of the Terry Fox Centre Archives

Watching him adjust to his newfound fame was interesting because he was still the same guy. So, [he] was "Aw shucks" and awkward, and it was refreshing because he could have been seduced by all that, and he wasn't. He was very focused on beating it again. We'd come back to my apartment and have some infamous moose roasts. So yeah, we all thought he would beat it again. Why would he not, right?

Rick's eyes tear up and his voice deepens as he explains why Terry is his hero.

People often see heroes as emulating aspirational qualities. And to me, Terry wasn't a perfect person. He was someone with those perfect qualities, the attributes of determination and resilience, being able to turn his [perceived] disability into ability, or tragedy [into] triumph, and paying it forward. I just think that everybody has that if they want.

I think that's the other thing people would want to know and be reminded of. For every big trauma that comes in, or every goal or dream, you see those endgames, but you often get seduced by them. In reality, there's little things every day that remind us of the goodness of things. The gratitude, the progress, those things are present.

PETER COLISTRO

Vancouver Cable Cars teammate, two-time Paralympic medallist in wheelchair athletics

In Burnaby, B.C., Peter meets me at a neighbourhood café. He comes in with a hop in his step, stopping to pull a few wisecracks with some regulars while getting his coffee. Peter's right leg is in a brace after contracting polio as a young child, but today it is covered under his jeans. He's a spirited man, speaking a lot with his hands as he tells stories with a mischievous grin about the shenanigans he got up to when he was younger.

His first impression when Terry came into practice at the Renfrew Community Centre was how scrawny he was. He thought, "How the hell did he play for SFU?" But he knew there was always more to someone with a disability; besides, Rick had recruited Terry, and he shouldn't be underestimated. Terry made a few layups and watched the others, and Peter knew he'd be back. He learned just how hard Terry was willing to push himself when he was told that Terry had been going outside during their practices and puking — an effect of the chemo Terry was going through in his battle against cancer — and then coming right back to continue practising.

Terry stands up from his wheelchair and reaches for the ball, during practice with the Vancouver Cable Cars.
Photo by Rika Schell

Terry fit right in with the competitive nature of this team. Peter says it was nuts how competitive they were. They would cry after losing. They weren't even being paid. They wanted to win the Canadian championship and then the North American championship, and they were going to have to work hard. Terry was setting an example for them in just what that entails.

> We were bitching in the changeroom, "Okay, well, do we have to come out for extra practice?" and this and that. All of a sudden, Terry comes in after one of his, probably, ten mile runs, and it was October or something, he's dripping wet, and then of course he's got the bloody stump. We looked at each other and said, "Okay, we're gonna sort this out. This is not a problem." So that's the effect.

With their team members set and the shared drive to become the champions, they realized they would have to come together and train even harder. Peter would join Terry and Rick running up Gagliardi Way, the hill to SFU. People in cars would roll down their windows and offer them rides, and they'd shout, "No, we're training!" Then they'd join practice for another two hours. The team was competitive, but Terry was competitive to the extreme.

Here's a story about me and Terry, one-on-one. He knows how competitive he is, and he couldn't beat me then because I had the chair skills, and he didn't. So, he decides, "Okay, we're gonna play standing up, just me and my leg hopping around." So, here's two guys, we're hopping; [if] people had probably come by, they'd say those guys look nuts. And we were kind of equal because my leg, I used to hop around, too, when I was a kid without a leg brace. So, my leg was pretty strong and his was getting stronger all the time. I'm thinking what the hell are we doing hopping around, trying to put a basketball in. At least he won half the times, maybe more, but I [wouldn't] admit that. I went home and I thought, "That guy will think of anything to try and get an edge."

Terry and Peter hanging out.
Courtesy of Peter Colistro

Although they pushed each other and were fiercely competitive, they still held a strong team mindset. It wasn't about one of them being a star; it was a community of like-minded people with the same challenges who wished the best for one another and held each other accountable. No egos. Only comradery, affectionate taunting, and an overall feeling of accomplishment.

None of our teammates will go look at a scoreboard to see [their] stats after a game. God forbid if you were caught doing that. We were about the group winning. So that's where Terry fit in — he was a team player.

This was a winning group of opposite personalities. Terry was serious in everything he did. While other teammates were going out and having drinks, he was studying and bringing his books on the road trips to games.

On the other hand, there was fellow basketball player Murray Brown. Peter describes him as a long-haired, marijuana-smoking guy, very laid-back. He had more of a disability being a paraplegic, but he was very competitive and just as committed to improving for the team — and Terry recognized that same drive in him.

Terry with fellow Vancouver Cable Cars teammate Murray Brown.
Photo by Peter Colistro

> After two years, [Murray] told me one time, "So you know what? Terry said I'm all right." I said, "What do you mean? You're *all right*?" He said, "He came up to me and he says, 'Murray, you're all right.'" He said, "It took me two years. I've finally convinced him." And [for] Murray, that made him [proud] because he had so much respect for Terry.

Strengthened by their mutual respect for each other, the Vancouver Cable Cars went on to dominate the sport. They won thirteen national titles between 1968 and 1983. But Terry still wanted more. He did not want to be limited. When Peter heard about Terry's dream of running across Canada, he didn't doubt Terry's ability or the effect he would have on the nation.

> When I heard, I just told him, "If you can make it to Ontario, if you can still run, it's gonna give you credibility." That's what I thought in my mind. I knew you had to make it a certain amount in a certain way, and you will make money. Because I knew Terry, he'd come across honest and not like it's a gimmick. But I figured he had to run a certain distance. I said, "Don't give up." No, I didn't say "don't give up," because I knew he never would give up. But I said, "Don't get discouraged, because when you start, you might

not get it. But once people realize what you're all about, and it's gonna take a while, you're gonna do all right."

If Betty couldn't stop him from running, nobody could stop him from running. These things [have] started to hit me now. And if I knew that he had a bad heart or something, I'd say, "Terry, it's not worth it." But would I have been able to? No. He'd already made up his mind.

Terry sent a postcard to Peter, updating him on the Marathon of Hope.
Courtesy of Peter Colistro

Survivors have a strength that comes from having to go through adversity. It's a strength with which you can more easily climb over the next hurdle. Peter felt it was easier for him because he had always had a disability. For Rick and Terry, their disabilities were something that they had to adjust to as teenagers.

Ending the Marathon and returning to the hospital to again fight against cancer, Terry did not give up hope or think he would fail. And his community of friends supported that.

> I think he had to think that he's still gonna beat it. So, we'd never say no. We just went on like, "You're gonna live." That attitude. So, we were positive, I guess, around

him. We didn't bring it up. But then when I saw him that night, when he opened his door to go [home], it just kind of hit me all at once. That memory, dropping him off and [Terry having to] open the door slowly. But he walked to the door and locked it, and I said to myself, "Maybe I let myself think that he's not gonna make it."

As invincible as Terry seemed, cancer was stronger this time. Most Canadians believed if anyone could beat it, it would be Terry. They had hope — the hope that Terry gave them —and they held on to that hope.

Peter doesn't remember where he was when Terry passed. A memory blocked away by anger and sadness.

All I remember is getting very drunk. So, I didn't handle it very well. I passed out somewhere. Never said that before. They should have said to people for it to take him, it's got to be really bad. Cancer is bad. For it to have finally got him. Even him. He never gave up. If you ever saw us playing one-on-one on one leg, the guy would trip you if you went in for a layup. But he was trying. I'd rather have someone like that on my team. I think the bottom line is that he's an ordinary guy; just through sheer hard work, everything he did, he earned. I think people related to him that way. That's why you say, "Well, I'm gonna work harder." You see him: "I'm gonna work harder. Look, he is running out there in the rain. So, if he can do that, I can do this." That's what the people see. That's what people resonated with. His honesty. If you're genuine, you can't fool people. He was genuine.

DARRYL SITTLER
Canadian NHL player from 1970 to 1985, Hockey Hall of Fame inductee

Darryl chooses his local McDonald's in Toronto as the meeting place for our interview. It is where he walks to get his coffee every morning, so he knows we won't be bothered by anyone because they are used

Darryl and Terry run down University Avenue, a major thoroughfare in downtown Toronto, headed to Nathan Phillips Square.

Photo by Gail Harvey

to seeing him. He gives me a firm handshake with a welcoming smile as though we were in his living room. He was pleased to hear about this project. Darryl is someone who often tells Terry's story and believes in the good that comes from sharing the hope of Terry Fox.

Darryl, like the rest of Canada, learned about Terry through the news and followed the media coverage. Then, out of the blue, he received a phone call from Bill Vigars. He explained that Darryl was one of Terry's favourite hockey players and asked if he would come and surprise Terry at the Four Seasons Hotel in Toronto.

I said, "What can I do for him?" So, I went to my house in Mississauga, spontaneously grabbed my All-Star jersey and threw it in a brown paper bag. I had my Terry Fox T-shirt that they gave me when I arrived downtown, and Terry had finished thirteen miles that morning, and they said, "He's up in his room. Just go up there and say, 'Would you like to go for a run?'" So, I'm nervous and excited, and honest to God, I don't know what's happened in your life, sometimes the vividness of something sticks out, and that happened [in this moment]. So, I walk in there, and I go, "Hey, would you like to go for a run?" I don't know who was all there, some of the family members and whatever because he just finished thirteen miles, and this was his position: he was kneeling down and he was tying a shoelace, and he looks up [with] a big freakin' smile.

Terry was happily surprised, and Darryl joined the group on their run down University Avenue to City Hall. As they left the Four Seasons Hotel, the media and the public lined the sidewalks.

The emotion just grabbed me. People were crying, people were cheering, people donating money and all that. And for me, this wasn't about me; this is Terry's thing. So, I didn't want to be front and centre. I just went behind him and let him go but absorbed all the stuff around him. And then we went into Nathan Phillips Square; I had no idea there was gonna be that many people there. It was packed: the stage, all the politicians, everybody was there. And I had my brown paper bag with my jersey in it, so I got up on stage and I took it out and gave it to Terry as a gift. That was kind of one of those overwhelming days.

Darryl continued to follow the run daily. Then on Labour Day weekend, Monday night, he got a call that he'll always remember: Terry's run had ended in Thunder Bay. A week later, Darryl and other stars pulled together and presented on the telethon that CTV hastily organized to keep raising money for Terry and cancer research.

When Terry returned home and was again battling cancer, Darryl gave Terry a call, and Terry was excited to hear from him. When the Leafs were going to play in Vancouver, Darryl invited Terry to come to the dressing room and meet all the guys. Some find it difficult in such times and don't know what to say or are too afraid of saying the wrong thing and don't say anything. Darryl believed in the power of positivity and just wanted to give him encouragement.

I tried to be encouraging to him, but uplifting. I mean, I guess what's happened in my life, by visiting Sick Kids Hospital and these [types of things], you never know what the situation is going to be, and the emotion.

Darryl presents Terry with his 1980 All-Star jersey at Nathan Phillips Square in Toronto on July 11, 1980.

Photo by Gail Harvey

149

But I'm fortunate that I can adjust or adapt or feel that there's, I believe, some positive hope or whatever it is. So, I've been blessed somewhat that I can do that, and I don't mind putting myself out there, because I know that person's reaching out or needs some help. You never know [what a] word of encouragement [can do] or just the fact that they've met you. If you have the time, and you have the spirit and heart to do it, why not? You can touch other people's lives. But the other part — you gotta keep your mind and your heart and your spirit open to it. Some people don't; they just close it out. They don't even let it come in. I let it come in not knowing where it's gonna go. Sometimes it's hard, sometimes it's emotional. And you say, "Why?" But that's what makes the difference in things. His spirit was very contagious, and that's what stories like this can do for other people.

To Darryl, Terry is the greatest Canadian ever. What he was able to accomplish in his short life, and with such humility, is truly spectacular.

I used to run ten, twelve miles a day, and I was working hard, but I did it because I was making a living doing it. I *had* to train. He was running in cold rain up and down the highway. There are trucks coming by. Next morning, get up, friggin' leg's bleeding, [does it again]. How the hell can somebody do that?

Darryl had a similarly powerful experience with fellow Maple Leaf Börje Salming. He was dealt a bad hand with an ALS diagnosis in July 2022 and called Darryl first when he got the news. Darryl went to Montreal to help guide and support Börje and his family through that time. Börje was determined to be at the Hall of Fame game on November 11 when three other Swedish hockey players were being inducted, and he wanted to bring his large family with him. So, Darryl spearheaded the effort with the support of Maple Leafs president Brendan Shanahan and organized all that was needed: first-class flights, medical staff, and oxygen tanks for the plane. With so many logistics, he wasn't certain that it would happen. But within forty-eight hours, it all came together. Being with Börje on centre ice, saying thank you to Toronto, was an emotional moment in Maple Leafs history, even if you're not a fan of hockey.

I see some people like Börje, like Terry, they have that . . . whatever it is. They don't quit. And it happened, and thank God it happened, not only for Börje's sake and his family's sake, but the awareness it raised for ALS. Our players put the patch on and sold the jerseys, and we gave a cheque to Mark Kirton, a teammate of ours who also has ALS. That never would have happened had Börje never [made it to the ceremony]. There would have been some degree of it, but not to that extent. The same as Terry.

November 11, 2022: Darryl and Börje Salming at the Hall of Fame ceremony.
Photo by Mark Blinch via Getty Images

The hockey community has come through for Darryl as well. As a young kid, Darryl received a Jean Béliveau jersey for Christmas, and he wore it everywhere. Years later, as a Maple Leaf, he faced off against Béliveau. They met only once more when Darryl was elected to the Hall of Fame in 1989.

When my wife died of colon cancer, at 10:30 the morning of her funeral, my phone rings. I pick it up. "Darryl, it's Mr. Jean Béliveau. I want you to know I'm thinking of you on your most difficult day of your life." He went and found my number to talk to me, to be there.

Darryl's wife, Wendy, didn't like the limelight, but she felt that she should share her story. She believed, "If I can touch one person's life — that they will have to go through what I've gone through — this is all worth it." Darryl has taken this to heart, openly sharing her story and listening to others. He's had a few interesting moments in his life where he feels the universe seems to step in briefly, nudging him and those around him towards each other.

> I'm at a corporate thing one night, and I'm sitting with seven, eight guys, and this guy beside me says, "I'm sorry, you lost wife to colon cancer. I lost my dad to colon cancer." I said, "Have you had a colonoscopy?" The guy's thirty-three years old. He says, "Oh, no." I said, "Honestly, somebody put you and I together for a reason tonight. You're going to shake my hand and you're going to promise me you're going to get a colonoscopy. There's a family history; you have a higher percentage." Six, seven months later, I'm doing another charity event for Baycrest Alzheimer's. This guy comes over to me, he says, "Darryl, I got an interesting story to tell you. Two months ago, a guy came into my office, and he says, 'The only reason I'm here is because Sittler shook my hand and told me to get a colonoscopy.' He had stage two colon cancer, and you saved his life." So, when that comes back to me, it's like . . . You sit on the sidelines, nothing will happen. I could go into a room of thirty people or a thousand people and tell Wendy's story. I don't know, but it might touch somebody. If I don't say anything, it's not going to touch anybody for sure. And that's what [the] Terry Fox Run continues to do and has done for so long and will continue to do it.

Who knows what effect our actions and words can have on others? A small act of kindness or a piece of advice can inspire people to do the same and spread the message, causing a ripple effect of collective good and change.

> I'm looking in the mirror one day, shaving, and I see this little mole on here. I picked up a Toronto newspaper, I started reading this whole thing: it was Melanoma Awareness Month. And I read this article, I'm thinking, "Shit." That

day, I'm going to a barbecue up by my cottage, and I drive in, and the guy that drives in behind me is a young doctor friend of mine. I said, "Doc, look at this." He said, "Oh, you better come in tomorrow so I can look at it." So he cuts it out, sends it away — melanoma stage two. I got it in time. But what I did, I went back to the *Toronto Star*. I said, "Listen, I read your story on melanoma. It touched me. I found it. You can write the story on me." Because when you get cancer, a lot of people want to keep it inside. Especially if you're a celebrity, you don't want to talk. I know you got to talk and make a difference.

Darryl has a portrait at home of Terry that is his touchstone. Ken Danby, a famous Canadian artist, was commissioned to do a piece depicting Terry's run, and Darryl didn't know about it until he saw it in the newspaper. It was a collage of pictures creating an image of Darryl holding Terry's hand and Terry wearing his All-Star jersey. Darryl phoned Ken and asked about it but was told there was only one in existence; it was one of a kind, just like the person it

Terry Fox by Ken Danby (watercolour, 1981). A reproduction of this painting hangs in Darryl Sittler's home.

Reproduced with permission from the estate of Ken Danby

portrayed. Darryl asked if there was anything Ken could do for him, as it was really important to him, so Ken took a picture of the piece, blew it up, signed it, and sent it to Darryl. Darryl feels its magic every time he looks at it.

If I get down a little bit, which I don't very often, I can look at it and say, "Listen, if this guy can do this . . ."

June 10: Day 60 (30 miles) Today, I felt good at the start. The only problem was my cysts are still bothering me. The first 9 miles took me to the Quebec/New Brunswick border. Here we said goodbye to Stan and Mr. Gordon, also to Bill Vigars for a while. Then I did 3 more [miles]. We stopped and slept well, 4 [provinces] down! Gained an hours sleep. It started to get hilly after this. We were by Notre-Dame du-Lac. I was dead the last 4 miles. We drove to Cabano.

June 13: Day 63 (24 miles) Today, we slowly crept out of bed. The wind is simply howling and shaking. It is terrible. It does this all day long. No way I could run against it. I had to get behind the van. It was hard on Doug trying to stay at a distance away. Terrible, ugly day. I got sick from the exhaust and fumes of the van. Somehow, we turned 0 into 24 miles. I was given a beautiful shower. Felt good. Exhausted.

June 22: Day 72 (15 miles) Today, the wind was out again. I did 11 miles and then we had to drive to the Jacques Cartier bridge. Here, with other runners and some wheel-chair guys, I ran to the Four Seasons Hotel on Sherbrooke Street. There was a warm reception here and lots of media. Here I also saw Clay [Gamble]. It was an enjoyable time. Then I went to the Canadian Open Golf Tournament with Clay, Darrell and Doug.

June 10, 1980: Terry, Doug Alward, and an unknown man stand at the border of Quebec and New Brunswick. Terry holds up four fingers, after having run through four provinces.

Courtesy of the Terry Fox Centre Archives

July 17, 1980: The last postcard Terry sent to Judith Ray in Papua New Guinea, updating her on his progress. His correspondence was limited during the Ontario portion of his Marathon due to the overwhelming support he was now receiving.

Courtesy of Judith Ray & Mission Community Archives [reference catalogue number: MCA-0183-PC19800717-005]

Hi.
How are you, Im fine
Now in London Ontario
and have now gone 2375
miles. The weather has
been hot and humid.
The response in Ontario
has been great. The
money raised has reached
3/4 million mark with 400,000.00
coming from Ontario
Bye for
Now
Terry

J. RAY
VATRABARA HEALTH CENTRE
BOX 90
RABAUL PAPAU
NEW GUINEA

August 7, 1980

Hi, Terry!

Thanks to my summer job at the local newspaper I was treated to the rare and rewarding opportunity of meeting and interviewing you. Through our encounter I felt I had managed to uncover a larger part of the Fox story than what the headlines gave us; like the warm and personable young man behind it!

From the interview I wrote the best article I could, and I enclose it along with copies of other area papers which feature your exploit.

In terms of response the story proved to be one of the best I've ever turned out. Since its publication, townspeople have shown their support of your cause through their comments and donations. You've done more for us than you could ever know.

I follow your story whenever I can, and I hope you arrive home safe, and happy. Good luck!

Yours,
Carolyn Edgerton
RR #1 St. Philippe D'aqpatin
Quebec

August 7, 1980: A young reporter from Quebec writes a letter to Terry, sharing an article she wrote about their meeting: "Through our encounter I felt I had managed to uncover a larger part of the Fox story than what the headlines gave us; like the warm and personable young man behind it!"

Courtesy of the Terry Fox Centre Archives

Bonne chance, Terry! Terry speaks to a classroom during his Marathon of Hope.

Courtesy of the Terry Fox Centre Archives

HARD WORK & DISCIPLINE

"I went through fourteen months of training. Physical training. I ran three thousand miles. I trained hard, very, very hard, in order to be able to do it. But it was a mental thing more than physical. I'm not a great athlete. I'm an average athlete in terms of physical ability, I think. What I'm doing I think I'm doing because of my mental toughness, desire, wanting to achieve, and having a good goal to fight for."

— Terry Fox
Quoted in *Terry Fox: I Had a Dream* (1981 documentary)

JAY TRIANO
Friend at SFU, former NBA head coach for Toronto Raptors and Phoenix Suns

Jay graciously speaks to me via Zoom for our meeting. He is sitting in his office, wearing a white Nike polo shirt, and looking very much like the sports coach that he is. Over his shoulder, I can see a whiteboard with drawings of basketball plays. His speech is forthright, and he is considerate with the words he chooses. He enjoys talking about Terry because Terry is his inspiration in life.

In high school, Jay accepted a recruitment offer from SFU to play basketball for them once he graduated. He would get updates from the SFU coach, so he knew about all the players and about Terry's amputation. Jay flew across the country from Niagara Falls, eager and excited, before it all sunk in, and his homesickness hit him.

> I was like, "Did I make the right choice? What am I doing here?" I went into the office and Terry was in with his prosthetic leg. I finally got to meet the guy that I had heard about. I couldn't even speak. I didn't know what to say. "I'm sorry" or "Good luck"? At the time, I don't even think he had talked about running across the country and I was just — [Jay widens his eyes]. Anyways, Terry left. I said to Stan [Stewardson, the coach], "I feel really bad. I didn't know what to say." He said, "Well, don't worry about it, you'll see him every day. He's gonna be a part of our team, a student manager, and he still wants to be around the team." So, I got to see him every day. And, obviously, the connection or the friendship that we had grew from that awkward first day to me being very inspired by him.

Jay was a young player, with dreams of going to the Olympics. He knew he had to work hard to get ahead of the rest and be noticed.

> I'm going up Burnaby Mountain to practise and thinking I got everybody beat. Nobody else is working out on a Saturday. As I'm taking the bus up, I could see Terry wheeling his wheelchair up the mountain. And I was just like, hold it. My motivation, my discipline to want to do something, is paling in comparison to this guy. We get up there, I'd be shooting around in the gym, and he'd roll in drenched in sweat. And I'd be like, "What are you doing?" He goes, "I'm gonna run across the country." And I was like, "Why are you wheeling up the mountain?" He goes, "Well, my upper body, I gotta get up the mountain. It's part of my workout. I gotta use my upper body to be

able to wheel because I'm gonna have to swing my arms more than the normal person [would] to move the prosthetic leg in front of the other one." It put everything into perspective for me. And I was just inspired and extremely motivated to see all this happening.

February 23, 1981: A letter from Jay Triano to Terry Fox, saying, "You worked hard, and I couldn't understand why. I couldn't see what you were working for. All I knew was that you had more determination than me and me being competitive, that bothered me. I had lots ahead of me with the Canadian National Team and I used you and the determination you had to force myself to work harder — to get the most out of my life . . . to me you are the most important person in the world . . . you have helped me achieve more than anyone else."

Courtesy of the Terry Fox Centre Archives

Terry was a strong-willed, positive person, and Jay realized it wasn't just for the dream of running across Canada. Terry wasn't dissuaded from failure, and that ethos seeped into everything he did.

He said, "We're gonna have a dance in the east gym this Friday night for students because I need help to purchase the vehicle or to raise funds. Because I'm gonna run across the country." And we all went, "Okay yeah, yeah!" Being close to him, we were like, "We'll be there." I remember the first dance we all got together as a basketball team. He had a band, and the place was empty. I'm like, "Man, there's no way you made money, not with us basketball players being the only ones here." He goes, "Yeah, I know, I think we're gonna have another one next week because more people will find out about it." I often parallel it to his run because he never stopped trying to fundraise and have these dances. Near the end of the semester, he was right because they got more and more popular, and it became more of a thing to do. Word got around and everybody came to these things. I may be completely wrong, but I believe they became a lot more successful. They were very much like his run. It was still his little vision of a few people believing in this, and him believing more than anybody that he was going to do this. And it became what it became.

Terry wasn't on the team as a player anymore, but he was part of the family. SFU had set up the athletic complex on one side of campus, so football players, basketball players, swimmers, and wrestlers were all there together and motivated by each other. Jay feels the dreamers and those who are successful are the ones who ask every day how they are going to accomplish their dreams. What step can they take today?

Everybody's got big dreams. I have [Terry's] quote right there. [Jay raises his arm and pulls back his short sleeve to point to the tattoo he has on the upper underside, "DREAM BIG DREAMS."] Everybody's got these crazy things that they're going to do, and they talk about it. As a leader, you always talk to young kids, and I had coaches do the same: "If you have a dream, write it down, say you're going to do it. And then when you tell more people about it, you become more convicted to it." Well, Terry just kept talking about this. He was like a chapter out of a leadership book, really, as to how to make a dream come true.

Jay was travelling with the national basketball team during the Marathon of Hope, so he would get snippets of information during phone calls home. Each time, he heard that Terry was still going and getting closer and closer to B.C., to his dream.

> When he was doing it, I said, "This is my friend. He's running a marathon a day. At some point in my life, I can run a marathon. I've got to do one." And I swore I'd do it before I was forty, and I think I did it when I was forty. But one of the reasons I was motivated to do a marathon in my life was because if Terry could do it every day, I wanted to see what that was like. And man, not being able to stand up afterwards and legs seizing up — and I have two able legs. It wasn't as inspiring as what he accomplished every single day and tried to do every single day, through hills, traffic, rain.

When Jay had a week off in the summer of 1980, he was home in Niagara Falls, and it coincided with when Terry was going to be there. Jay didn't think about the Marathon; he thought about how he was going to see his friend. He went to City Hall and sat down with Terry after a small event hosted by the mayor. To Jay, they were just two friends talking, catching up on the details of their lives.

> Maybe it was a sense of just a connection, too, a sense of being able to connect with somebody because all you're doing all day long is meeting stranger after stranger and they don't know you. They didn't see all the prep, and the training, and the wheeling up the mountain to prepare for the run, and the dances that failed and then became successful. They didn't see any of that. They see a guy on the side of the road for a fifteen-minute glimpse of time. But when you know the story behind it, it's pretty crazy to think that I did get to spend some time with him on that

run. And some of the pictures I have, he and I on the steps of City Hall just talking, kind of looking at each other, and you can tell it's not about "What are we doing here in Niagara Falls?" It's "Yeah, what's going on?" We're just understanding each other.

Jay wishes they could have spent more time together that day, but Terry had to go back to Toronto, and Jay had a banquet to attend that night. Jay knew Terry was a focused and driven person, intent on making a difference with the Marathon. His determination was part of his makeup, and then his amputation and cancer made that motivation even stronger. He was never going to quit.

July 12, 1980: Jay and Terry chat on the steps of Niagara Falls City Hall during the Marathon of Hope.

Courtesy of the Terry Fox Centre Archives

You can tell when he was interviewed, even if you see old interviews now, it's never about Terry. He didn't want that. He cared more about making sure that he finished or tried to finish what he started and that he was going to be disappointed [if he] let people down. It wasn't even about letting himself down. It was more how he felt about everybody else. So, I think his relationship with people magnified the desire that he had, and you don't see this in today's athletes. It's more selfish. The word for Terry, when you're talking about him, was *selfless*.

When Terry returned to B.C. for treatment, Jay was still playing with the SFU basketball team. In the locker room, they told him Terry was in the stands. Jay ran out to go sit and talk with his friend.

And I remember sitting there talking to him, and just, "How you feeling?" and he goes, "I'm feeling good." You know, he's always still super positive and everything. And I think he asked me for an autograph. And I was just like, "Are you kidding me? You're, like, the greatest

Jay gave Terry a signed picture of him playing for the SFU basketball team. He wrote along the bottom of it, "Thank you for the inspiration — your [sic] a good friend."

Courtesy of Jay Triano

hero of all time. What are you talking about? You are one of the most famous people in Canada right now. I'm a college basketball player who's your friend; you've got Bobby Orr's autograph. You've got Darryl Sittler's autograph." I was like, "Come on, man." We just were like friends again.

He did eventually give Doug Alward a picture to personally pass on to Terry when he was back in the hospital. Jay had autographed a picture of himself in action on court with the SFU basketball team.

In 1981, Jay was at training camp with the Lakers when he got a call in his hotel room in the middle of the night. He didn't know anyone in L.A., so he wasn't sure what it could be about.

It was a TV station in Vancouver who had tracked me down. They said, "Didn't know if you were aware that Terry Fox passed away last night." And I was just like, "I wasn't." And they said, "Do you have any comment?" "I can't. I can't comment right now. I don't want to comment." I was blindsided by it. And that's how I found out.

Jay was the emcee at the unveiling of Terry's statue at SFU, and when he comes back to Canada, he is involved in the Terry Fox Run and speaks to elementary school students about Terry. He tells them that they will go through tough times, and even if something sounds impossible, try it anyways to find out.

Obviously, there was a mental toughness inside of Terry that was probably unparalleled: to never quit, to never give up on his dream, and to keep going every single day. Any goals or any challenges that I've had in my life, I use him as motivation to just keep going. Hard work and being a nice guy, I think, are two of the things that I would want people to say about me, and those are the two things that I said about Terry. I've been very blessed to have a crazy sports career, and I don't know if any of it [would have] happened without the fact that I had him as a friend and him as a light to see how to attack challenges.

DOUG ALWARD
Best friend and van driver during the Marathon

Doug is waiting for me out on his driveway on a hot, humid day in B.C. He has the build of a runner and is dressed like one, too. Not surprising for the man who became a gold medalist in the Vancouver Sun Run at age fifty-six. He lives a fairly quiet, remote life by the water and sometimes spends nights and early mornings taking long walks through the neighbourhood, undisturbed by people. Years after the Marathon of Hope, he went on to run marathons himself, and he has many bikes that he often uses for errands. He keeps so many on hand in case someone ends up stealing one — he'll just grab another. The Marathon may have

April 27, 2014: Doug runs the Vancouver Sun Run at age fifty-six, winning the gold medal.

Photo by Rita Ivanauskas

come to a stop, but the always-prepared driver of the famous van has continued to keep moving, one way or another.

Many have said that there would have been no Marathon without Doug. He was the only one who could have done it. Not the driving of the van, but the driving of Terry. Being a hard worker was as ingrained in Doug as it was in Terry. They had known each other since childhood and had a bond and an understanding of what made each other tick.

Doug and Terry in their peewee soccer team photo.
Doug stands in the middle, with Terry to the right of him.
Courtesy of the Terry Fox Centre Archives

From the soccer pictures, we are like best friends at eleven years old. And yet I don't remember anything about Terry in soccer except he was the right winger, and I was jealous at how far he could kick it, and I was a left winger. It's interesting that we latched on to each other even though we were on different ends of the city. There must have been something we saw in each other — like a determination — that hooked us together right from the very beginning. I think our values were very similar. Solid families — parents are involved as they can be, siblings that are into sports. And academically, even from grade eight, we were always getting together. I was always trying to sneak a few extra hours of studying in to beat him all the time. I didn't tell him that. Actually, he was trying to do the same thing, but I was more devilish about it. He had a purer heart than I did. We always wanted each other to become as good as we could.

They pushed each other in everything, schoolwork and sports, and got results. Their last year of high school, they tied for the Athlete of the Year award.

We were probably in the top five percent of all kids who played sports — that's how you'd rate us. It was the competitiveness!

Terry was always thinking about how to be the best, how to improve, and what was the right thing to do. He wasn't embarrassed to be the worst player on the team, sitting almost all season on the bench. It just meant he was going to keep practising and improving his skills. He had this same reaction when he got cancer. No one spoke about cancer back then, but he would. He didn't care what people thought. He was going to show what cancer does because it was the right thing to do. Doug shared when Terry called him and spoke of his plan to run across Canada.

I really didn't have any doubt in my mind that he could do it. None. I think it was in March [1979], and he phoned me to get advice. The only advice I could give him is like [as] a regular athlete: start a little bit, add a little bit every day. I thought it would take two, three years to get through the injuries. But Terry had that "one in a hundred" body that he could punish to the limit, and it wouldn't crack.

1979: Terry successfully finished all seventeen miles of the Prince George run, though he'd originally intended to run half.
Courtesy of the Fiddick family

The Prince George race was Doug's idea. It was the best run in B.C. at the time. They were sitting on the back steps of the Alwards' house, and Terry was running eight or nine miles by that point in his training with Mitch Fiddick. Doug signed up to run the 8.5-mile race. Terry said he would sign up, too, but Doug pushed him and said he was already running that in training, so he should sign up for the full seventeen miles. Doug knew Terry, and he knew he could do it. Ultimately, Terry did complete the race. It was on the drive back from Prince George, Terry driving his modified car with Doug as his passenger, that they locked eyes and knew. It was time to get ready for the run across Canada. It was just assumed that Doug would go with him on the journey — it was automatic.

Terry was very scientific about everything. He knew he couldn't just go out and run; he had to be in unbelievable shape. He knew there was hard work to be done, but he was smart about it. He talked to trainers, focused on building muscles, endurance, and strength, wheeling up mountains, rain or shine. Running wasn't just about his legs — he also needed a strong back for the punishment it was going to endure, the core strength that would be involved. He was meticulous and devoted.

Doug shares that he had no idea what he had signed up for. It took them many flights just to get to St. John's, Newfoundland. First to Penticton, then Cranbrook, Calgary, Regina, Winnipeg, Toronto, Montreal, Charlottetown, Halifax, and finally St. John's. It was stressful just to get to the starting point, and there were other realities to come. It was going to be way harder than they ever thought.

> You look at a little map and it looks all nice and rosy. Coming out of St. John's, the biggest city in Newfoundland, once you're five miles out there's not a store. Nothing. And it's winter and you're half freezing. People seem to understand that it's pretty hard to run a marathon. But it's like doing a double marathon a day when you're out there on the road. The rolling hills, the weather, and the wind. Virtually every marathon that's ever done anywhere, they pick the best time of year, the best weather, the easiest course they can possibly do. And even that's a killer for ninety-five percent of people.

There were other difficulties outside of the running, such as gathering supplies, food, and where to sleep each night. Doug believes they spent the night in people's houses for most of Newfoundland, either with Canadian Cancer Society (CCS) volunteers or total strangers who opened the door to them. And then there was being in the van together.

Even the closest of friends can get on each other's nerves. Add stress and isolation into the mix, and it was no surprise that irritation grew.

Doug feels he didn't really understand. At the time, he thought, "Well, the record is two marathons in a day for a person with two legs. So, what's the problem here?" Doug didn't see Terry walk one step. Not one. Now he knows how impossible that is, having become a marathon runner.

> I remember sitting in the van. Terry had taken off about fifty yards ahead, and some guy's standing there with money, handing it to him, and Terry yells at him. I was embarrassed to be there. But, you see, you don't understand what's going on. He's totally exhausted. I didn't really understand until I was running a marathon. I'm ten miles out, running my guts out, and the guy at the water station, hands the water to the guy ahead of me, but he doesn't have a water ready for me. I [swore] and I thought, "Oh, I understand now, Terry." It takes very little to get you irritated and totally become a different person. When I look back on it, we were two grumpy guys.

By the time they were halfway across Newfoundland, they weren't talking to each other. Just like anyone who is exhausted and crammed into a small space, it became all about the little things. Setting the alarm clock correctly, driving back to find the bag of rocks that marked the spot they had stopped at, sometimes in pouring rain, and then Doug converting the kilometres on the van odometer to 1.6093 kilometres to mark one mile, even if that meant getting as close to a cliff edge as possible. Terry wanted everything done a certain way and it had to be done that way. Doug agrees now that it did.

> I discovered this especially when I was running a marathon. Your brain is programmed, and you don't want anybody getting in your way. You're going flat out mentally, physically. If somebody wants to shake your hand, you're miserable. You don't want to shake their hand. You're in your zone. When I look back on it, I understand. His parents flew to Halifax and drove up to talk to us, because Terry phoned and said, "This isn't gonna work. We're ready to kill each other." I remember talking to Betty, and

then she'd go talk to Terry privately. We weren't getting together to discuss anything. Something's wrong, but you can't quite pinpoint it, and you almost need a mediator, sometimes, to help each of you understand how you can get back together. I knew I was miserable, sitting in that van all day, and I didn't realize how miserable he was out there running all day.

I'd get out at the end of every two miles, he'd do a mile, he'd run right by the van and at two miles, I'd be out here with a piece of orange and water. We wouldn't even talk. Things got so bad once he drank a little bit then threw the water in my face. But we were both totally miserable, and I deserved to have the water thrown in my face when I look back at it now. Because the problem was we didn't understand the hell each of us was going through.

A protective Doug watches Terry from the Marathon van as Terry prepares to set off after a break from running.

Photo by Gail Harvey

Just before they had arrived in Port aux Basques, at their midday break, a CCS volunteer, Gladys Willis, took them in at her cottage. Many runners, and their drivers, attempting to run across Canada had stopped there.

> So we stayed there, and all across Canada these runners had signed [the wall] there. And the lady said then, 'The [other] drivers had all quit by now. How come you're still going?" [Doug lets out a deep belly laugh, at the irony of it all.] Terry and I looked at each other, and we weren't talking at all then. I never forgot that old lady!

Doug recalls one time in Grand Falls, Newfoundland, when they were at dinner at another CCS representative's home. It was brought up that there were three high schools they could visit the next day, but it would be during Terry's morning break. Doug didn't want to ask Terry out loud in front of the rep, so he wrote on a piece of paper asking if Terry wanted to do that. Terry agreed. The next day, they went to the three schools, and it was good, but Terry was miserable after. Doug didn't realize how much he needed that morning break each day. But in this area of Canada, there was only one city every 150 miles — this was his only chance to try to raise funds.

> I think a lot of our problems maybe started because I thought, "Is he really running across Canada for cancer research or is he just running across Canada?" I wasn't sure in my own mind yet. I didn't know how much cancer had affected Terry because he always hid it from me when he was going through chemotherapy. He'd always put on a show, wear his blue jeans and dress up whenever we went to see him. He never talked about it to me. But after I'd seen him speak, and he'd break down and cry, I think that's when I thought cancer's bigger than the run, and that's when I got behind him. I thought, "He's willing to die for this. If he's willing to die, I'm willing to go to the limit, too."

Running with Terry

One-legged runner has pal at his side

By Leslie Scrivener Toronto Star

If old friends are gold, a friend like Doug Alward is pure platinum.

Alward is a soft-spoken, publicity-shy 21-year-old who has been thrown into the spotlight as driver-companion to his childhood friend, Terry Fox.

Alward was by Fox's side when doctors told him his right leg, infected with cancer, would have to be amputated from above the knee.

That was three years ago and he's at Fox's side today, as patient and faithful a friend as anyone could wish for.

Alward drives the van accompanying Fox on his 5,200-mile run across Canada, raising funds for the Canadian Cancer Society. Already, Fox has achieved what many thought would be impossible: He's at mile 1,711, just 80 miles east of Montreal, and by early next week he will have completed one-third the distance across Canada.

But Alward is much more than a driver. He's learning to be a publicist for Fox. He swallows his natural reticence and bravely phones radio stations and newspapers, asking for support for the run. It's agony for someone who would rather be in a quiet corner reading a good novel, but, as he says, "I made a commitment to do this and I'm doing it."

Plans daily schedule

He's also becoming an organizer, planning Fox's daily schedules and making sure he's at his fund-raising appointments at the right time.

Alward is giving up his next semester at Simon Fraser University (where he plans to study to be an elementary school teacher) because no one expected it would take Fox such a long time to cross Canada. At his pace of about 28 miles a day, it's unlikely they'll reach their Port Coquitlam, B.C., home before October.

Alward, who worked as a psychiatric aide before joining Fox on this journey, says he has never been outside of British Columbia and that it's the chance of a lifetime to see the rest of Canada.

He may be seeing Canada, but he's seeing it very, very slowly. He drives the van at a pensioner's pace or drives a few miles ahead and waits for Fox to catch up. It's tedious, but gives him a chance to read a mountain of books. Appropriately, the most recent was *Intrepid* by William Stevenson.

Both Fox and Alward are anxious to arrive in Ontario. Besides fighting the wind, Fox is running in virtual anonymity in Quebec. No one knows who he is or why he is running.

As a result, pledges are merely trickling in. They raised only $35 in running 100 miles, which takes about four days.

Offered a ride

"A lot of cars have stopped and offered him a ride and asked if something is wrong with him," Alward says.

The poor fund-raising of the past week has been very disappointing for Fox and he's the sort who usually bubbles with an enthusiasm that would leave Dale Carnegie speechless.

"You know, anyone can get cancer, I'm running across Canada and Quebec is a province in Canada," he says. "With me it isn't political or racial. I'm just a human being and cancer can strike anyone and I'm trying to help everyone on my run."

Fox is continually cheered by news of Ontarians' innovative fund-raising efforts on his behalf. He learned this week that Toronto's Take One Singers, led by Nancy Ryan, are recording a song for him — Run, Terry, Run. Written by Vern Kennedy, the song will be distributed to radio stations on Fox's route in Ontario and Quebec.

All royalties from the single will be donated to Fox.

Anyone wishing to support any of the fund-raising activities in his name should phone the Canadian Cancer Society at 923-7474 or write 185 Bloor St. E. Toronto, M4W 3G5. Donations can also be made through the Four Seasons Hotel. In Toronto, phone 445-5051 or the toll free number of 1-800-268-6282.

The Star is carrying a report on Terry's progress every Friday in the Family section.

Commitment: Doug Alward, right, swallows natural reticence to publicize Terry Fox's run.

It was difficult to comprehend what he was doing, but once people saw him, they understood. To Doug and the country watching, it wasn't just about cancer. Terry was demonstrating that everybody struggles, but you can try a little harder to push through those challenges. That's why the Terry Fox Run is still going today and why it's so entrenched in the school system. The concept that anyone can be capable of incredible feats, like Terry and the athletes he was inspired by, has resonated deeply with people all over the world.

> It inspires you to be better, too, doesn't it? That's why I think it's so neat that when his family has gone around [to communities], Betty always made a point of saying, "He's just like you. Everybody's got some gifts to give. You've got to find what you're gifted in, and you can do amazing things." Not everybody can be a runner or a basketball player. I think the message is "Don't limit yourself."

Doug never doubted that Terry could run across Canada. He knew when Terry said he was going to do something, he'd do it. He saw the awe that Terry produced in people all along the roads, but Doug didn't feel the same awe. To him, this was Terry. It was always what he had done, even though it was the most extraordinary thing anyone had seen or done before.

Doug is a Christian, and he knows Terry believed in God. He knew Terry was reading the Bible,

A June 20, 1980, *Toronto Star* article by journalist Leslie Scrivener describes Doug's crucial support in Terry's journey.

although he didn't know where Terry had it hidden in the van, and they never really spoke about it. When Terry died, Doug went to see his body; it felt important to him.

> I touched the body, and all of a sudden, it's not an audible voice, but it's a voice that penetrates right to your soul. I started laughing. Terry was laughing, and Terry said, "I'm up here, Doug." It was so powerful. Even Leslie Scrivener [the *Toronto Star* reporter who covered the run] commented at the funeral the next week, "How come you're so happy, Doug?" It's hard to explain. It's like you've experienced heaven.

GARTH WALKER & JIM BROWN
Cyclists who biked from Toronto to Ottawa to raise money for the Marathon of Hope

Garth Walker had gotten heavily into cycling after meeting a promising young cyclist in Hawaii in January of 1980. This man loved cycling but was tragically hit by a truck and was now a quadriplegic. He implored Garth to discover the magic of the sport, so he threw himself into it, changing his diet, exercise, and habits to get into the best shape of his life.

In the spring of 1980, he wrote to his friends that he would be visiting Toronto. He told his friend in Kingston, Jim Brown, to get out on a bike, and when Garth arrived, he bought a new bike, sturdy and built for touring. They decided to ride from Kingston to Ottawa to visit with Jim's brother. They felt exhilarated, with Jim saying to Garth, "I need more of this."

> Garth: The next day we started out on our adventure — making it up as we went along. We settled on riding up to Mount Tremblant. It was a painful trek, but we were young and seemed to ride ourselves into shape. The day we

left Tremblant we happened upon the autoroute highway, which was a direct route to Montreal. It had a very inviting wide shoulder, so we decided to take it. Riding down that mountain highway felt like we were flying. We were going so fast we were passing cars. Every time we came to a French-Canadian toll booth, the operator would jump out and wave his arms frantically at us as we flew past them without stopping. Jim just said, "Smile and wave back at them."

They ended up at the Four Seasons, walking into the ornate lobby in cycling shorts, carrying their bikes on their shoulders. They didn't have a lot of money, so Jim talked the staff into allowing them to stay the night in a meeting room with a pull-out couch and an extra cot. The next morning, when they were at the checkout desk, Garth saw the Terry Fox Marathon of Hope poster asking for support.

Garth: The poster was a call for people to organize their own community events and spread the word and hype about Terry's Marathon of Hope. I remember Jim's reaction being something like, "I've run marathons, and it took a lot out of me. He's running one every day on one leg." It seemed unbelievable to us, but then we came to the conclusion that he must be doing it, otherwise why would a hotel of this stature be promoting it? We were totally stunned by what we had just read.

On their ride back to Kingston, they kept talking about Terry Fox. They were brainstorming ideas for how they could help. They parted ways in Kingston, and Garth continued to Belleville to his aunt Shirley's farmhouse. On Highway 2, he had an epiphany. They could spread the word that Terry was coming by riding from Toronto to Ottawa in just twenty-four hours. The next morning, he called Jim, who assured him he was on board. His aunt, who was the past president of the local CCS chapter, called the group in Toronto to let them know of Garth's idea.

Garth: Shirley was a force to be reckoned with, and she wanted them to listen to the idea. Next, I had to face calling my dad. That was a really tough one. As soon as I told him, he was really exasperated. My dad was vice president of corporate affairs for Gulf Oil, and all this time off work wasn't sitting well with him. "Son, you need to stop this. That's impossible! Why would you want to do that? You could really hurt yourself!" It was a total beat-down of the idea, but I knew it was because he cared so much about my well-being. I wasn't even sure at that point whether we could do it, but Jim and I had done some calculations and figured that it was possible, and we were up for this gonzo act. That was the name we gave crazy physical challenges back then.

In Toronto, with an enthusiastic Bill Vigars at their side, they did the publicity circuit. They were introduced to Leslie Scrivener from the *Toronto Star*, and Garth felt he was among the Terry Fox disciples.

They set up in Nathan Phillips Square, and it seemed any roadblock was removed for them. They wanted to collect donations and have people sign a giant roll of paper with personal messages, so the City allowed for an exemption to the no-solicitation rule in the square, and the mayor came out to cut the ribbon. They had flags, donation boxes, and tables with the help of volunteers from the CCS.

Garth: One of the most moving things for me was when I spotted my dad walking across City Hall with his executive secretary in tow offering to help that day. Then he told me that he had asked for

June 26, 1980: Garth and Jim pose at Toronto City Hall with a Marathon of Hope poster after collecting pledges.

Photo by Colin McConnell via Getty Images

a special meeting of the directors at Gulf Oil to get Terry $1,000 of gas for Terry's van, and sure enough he got it. Well, the response was unbelievable from the people of Toronto. They came in droves to support Terry. We stood there day after day with our bikes speaking to people who often had their own cancer stories. As Jim would often say, "Cancer will touch someone you know in your lifetime." I recall one man endorsing his paycheque and putting it in the box after telling me about his family's ordeal. It was one of the most memorable and moving experiences in my life to see that outpouring of love for Terry.

They continued to promote their ride, but in doing so, they hadn't left much time to train *for* the ride. They were a little concerned, but as planned they started off on the afternoon of June 30, 1980, with support vehicles in tow. They were supposed to have a westerly wind as they headed east, but instead faced a headwind, then rain, then sleet and hail. Garth remembers Jim calling out into the sky at one point, "Is that all you've got?"

In Belleville, they stopped at the Bay of Quinte golf course where Aunt Shirley had organized a reception. Garth headed straight for the shower, standing under hot water in all his riding gear until he stopped shaking. Then they hit the road again.

Garth: Now we turned north to Smiths Falls and that's when things got grim. I can't recall the hour, but suddenly Jim was saying "Scream at me" as he weaved along the road. Jim was on a thyroid replacement, and he wasn't doing well. Then my right knee, where I had an operation ten years previously, suddenly became extremely painful. The pain was so intense that I couldn't put any pressure on the pedal. Peter Kingston, one of Jim's friends was hanging out the window holding a Terry Fox poster and screaming, "*He's* not going to quit! Are you going to quit?" That worked.

Jim then came up with an idea to duct tape my right foot to the pedal and just use my left foot to pull up and push down. That night was really bleak. It was a really difficult ride in those early hours of the morning. My next memory was the team calling out regular distances now that we were approaching Ottawa and then the police escort to the Four Seasons. The duct tape idea had worked incredibly well. The pain let up, and somehow, we got there just under the twenty-four-hour wire.

Everything was a blur after that until they met Terry. All the pain was worth it to meet their hero. They went up to release some balloons from the roof of the hotel, and then they sat down to dinner with Terry.

Before Terry left to do the kickoff at the Ottawa Rough Riders game, he asked the two to join him on his

July 1, 1980: Terry and team release balloons off the roof of the Four Seasons Hotel in Ottawa.

Published in *Terry Fox* by Jeremy Brown and Gail Harvey

run in the morning. Garth was excited but was unsure he would be able to do it with his knee. A determined Jim woke him the next morning, pounding on the door, drinking coffee mixed with granola and honey, a concoction they had developed for their ride. Jim describes it as the "original power sports drink." They let Terry set the pace, which was fine with Garth who wasn't sure he was even going to keep up. Jim was a runner and had done marathons, but he was still exhausted from the bike ride the previous day.

> Jim: I mean, we were pretty darn tired. But it's one of those things where something happens to your energy and you just go, and then you crash later. He was a sturdy, doggedly determined guy. Pleasant, but not wasting a lot of energy on anything other than moving and keeping the message going. That's how he struck me.

July 1, 1980: Jim Brown and Terry meet.

Photo by Richard Walker

When they had run seventeen miles and stopped at a diner, everyone was cheering. Garth went to the bathroom and had a good cry. It was an intensely emotional experience. Later, they were asked to join Terry on the run down to Nathan Phillips Square. They watched Darryl Sittler present his jersey to Terry, then met the Fox family at the Four Seasons. The last time Garth saw Terry was in Gravenhurst on Terry's birthday, July 28. He was there with his brother and a friend, and they had brought a cake, one of several Terry received that day, which led to an eventual cake fight.

Jim doesn't think what he and Garth did was that amazing. He's travelled the world and has seen people go through horrible things, facing challenges we couldn't even imagine, just to get through life. If we're talking real guts to keep you going, what they did wasn't even close. To this day, Jim believes in taking action, his attention now having turned to climate change.

Jim: It starts here. [He points emphatically to his chest.] There's no one coming, and I think that whatever it was in Terry, he said, "This is what has to happen; this is what I have to do. Nobody else is going to do it." Despite all the discouragement and physical pain and discomfort, he kept doing it, and that's the challenge of life: pick it up, put another foot in front of the other. And if you do, others will, too. There are others that struggle to do that, but if you do that, and you hang out with people who do that, we give each other strength.

Those are acts of love, and love is a verb. As they say, if you're gonna pray, you've got to move your feet — and that man moved his feet. And there is another choice, and that is you capitulate to whatever life throws at you.

July 1, 1980: Terry, Garth, and Jim chat in Ottawa.

Published in *Terry Fox* by Jeremy Brown and Gail Harvey

The two were incredibly moved by their time with Terry, and Garth shared just how deeply it impacted him.

> Garth: Terry gave me many gifts — strength when I didn't have it, focus when I needed it, and awareness of the need to help others who are less fortunate than I am. He showed me how to conquer tasks that seemed impossible and reinforced my belief to speak up when confronted with other people's incorrect assumptions. I have so much respect for what Terry achieved in following his dream.
>
> I asked him how he attacked such a large task as running across Canada. Terry said that he looked at each day as twenty-six pieces. He would have his best friend, Doug, drive the van one mile and he would run to the van. Terry said that one day, Doug drove over a bridge out east because it was too dangerous to stop, and he got really mad because it was more than one mile. That's how amazing Terry's focus was. He knew the number of steps it

was for one mile. For the past forty-three years, every time I have had a large task in front of me, that's how I have attacked it. Terry gave me so much that I am thankful for.

MATTHEW REID
Terry Fox Foundation volunteer in Australia

Matthew and I connect over the phone, after navigating the drastic time difference between us. He is *the* Terry Foxer in Australia, and he has taken it upon himself to be the person who will ensure that Terry, and his message, stay alive on his continent. He starts by sharing how he first saw Terry: on television, of course.

> In June 1981, *Wide World of Sports* started in Australia. I walked inside my house, looked at the TV, and saw this guy running on a prosthetic leg. I sat down and watched the whole story. I just couldn't believe what I was seeing; I was glued to the TV. And then I heard that the run had stopped. When the story was out, Terry hadn't died yet. I knew that he got off the road because the cancer returned, and I remember feeling that was a shame, not having the full gravity of what was happening because I was only thirteen. So, I went outside and played and forgot about the story. Thirty-five years later, I picked up a *Reader's Digest* magazine, opened it up, and I saw his name and his picture on there. I knew straight away what it was and who it was and where I saw it. I couldn't believe it. I said to my wife at the time, "I remember watching him run as a boy."

He read the article and then went online to find more information and videos. Becoming an athlete himself, Matthew understands the physical achievement and effort Terry's Marathon required.

> I'm a former fighter, and I appreciate gutsy efforts, hard work, and dedication — doing things that are impossible.

Just reading about Terry was amazing enough that it inspired me to run from Melbourne to Sydney in 2015. It's nine hundred kilometres, give or take. I organized talking to schools on the way up, talked about Terry, and then I finished the run and raised about $35,000 in his name. Then I started trying to get with politicians to get the Terry Fox story in schools to inspire the kids, and I hit a dead end. Politicians talking rubbish, as per usual. But that was okay because I'm stubborn in my sport. When I believe in something, I don't give up very easy. So, in 2018, I was able to organize my own Terry Fox event for the community.

Matthew started a Facebook page for the Terry Fox Run and held his first event in 2018 in a suburb of Sydney. Three hundred and fifty people attended. The next year, he went to the Canadian consulate in Sydney and got a big Canadian flag. He organized a school band, and they played the national anthems of Canada and Australia. About five hundred people participated in 2019, and for both years he raised around $20,000. Speaking to students in schools, he shares how Terry ran with a weakened heart and a prosthetic leg weighing six kilograms, and the reason why he did it and kept going.

When I do the school Runs, I say, "You kids are well and healthy, and we're all going to do something to raise money for sick kids your age." It's this spirit of Terry Fox, his achievements, and his legacy. Adults are there, too, when I'm talking, but I try to direct everything to the kids.

Matthew visits a school in Australia, raising awareness of Terry's story.
Courtesy of Matthew Reid

Many of them have never seen Terry Fox, the Marathon, the story. Matthew knows they don't believe him when they hear it for the first time, thinking that he is exaggerating.

> That's the beauty of it. People don't believe it. And then what happens, I'll put footage on of Terry, the whole story, and they are glued to the TV screen. They cannot believe it. Every time, I have a Terry Fox shirt on [when I talk to them]. He's been my inspiration as a fifty-five-year-old. You can still be inspired, and you can always check yourself when you have a bad time or you're getting a bit loose. Anyways, he always checks me. He always puts me back on the right track, because there's more important things in life, and he's made me a better person.

Matthew considers this his life's work. COVID forced him go virtual, but he was still raising donations, and because of him thousands of people have become intrigued by Terry and learned about his story.

Darrell Fox and Matthew pose after hiking Mount Cheam in Chilliwack, British Columbia.

Courtesy of Matthew Reid

> I'm just glad that they see for themselves why I'm doing what I'm doing. It's one of the best stories you'll ever hear, and I feel like he's one of the greatest athletes of all time. I wish the Americans would acknowledge that a bit more, but what he did is top shelf and it's right up there. I think, personally, it should be told all around the world. He was the only person in history to do what he did, and even doing it on two legs is terribly hard.

As a boxer, Matthew has sustained his own share of injuries, and he drew on Terry to overcome those. But he feels he is like Terry in the sense that he doesn't give up. In 2017, he went to B.C. and stayed with Terry's brother Darrell Fox for a few days. Darrell took him on the Terry Fox tour to see where Terry trained and went to school. They also did a lot of walking, running, and climbing, which gave Matthew the time to ask Darrell about some of the details of the run.

> When I did Melbourne to Sydney and I was training, I used to have ice baths, massages, because I was forty-seven at the time. I said, "Did Terry do anything?" And [Darrell] goes, "Nope." He had junk food. No massaging. No ice baths. None of that. The shoes were average at the time, so it shows you even more what he did because he did nothing to help himself each day, in the sense of being loose for the next day or stretching and all this sort of stuff. He just ran and that's it.

Matthew will continue his work of sharing Terry's story and motivating people. He says it's hard work, but he knows how many people can be helped or inspired to get through their troubles. He wants his fundraiser to get bigger and bigger every year. He had the acting high commissioner for Canada, Isabelle Martin, present when he finished his 2022 walk in Canberra. Since it was featured on TV, he feels now that the Canadians in Australia recognize what he is doing and will help it grow.

Matthew and acting high commissioner Isabelle Martin after the Canberra Terry Fox Run in 2022.
Courtesy of Matthew Reid

> That's my goal. I don't muck around. I don't take any nonsense either. I don't like to hear no. I'll always find a way. I wrote something once, I said, "What Terry does just shows you that everything is possible. So don't say no."

June 27: Day 77 (22 miles) Today I ran to the exit that goes to Hawkesbury, Ontario. The miles went easy and fast. I did 12 in the morning when there was very little traffic. Then I did numerous phone calls. I had a police escort in the afternoon and boy did I need it. A lot of people honked, waved, and gave money. At night we went back to the hotel in Lachute. Then I spent 45 minutes [driving the van] finding the Ottawa river.

June 29: Day 79 (26 miles) Today CBC was there to film as I walked out the door at 4:30 a.m. They followed me for the first 10 miles then left me for the last 2. I ran very, very well. Felt really good, no wind and not hot or cold. I took a break during which I couldn't sleep, too hot, then tore through 14 more miles. I made it through Cumberland County. I had tremendous support from the OPP. It was easy for me because I didn't have to worry about traffic.

July 1: Day 81 (15 miles) I was sore and tired because I didn't sleep last night. I took a break at 7 miles and then did 8 more. After that I went to the Ottawa/Saskatchewan football game where I kicked off the opening ball to a standing ovation.

July 2: Day 82 (20 miles) Today I ran with Garth [Walker] and Jim [Brown] in the morning run — I did 10 ½ miles. After that I did 9 ½ more miles then met Mr. Trudeau. It was an honour, and he is a very nice man. I needed more repairs on my leg — my stump is 2" wider than my leg.

July 2, 1980: Terry meets Prime Minister Pierre Elliott Trudeau.

From the Canadian Press

July 1, 1980: Terry shakes the hand of Rough Riders' tight end Tony Gabriel.

July 3, 1980: Terry runs past the Peace Tower of the Parliament Buildings in Ottawa.

Young hero welcomed to Ontario

By Leslie Scrivener Toronto Star

HAWKESBURY, Ont. — It didn't matter that the Welcome to Ontario sign had fallen down and stayed down.

It didn't matter that the brass band played Georgie Girl off key.

It didn't matter that MP Albert Bélanger goofed by describing Terry Fox's 3,200-mile cross-Canada run as a walk.

What did matter was that Fox had crossed the Perley Bridge into Ontario. He was flanked by two flag-bearers and was welcomed with thousands of balloons, cheers, and hip-hoorays from a crowd of about 200.

They were touched by what they saw: A small, sun-burnt young man with a glorious crop of curly brown hair running on one muscular leg and one artificial leg. Gritty determination and concentration were carved on his face. There was no doubt, every step was a struggle.

No one's immune

They were also touched as they heard the story of his battle with cancer: "One morning I woke up and the pain in my leg was so bad I couldn't get out of bed. The next day doctors told me I had a malignant tumor and in four days I'd have to have my leg amputated. Losing my leg was never a problem, going through cancer was a lot harder and no one is immune to it, nobody here, nobody in Hawkesbury."

The effect was spell-binding. The crowd, mostly families, was silent. Men and women stared at, the greased Children's eyes grew large and fixed on the 21-year-old speaker from Port Coquitlam, B.C.

I've spoken to Fox regularly on the telephone for the past 2½ months, since he left St. John's, Nfld. and this was our first meeting. I travelled with him Saturday and Sunday in a van driven by his friend, Doug Alward, 21, and his brother, Darrell, 17, through Hawkesbury, L'Orignal, Plantagenet, and Rockland, Ont.

My first impression was obvious. Fox seemed so small and the country so enormous, how could he do it? On closer look I knew how. He was putting so much of his heart and soul into every step I knew someone would have to tie him down to stop him from running.

Since our first conversation in April I'd been thinking about his impossible dream, even dreaming about his run in my sleep.

When we met I suspect I had the same feelings as the L'Orignal motel keeper who solemnly shook Fox's hand and said, "Sir, it's a pleasure to meet you."

He has that effect on people. The boys from the Fournier Vets peewee baseball team proudly presented Fox with their $6. They were simply unnerved. The organizers of the Plantagenet fair got together and raised a couple of hundred dollars to put a few hours. Blushing teenage girls wanted his autograph and I'm sure they noticed he has the same good looks as a young Paul Newman. Pensioners threw in $10 and wanted an autograph too.

What was most inspiring yesterday was the sight of Fox, who seems more frail, and boyish than

Running with Terry

in his photographs, pushing himself hard along Rockland's main street. It was lined with people who had poured out of their houses, drawn by the wailing of Ontario Provincial Police sirens. Their cruisers are escorting him through Ontario and protecting him from erratic highway drivers.

The day had begun early; we were on highway 17 at 4:20 a.m. yesterday. Fox lay in the back of the van, wrapped in a sleeping blanket. No one spoke, but we looked at the night sky and the moon shaded by clouds and wondered what the day would hold.

By 4:45 Fox was running on the deserted road. We slipped ahead in the van exactly one mile to a marker so he knows exactly how far he has to run. It was his favorite time of day.

"I really enjoy these mornings," Fox said. "There's no wind and there's no one around. It's not hot and not cold. I'm on my own. There's nobody to talk to to block my concentration."

As he ran, we listened to his favorite Hank Williams tape featuring, Your Cheatin' Heart and Jambalaya. He said he would take a drink of water after 5 miles.

At his breaks Fox was even more tense than usual. He would drink the water and maybe have a quick "tube," an application of skin cream to ease the chafing of the belt attached to his artificial limb.

Mental toughness

While I had known of Fox's very strong will, I wasn't prepared for his mental toughness. He comes from the armed forces' accomplishments in life are the result of steady, sweaty hard work, not natural gifts.

He did well in high school graduating with straight A's and one B, because he memorized and studied hard. He did well in sports because he tried harder than anyone else.

"I'm just an average athlete," Fox said during his breakfast break after he'd run 12 miles. He lit into a bowl of cereal, a couple of weiners and peanut butter sandwiches, a tin of beans — "they give me a lot of energy" — and a soft drink.

"It's more effort than ability. I was on a basketball team in Grade 8 and I played for one minute of one game for the whole season. When I got on the floor, everybody laughed at me, I kept working and made second string, then first string, then I was on the Junior Varsity team at Simon Fraser University."

He was taught by his parents, Betty and Rolly, to be hard working and competitive. He inherited a little extra stubbornness from his father, a Canadian National switchman.

"When we were kids, my older brother, Fred, and I used to have fights with my dad. We really fought dirty," Fox said. "We'd be hurling our eyes out, but we'd come back for more. Even to get

one more shot in, it was worth it."

Fox wants to set an example, to show the rest of us that human endeavor is worth something and that we all have a part to play.

"Man is supposed to be an intelligent species. Yet we keep polluting the earth, we're heading right into a war, we seem to want to wipe

ourselves off the earth and no one is doing anything about it.

"That bothers me. Everyone seems to have given up hope of trying. I haven't. It isn't easy. It isn't supposed to be. But I'm accomplishing something . . . so many people are thinking about themselves. You might say I'm a

dreamer, but how many people would have thought I could run across Canada?"

Fox says he can run the distance. "That doesn't mean I will, but I know I can. I've made it this far." For once, his usually sombre face isn't lined with concentration and he breaks into a joyful grin.

It isn't easy: Determination shows on the face of Terry Fox, the 21-year-old cancer victim who's running across Canada to show that human endeavor is worth something. His mental toughness helped him adjust to losing his leg to a tumor.

Hero's welcome: Young runner Terry Fox crossed from Quebec into Ontario at Hawkesbury yesterday. He was flanked by two flag-bearers and was welcomed by thousands of balloons and cheers from a crowd of about 200 people. OPP cruiser will escort him.

A June 30, 1980, *Toronto Star* article by journalist Leslie Scrivener describes Terry's entry into Ontario. He arrived in Hawkesbury to enthusiastic supporters ready to cheer him on.

SUPPORT

"They told me I had a malignant tumour and I had to have my leg removed in four days. It was a terrible shock, but I had encouragement and support from all kinds of people. So right from the beginning, I decided to do my best and show people what can be done on one leg. I would try to run across Canada and raise as much money as I could. You know, sometimes I have to run in a lot of pain, and I get pretty tired, but I don't feel any pain when I get support like this. You're fabulous and I'd like to thank you for that."

— Terry Fox
Speech in Grand Falls-Windsor, Newfoundland, April 23, 1980

DONNA BALL
Pen pal and former worker at the Canada Games for the Physically Disabled

Right at the beginning of our Zoom interview, Donna apologizes in case she becomes too emotional. It has been many years since she met Terry, and she is a grandmother now, but it still makes her tear up. Sitting at her computer in her home office, I can see she is wearing glasses and has short, cropped hair. She is unassuming, and when she smiles, you can still see a dimple at the corner of her mouth.

Her relationship with Terry started in 1978, two years before the Marathon. On Terry's first visit to Newfoundland, he was representing British Columbia at the Canada Games for the Physically Disabled. St. John's was the host that summer, and Donna, eighteen at the time, had gotten her first summer job working the event registration. The headquarters were on Memorial University's campus, and they had set up four long tables for the players to register at. The B.C. team was the first to arrive, and with the greatest luck of her life, Terry stepped up to her registration desk. He was with Dan Wesley, who was a double amputee. Terry was in jeans and walked well, and Dan was in a wheelchair.

> They're both very good-looking young men. So that sort of sticks out in your mind, and I think Dan is probably about the same age as Terry. I remember both of them having a lot of fun with each other. Terry was shyer than Dan — Dan did most of the talking. But in the meantime, there was a charisma about Terry. You could tell, even though he was shy. And they both obviously had a sense of humour because they were joking back and forth. I don't even remember what they said, just them laughing so much. And of course, I was doing my Newfoundland and Labrador thing where you're welcoming, [and] everybody is friendly. Throughout the games, I saw Terry a couple of more times.

Having met so many wonderful people, to keep in touch, Donna went through the files and found the addresses and phone numbers of a bunch of athletes — a time when privacy issues weren't in the minds of many. She wrote twelve letters, handwritten on nice stationery, and two people wrote back. One was Terry.

> He didn't write me for six months, and in that first letter, he explains why it took him that long to write back. He also talks about how he has begun training, but he doesn't

explain what for, [and shares] details about the lead-up to his running and training. He did talk a lot about his cancer experience in the letters and how the experiences of being in the hospital really changed him, in particular seeing children with cancer. The thing about these letters is that they were written in the spring of 1979, so they predate the letters that he would have written to Adidas and Ford Canada to ask for support. You know, he was not a famous person. For me, he was a friend on the west coast of Canada writing letters back and forth, just talking about things young adults talked about. And I kept those letters, obviously at the time having no idea what would become of him, or what those letters would mean, or what his life would mean.

The writing stopped in 1979, but in 1980, they reconnected. He had returned to St. John's and was training in the days leading up to the run. The local paper had printed an article and a photo, and her mom said, "Isn't that the fella you used to write letters to?" There was no "Marathon of Hope" in the media at this point. He was still just the person she met a few years ago.

Donna called the Canadian Cancer Society (CCS) to find out where Terry was, and they told her the Holiday Inn, so she called there and was connected with Terry. She doesn't recall if he invited her, or if she invited herself, but on the night of April 11, the day before the Marathon began, she knocked on their door. Doug Alward answered, and he was extraordinarily shy, but she sensed the relationship between him and Terry was special, full of loyalty and protection.

Terry and I sat and talked. Overlooking the window of the hotel, you could look out to the street below. Doug was sort of hovering around, protecting almost. And, of course, I always refer to Doug as Canada's greatest unsung hero. We think of Terry, but Terry could not have done what he did without Doug for sure. So, we sat there in the hotel room. Terry just talked about what he was doing, and why he was about to run across Canada on one leg. And he did speak about children that evening again; he had done that in the second letter. I'll just read that quote: "I really love kids, too. They are so carefree and lovable, without any worries in the world. Quite often, when I am running, kids will run and ride their bikes along-side me. They are always full of questions and encourage-ment for me." So, it's very clear, even as early as the spring of '79, that children played a very big role in the Marathon of Hope.

That night felt normal to her. This man was going to run across Canada on one leg, but the enormity of that didn't sink in. She thinks it's partly because Terry had the feeling of invincibility as a young man, but it was also that he was so deter-mined. There was a confidence and a conviction.

Nothing will stop him

Terry Fox has decided to run across Canada and nothing will stop him, even the loss of one leg. Three years ago Terry was told he had cancer in his leg, and three days later it was removed. After seeing the suffering of other patients he decided to raise money to help them. As a result, he will be leaving St. John's this Satur-day on a "Marathon of Hope" run for the Cancer Society and those who wish to make pledges can contact the nearest Cancer Society office.

April 10, 1980: This article in the *Evening Telegram* brought to Donna's attention Terry's plans.

From Saltwire, *Evening Telegram*

I think the biggest thing, though, is this kind of integ-rity of purpose that was there from the beginning to the end. He never wavered from that. Despite the early days, when there wasn't a lot of interest; despite the alleged or presumed negative reaction he had in some areas, particu-larly Quebec he would say sometimes. Despite all the heat, the summer, all those things, he never wavered from what I call the integrity of his purpose. And he didn't that night in the hotel room. It wasn't like, "Oh, I hope I make it," or "I don't know. I'm gonna give it a try." There was none of that. It was just his confidence that "I'm doing this."

Before leaving that night, Donna asked if they needed anything. They told her that they planned to collect pennants from everywhere they visited, and they had some from Newfoundland and Labrador but none that said *St. John's*. So the next morning, having never been in souvenir shops as a local, Donna went on the hunt for a pennant.

> I went driving all over downtown St. John's, trying to find a souvenir shop! So, I did find one, and I immediately saw one right up above the cash register, and I just shouted, "I need that pennant right there!" I bought that, went up to a shopping district called Churchill Square, and purchased a good luck card, and then I drove back to the hotel. Doug and Terry were outside in the parking lot with the van, loading things in and getting ready to go on. This is the morning of April 12 now. They gave me what I call a "tour" of the van. Bucket seats in the front, everything was sort of brown and orange, wood panelling, shag carpet, plaid seats. It was a camper van, so it didn't look like a luxury vehicle or anything like that.

In 1980, driving down Temperance Street in St. John's, you could literally drive into the harbour. It's technically where the Trans-Canada Highway starts and was chosen as Mile Zero, where Terry dipped his foot in the Atlantic Ocean. Donna recalls the road up from the water being so steep that it seemed impossible for a man with one leg to make it up. If Terry could do that, then he could probably make it across Canada. He ran the first mile to City Hall, in an area which is now often referred to as Mile One.

Donna was there with about thirty or forty people. There were volunteers, CCS representatives, and locals, all curious, amazed, and applauding. The flag was raised, and the mayor, Dorothy Wyatt, ceremoniously put her robe of office on Terry.

> At the time, I just thought this was an eccentric thing, to throw a robe on somebody. Years later, I came to understand it was quite different. She was a nurse before she was a mayor. It was so cold that day. I believe now that's

why she put the robe on him, to warm him up a little bit before he was going to head out on the highway. Terry had on a pair of shorts and a long shirt with a T-shirt over it. It was part of Terry wanting to show amputees in the mainstream. In 1980, you didn't see amputees' prosthetic limbs, and he wanted people to witness that. He advanced that issue but also kind of advanced parasports, too. We think of him as fundraising for cancer research, but there's so many other things that he advanced in the way we think and the way society is.

After he removed the robe and continued his run, Mayor Wyatt ran behind him for a while. Then Donna got in her dad's car and slowly drove behind him. She tooted her horn, waved goodbye, and he was on his way. He waved back to her, and she never saw him in person again.

A couple of days later, my dad was driving from Gander, coming home from a business trip at 5:30 in the morning, and he saw Terry on the highway running in the snow. This time with long pants on, a toque, and gloves. I mean, Terry had no idea what Newfoundland weather might be like in April. And as soon as Dad got home, he told me, "Oh, I saw Terry out there!"

I just became this sort of media junkie. I started listening to the radio every day and television every night to follow the news, collecting every newspaper clipping I could find. I started a scrapbook, and then a second scrapbook, a third scrapbook. I ended up with a suitcase full of various things, just kept following him all summer, really. Then along comes September 1, 1980; things are brought to a halt, and I remember being incredibly angry. I watched the news, and I wanted to throw something at the TV. At that point, I went back to the way I had known Terry, and that was writing letters.

Donna knew he was probably getting thousands of letters from people, expressing their sadness and support for his second fight against cancer.

I decided to do something totally different, so I wrote him letters as if we were just continuing from 1979. My letters were things about what university courses I was taking, dance classes, my part-time job. I just wanted to normalize his life in some way. I think I wrote thirteen letters over that period. In my mind I kept thinking, "Oh, one day he'll write," but of course, he never wrote. I did get a letter from his mother eventually and met his family. His mother and I corresponded over the years, and we met a number of times in person.

When it was the twenty-fifth anniversary of the Marathon, the whole Fox family was in St. John's for the celebration and unveiling of a Terry Fox special edition loonie.

At the end of Betty's speech, she went over and sat down with her family. The proceedings were closing, and I went over and said hello to her. "Hi, do you remember me?" I had not spoken to this woman in nineteen or twenty years, and she, meanwhile, had been all over the country meeting hundreds of thousands of people. I'll never forget it. She stood back, she looks me up and down, and she goes, "Donna?!" She definitely remembered me. The other interesting reaction that day was Doug Alward. I went over to him, and I said, "Do you remember me?" And he said, "No." Very quiet, very shy. And I said, "Well, I met you on April 11, 1980." And he wanted to correct me and say, "No, April 12," and I said, "No, no, I went to the Holiday Inn." And suddenly a light bulb went on, and his eyes — it was just phenomenal to watch his face. He goes, "Oh, my God. I do remember you. I remember you coming to the hotel."

Donna's children have been involved with the Terry Fox Run since they were infants. When she was invited to the announcement of a Terry Fox statue being installed at Mile Zero (as a result of her letter to Environment Canada requesting such), she pulled her younger kids out of school to be there. Normally, she wouldn't do that for anything

Many people donated money for me to continue school, and for instance my university team played my old high school team in a benefit game.

With help from so many people I had always a positive attitude towards the outcome of treaments and I was able to go on living happily despite the circumstances. I have know been off treatment for a full year. My hair grew in curly when before it was straight. I have decided to major in Kinesiology (study of human movement).

I really can't explain what impact the hospital atmosphere has had on me I hiew have an inner drive to try and help people in terminal situations not only in diseases such as cancer but do all those people who are having problems grasping the meaning of life.

It really bothers me to see people living their life away, with no desires or hopes. It bothers me to see people who hate life, and it bothers me to see people in such pain and anguish as those with terminal cancer are.

The first 20 years of my life I had been very self orientated. I had no concerns for anybody but my own well-being. It took cancer and helpfull, loving people as yourself to realize that been self-centered is not the way to live. The answer is to try and help others.

My problem was that I didn't no how to go about doing it, or how to get started. I think that now I am slowly finding the answer. I guess if you want something bad enough you try harder and harder to get. I've always wanted to be a more loving helpfull person.

I Know that I have inspired many of my former old teammates and friends. So I think through athletics I can also help other people in troublesome situations by showing them courage and strength to get over the roughest situations.

I have started running with my artificial limbs. Every 9 days I add on another 1/2 mile. Right now I am up to running 4 miles a day. I try and run every day of the week but occasionally I miss out. Since my body is very prone to injuries because of my running tecnique I have started to weight lift every second day to build up my muscles, so they

can take the stress. My first goal is to run in marathons. My second goal is to try and raise money for disabled sports as well as cancer research. I hope through my efforts I can inspire and help all those people in stressfull life situations.

April 20, 1979: Terry writes to Donna, sharing that the reason his response was delayed was due to his running training. He says, "I really can't explain what impact the hospital atmosphere has had on me. I now have an inner drive to try and help people in terminal situations not only in diseases such as cancer but also all those people who are having problems grasping the meaning of life." He also shares his training method, saying, "I have started running with my artificial limb. Every 9 days I add on another ½ mile. Right now I am up to running 4 miles a day . . . My first goal is to run in marathons. My second goal is to try to raise money for disabled sports as well as cancer research. I hope through my efforts I can inspire and help all those people in stressful life situations."

Courtesy of Donna Ball

other than medical appointments, but she felt it was important to show them why they should take action when they believe in something and what they can do to help others.

> Terry's definitely a part of our family life. Even before I had kids, I'd think of Terry all the time. Whenever there's a challenging moment in my life, I think of his strength and that helps. In one of the letters, he writes, "I have nothing but admiration and respect for people such as yourself. You live your lives to help others." So, it's an extraordinary set of handwritten words by the man that he became. Those words, along with my parents as models, I try to live a life of service based on those things.

BILL VIGARS
PR coordinator for the Marathon of Hope, author of *Terry & Me*

I meet Bill at a popular restaurant in Vancouver. He is an easygoing and gregarious man, apparent at first glance and in his warm handshake. Bright-eyed and bushy-tailed, he has joy in telling his stories from the run and the once-in-a-lifetime experiences with Terry.

Bill was hired in February 1980 as an Ontario representative for the CCS. He had volunteered for them before, but when a paying job became available, he took it. He recalls being hired because someone at the CCS had told the hiring committee that Bill thinks outside the box. "What box?" Bill says with a smile.

> My boss, Harry Rowlands, came and literally handed me a sheet of paper and said, "There's a kid running across Canada with one leg. You want to go see what you can do for him?" I don't think they thought I was going to get as involved — nor did I — as I actually did. And so, initially, I just followed him from afar. I didn't reach out. I just was reading what Leslie Scrivener was writing once a week, but then getting all this other information from mostly the national office.

Bill was thirty-three at the time. He was just the type of person who was needed. Someone younger, not bound by the rules, who could make things happen on the fly and clear the way for Terry on his Marathon. He didn't think that the others involved in the CCS were "getting it" because they were all in their fifties and sixties.

Bill poses on a motorcycle on the Lott family property, summer 1980.
Courtesy of the Lott family

Terry was refusing to get a medical check-up in Newfoundland and Nova Scotia, and they needed someone to go and speak with the boys. Bill agreed to meet Terry, Doug, and Darrell at the border in New Brunswick. He had to see for himself "if this kid is for real."

He didn't know what hotel they were at, so he drove down the road until he saw the famous van. It was cold and late, so he climbed into the backseat of his car to rest until morning. Early the next morning, he heard the motel door open, and the three boys walked out. Doug, who was the first one out, looked at him questioningly and asked, "You're the guy from the Cancer Society?" Bill shrugs his shoulders and figures they probably had different expectations. He gave them some cassettes they had requested and brought some mail from home.

> It's five o'clock in the morning. Pitch-black still. We all pile in the van, and we drop Terry off, and I get into the routine. There's no traffic on the road other than transport trucks and the odd car, and you could hear the transport trucks coming from miles away. So, we've driven ahead a mile, and the transport trucks would come by and shake the whole van. Like, the whole van would rock, and it was pitch-dark. So, at first all I'm seeing is him in the headlights. You can't hardly see him coming from behind in the passenger mirror, and the headlights, and then you pull ahead and give him a break. Nobody talked. I'm following everybody's lead.

That was the morning for twelve miles. Terry would run his first couple of miles before taking a break and then continuing on.

At one point, I remember I was in the passenger seat, watching in the rear-view mirror when it was light as he was coming towards us. At some time, before the morning break, I turn to Doug and go, "How do you watch him do this?" And he said, "I don't," which I thought was odd, but then I realized very quickly that it was too painful for him to watch.

Watching Terry, Bill was immediately inspired. He knew he was going to do anything and everything to help Terry. He was all in. He had worked for radio stations and community organizations before, so he understood small towns and how the media worked.

[Those] two days that I spent with him in New Brunswick, I was so sold on it. Like, there wasn't anything I wasn't going to do to make this work.

John Simpson, a documentarian, recognized that Terry and his run were going to be something big. He came out to Nova Scotia with a cameraman to start filming them on his own dime. Bill joked a lot while the camera was rolling, and Terry had an incredible sense of humour.

There were a few times where John would say, "I want to set up a shot of Terry coming and getting into the van, and having a conversation with you, Bill." Terry did this several times for John. John would be shooting, Terry would run up, and you could see the setup [of the camera]. And he'd get up in the van and he'd go, [Bill begins impersonating Terry using a robotic voice] "Well, I'm here to talk to you, Bill. Jeepers! There's John." [Bill shakes his head and switches to a sillier voice as Terry.] "So John. What do you think I should be talking about today?"

The staged moments didn't work, and the boys and Bill enjoyed ruining them for John. One time, John had gone to great effort, going down the road, scaling a cliff to get the shot of Terry getting out of the van and walking around and running. The police are there, Darrell, Doug, and some kids. Terry gets out, and he and Bill just shuffle about, oddly hunched over. John's out there yelling, "This is not funny! Not funny!"

Bill returned to Ontario, but one Sunday night, John called and raised some concerns:

> "This thing is going to fall apart. He's not going to make it to Ontario. The guys have run out of money, they all have colds, they've all been sleeping in the van. I've spent my own money to put them up in a motel tonight. They haven't been showering, and you have to do something, or this thing is going to collapse."

The CCS came together for an emergency meeting, with all the district reps and the national office. Terry was in Quebec, and the police were trying to move him to another highway. They wanted a sign on the back of the van that said *Slow runner ahead*, which Terry was never going to allow. Bill got the approval to go back out and called on his friend Ray Bagar, who spoke French, to join him.

It was an early morning in Drummondville, and the crew was on a rest break at the side of the road. Ray, unaware of what would be needed of him, showed up in a suit. Police had shown up, and Bill was trying to talk to them. They wanted Terry to move to another highway, and the crew didn't want to.

> [I said to Ray,] "You gotta talk to them. I don't care what you say to them, you have to keep us on the road." So, Ray goes over, and about fifteen minutes later, the police get in their cars and drive away. Ray comes back and goes, "Okay, we're good, let's go." I have no idea what he said to them. Twenty-five years later, we're having a beer, and I said, "Remember that day in Quebec, and the police and everything? What did you say to them? What happened?" And he said, "Well when I first went over, they were adamant. The moment I started speaking French to them, their attitude changed. Remember I was wearing a suit coat? I don't know where it came from, but I told them that I was from the Prime Minister's Office, and that the prime minister

had sent me personally to assure that Terry Fox gets to Ottawa on July the first, and we need the cooperation with Quebec police. They bought it!" First the older policeman left, and then the younger policeman said, just before he drove away, "We just don't want to come out here for a dead body on the road." So it wasn't that they were being obnoxious. They were concerned that he was going to get hit by a truck or a vehicle.

Once into Ontario, though, the OPP was on board to offer support.

I wrote the commissioner of the provincial police to ask for an escort. At home, he'd talk about work, and he talked about this kid who was running across Canada, and [that] they'd been asked to escort him. His kids had heard about Terry and talked their dad into providing the eventual police escort. And that's how the Ontario Provincial Police got involved.

They made plans for the run and for events, but things changed quickly, and they would have to adjust as they went. Part of the appeal to so many was that the run itself was a genuine grassroots endeavour. These were just some kids on a quest that started out with no corporate sponsor and no large organization backing them up. Bill described his briefcase, or rather lack thereof.

You get some coasters, scraps of paper, some napkins, and you carry them around in your pocket. That was my briefcase. On the run, that was how it went. There was a plan, but you could never stay to the plan; it changed almost every day. One moment it would go this way, and the next it could go this way. And over the time I was with him, there were so many times where we could have turned left or we could have turned right. It seemed, in almost every instance — I call it the Terry Factor, and it still exists today — every time he made a decision, it turned out to be the right one.

One of the best examples was when they were scheduled to be at Parliament Hill. The governor general was supposed to do the kickoff for the Ottawa Rough Riders football game. When they had to cancel, the PR man for the Rough Riders was in a panic.

> So, they come down to the hotel, and Terry was on his sleep break. They asked me, "Would he do the kickoff?" And I said, "Well, he's supposed to do this, but I'll ask him when he comes down." So, he came down and I said, "We could do this, and here's the circumstances, or we can do this." And his immediate reply was "I'd rather go to a football game." And the football game turned into a pivotal moment for many reasons. One, it suddenly had gone from nothing in Quebec to a standing ovation. And probably more important, the recognition he got at centre field from the football players, from athletes, big guys, [and one of them] said, "We were talking about you in the dressing room before the game. We're professional athletes. We train every day, and none of us can figure out how you're doing it. This is the most unbelievable athletic feat we've ever seen." So, it was two-fold. Terry was getting a boost. His message is getting out and being recognized for what he's doing. It was really, really important.

From the early days, Bill could see how Terry affected people. He wasn't well-known, but the news was quickly spreading by word of mouth, and more people were gathering at the side of the roads.

> At the end of the concession road, five or six cars, two or three families maybe, they were mesmerized. Transfixed. Emotional. And then the next concession, same thing. They've obviously come from down the concession. They heard he's coming; the message is going down the road. And then when he spoke, I saw the emotion, and how sincere, from the heart, and focused [he was] on what he was saying. He had one message. It was talking about the kids, how it affected him, and the need to find a cure for cancer.

He was eloquent in a very simple way. Literally, every time he talked from the time I met him to every speech we ever did — not a sound [as the crowds listened to him].

Bill was laser-focused on finding support for Terry. On his way to work one day, Bill was driving down the Don Valley Parkway, listening to Jeremy Brown and Don Daynard on CKFM. They were usually the morning's comic relief, but this time, they were talking about Terry. Touched by Leslie Scrivener's articles, Jeremy wanted the station and their listeners to get behind Terry's cause. Ready to take any opportunity to get the word out, Bill sidetracked to the radio station to give

July 11, 1980: Thousands of fans cheer on Terry at Nathan Phillips Square in downtown Toronto. It was the largest reception Terry received on his Marathon of Hope.

Photo by Gail Harvey

them his spiel. After a meeting with the GM, marketing managers, and PR people, they told him, "Don't worry about Toronto. We'll take care of Toronto." Bill left it in their hands, but he had no clue what would be waiting for them. A few weeks later, Terry arrived at Nathan Phillips Square to a cheering crowd of ten thousand people — his largest reception yet.

When Terry was getting in his miles, he wouldn't stop. He wouldn't talk to people, just wave. So, Bill and the volunteers would collect the money on the road, but they would have to be smoothed out because people were donating crunched-up balls of bills.

> And we figured out what it was. The people are standing there with their dollar, they're watching him coming, and they're subconsciously doing this [Bill tightens his fist] because they're so moved by what they see. I think it was very clear to people watching him run that he was in pain, that it was hard. They were amazed that he was doing it. They were amazed that they were looking at somebody with an artificial leg, which back in those days was very rare. The effort, the focus, the look of the face. I think people could feel what he was feeling, amazed at what he was doing and wondering, "How are you doing that?" That was my reaction.

Bill still doesn't think he knows the answer, at least not exactly.

> I can only go back to what he must have experienced in the hospital and how it affected him immediately. I don't know whether it was his nature before that. From what I understand, from the moment he was in the hospital, he was very compassionate towards the other patients. Initially, it was the children, but then it was the cancer

A volunteer smooths out crumpled bills that were held tightly in the hands of emotional supporters along the road.

Photo by Gail Harvey

ward. So, it was everybody. And one thing that he said —
and it was something he said all the time, I think it's one
of his famous quotes — "I couldn't leave that ward and
put those people out of my mind."

He said so many things, like "I run one pole at a time.
I can't possibly run a marathon a day, but I can run to the
next pole." And there were so many times I think where
he used the image of what he experienced during his treatment to take him above the pain. And the pain became
much worse — but he just kept going.

Terry had the support of so many people, and with each mile it seemed
that more and more people became involved, giving their time, energy,
and focus to help a young man achieve his dream for everyone else.

He was so real. He was so dedicated. He was so focused. So
self-effacing. He was so humble, but he was so normal.
Eloquent speaker. Great sense of humour behind the scenes.
Focused when he talked; to everybody he talked to, he was
never looking around. And there was no ego. None, zero.
He was never once looking around for a camera. He just
was trying to get his message out. At one point, I had a
conversation with him later on: "Maybe you want to take
some of that money and put it in education or —" He was
emphatic. "No. Research. Nothing but research."

LESLIE SCRIVENER
Toronto Star reporter, author of *Terry Fox: His Story*

I arrive at Leslie's home, a tall modern industrial-looking building in
stark contrast to a neighbourhood of older smaller homes of generations past. But already there are shrubs at the front and greenery
growing through the cobblestones in the driveway. A bit of nature
rebelling against industry — an apt description of the woman herself
who answers the door in a white flowy long linen shirt with a '60s

naturalist aura. She welcomes me upstairs to the open living room and kitchen area and has breakfast already on the go. Leslie is happy to talk about Terry, having been there, reporting on the run, and writing his story. She is still fascinated to hear and discover more about him, having become a fan within the first five minutes of meeting the young man.

Leslie was assigned by the *Toronto Star* to cover Terry's story a few days after the run began. The assignment editor, Bonnie Cornell, had a mother who was fighting cancer. She brought it up at a story meeting, but others laughed about it, skeptical of his goal. But Leslie was assigned the story and had to find Terry that day to talk to him. She was in Toronto, but operators couldn't find him anywhere. Luckily, Terry was located at the mayor's home in Come by Chance, Newfoundland, probably having his mid-afternoon break.

He runs a campaign of courage

By Leslie Scrivener
Toronto Star

Running with Terry

□ *Terry Fox is a living lesson in courage and determination. Last Saturday, the 21-year-old cancer victim with one leg set out to run 5,000 miles from the Atlantic to the Pacific oceans to prove that cancer can be beaten. The Toronto Star will be running with Terry all the way. Terry will be checking in weekly with The Star. You'll read his progress every Friday in the Family Section, starting next week.*

Nothing, not gale force winds, not pouring rain nor last spring snowstorm, not even the lack of a leg is going to stop Terry Fox from running across Canada.

"I come from a competitive, stubborn family," says the 21-year-old university student from Port Coquitlam, B.C., who lost his right leg to cancer three years ago. "I have to prove to myself that even though my leg was amputated, I am not disabled. I am not going to let myself down."

His journey, to raise pledges for the Canadian Cancer Society, has only just begun. Terry spoke to The Star yesterday from the home of the mayor of Come-By-Chance, Nfld., 93 miles north-west of St. John's where he started his run last Saturday afternoon.

A Simon Fraser University student and former basketball and soccer player, Terry hopes to dip his artificial leg into the Pacific Ocean next fall just as he dipped it in the Atlantic last week. If he keeps a pace of 20 to 30 miles a day he should be on the cedar-lined shores of Stanley Park next October.

Terry says he feels "pretty good" even though his first four days of running on the Trans-Canada Highway were slow, marked by heavy rain, a snowstorm, 40-mile-an-hour winds — "they held me to a standstill, I couldn't move" — and very steep hills.

Glimpses of sea

"But I've heard the hilly country is pretty well over," Terry says in a voice bubbling with confidence. He says the route has been at times barren, at other times heavily treed; occasionally he has had glimpses of the sea. "Tell my Mom we're having some Vancouver weather here," he says.

He also has had to sleep in a bone-cold camper, supplied by the Ford Motor Co., because the propane tanks can't be filled until Clarenville, a town 26 miles away.

The setback he expected, a break-down in his artificial leg, hasn't happened. He's carrying two spares with him and hopes they will see him through the 3½-week crossing of Newfoundland. The War Amputations of Canada organization is supplying and servicing the legs in centres where they have offices.

His only physical complaint so far is a tightening in the thigh muscles.

But Terry is being cheered by motorists, who honk, wave and wish him well, and is warmly welcomed in the tiny Newfoundland whistle stops along the route.

Betty Gilbert, wife of Come-By-Chance's mayor George, stood on the road yesterday and waved Terry down, offering him a hot shower, home-cooked meal and a good bed for the night. She said the town's young people were baking him a cake, buying a gift and planning a surprise party for the brave young runner.

Terry is accompanied by his childhood friend, Doug Alward, also 21 and a student at Simon Fraser University, who drives the van, prepares meals and has fresh clothing laid out. Terry says he wears four shirts, sweat pants, a rain top, toque and gloves in the cold weather. "That's really draining, but I should be really trucking on pretty soon."

Terry's determination dates to 1977 when he was an 18-year-old student in first year kinesiology who learned the pain in his leg was bone cancer. Within a week, his muscular leg was gone from six inches above the knee.

Diagnosed as cancer

The suffering and cancer deaths he saw during follow-up treatment made him all the more determined to help fight the deadly disease that claims one out of every six Canadian lives. In the time it will take to complete his run, it's estimated nearly 40,000 Canadians will be diagnosed as cancer cases.

From sea to sea: Terry Fox has come 93 miles; he still has about 4,900 to go in his journey from Atlantic to Pacific ocean. But the 21-year-old who lost his leg to cancer three years ago is determined to prove he is not disabled.

coach about a one-legged man who ran the New York marathon.

"I decided if he did it, I'm going to do it too," says Terry.

He started training 14 months ago, walking a quarter-mile a day, enduring great pain and blisters, sores and the loss of toenails on his good leg because of the pressure on it.

But he ignored the discomfort, his father says proudly, because at the back of his mind was the single thought of the strong-willed New York runner.

In 1974, Mark Kent, a 17-year-old North York high school student was the first person to run across Canada from coast to coast. Terry will be the first person to run across the country with only one leg.

Last year, Terry ran for 101 consecutive days, training for this cross-Canada endurance test, and stopped only for Christmas Day, his father says.

"It convinced him he was in very good shape mentally and physically to complete the run," Rolly Fox told The Star from his Port Coquitlam home.

His mother Betty, who manages a card shop, says she worked with her son, laying the groundwork for the journey. He wrote to businesses asking for sponsorship and received support from such companies as Esso, which supplied gas money, Adidas for running equipment, Safeway and the Four Season hotels, among others.

His parents say they believe he can cross Canada if his health endures. His mother, showing a lively maternal concern, says, "I just hope he doesn't push himself too hard. But because of the type of person he is, I think he'll make it."

She says Terry was deeply affected by his experiences in chemotherapy. "He wants to help cancer research. He's seen a lot of young people stayed with him — and that impression stayed with him — of all the suffering he's seen in others."

She proudly adds that throughout the rehabilitation, Terry kept up his school work, receiving all As and Bs and somehow managed to get on the golf course within a month of his operation.

Says his father, simply, reflecting the confidence that seems to be a family trait: "He was brought up to finish what he starts."

The first of Leslie Scrivener's column "Running with Terry," printed on April 17, 1980, five days after Terry began his Marathon of Hope.

I still remember the tone of his voice — youth and hope and optimism and "I will do this." And I believed him. His voice still stays with me. I can see [it] as clearly as I see you, where I am at my desk on the phone. And then I had to write it right away for the weekend paper.

He was a great natural communicator. Bonnie decided that Leslie and Terry would keep a weekly call, although people at the paper didn't care for it; they thought it was boring. But it became the best part of Leslie's week, a little column at the bottom of the page called "Running with Terry." She was happy to have regular contact with him, and he was happy to do it because it would promote his mission. The *Toronto Star* at that time was the largest circulation paper in Canada.

On June 28, 1980, Leslie first saw Terry in person when she travelled to the border of Ontario and Quebec.

Oh, was I nervous and excited. That first look at him on the road. [Leslie pauses, as if the memory takes her breath away.] No one else on the road, no other cars. He's

Leslie speaks with Terry Fox during the run.
From *Toronto Star* Archives via Getty Images

running toward me, and it is electric to see. He looked very small. He was really just a kid. I knew that he would be coming along; I was just shocked that he was so alone. He was a beautiful, beautiful young man. And he had all of these fine qualities. Noble, self-sacrificing, humanitarian-oriented person.

As he crossed the border, there was a festival atmosphere with balloons, a local MPP, and many awestruck, happy kids. Leslie had driven out in a car, but she did get to join the crew and spend time with them in the van. She says that people talked about the loneliness of the long-distance runner, but Terry didn't feel that — he liked it. Leslie was with them for about two days, interviewing Terry when she could. To Leslie, he talked about his views on things, asked a lot of big questions like "Why did Canada want to break up?" and was always positive. He would be courteous with bystanders who had gathered or when meeting officials like mayors, but Leslie could tell when he was doing things he didn't really want to do, a slight clench in his jaw, especially when he was tired and needed to rest. By the time they had dinner, after 7 p.m., he'd go to his room to rest, and Leslie would walk back and forth thinking that it would be a good moment to have an interview, but she couldn't bring herself to knock on the door, wanting to give him that peace. She describes the reaction from people on the side of the road watching him running, step by step, towards his goal.

Eyes of disbelief, really. And that look is almost a transformative look in a person. By seeing him do this, you could actually see the look — jaw-dropping disbelief that a person is doing this, giving all that he has. And it showed on his face. His face was not calm and easy. It was effort. But you could see this physical impact on people. That to me is still the most astounding. You could visually see some change of spirit.

Once Terry hit Scarborough and was coming to Toronto, the attitude of the people at the paper changed. It was the *Toronto Star* who paid to have the family flown in from B.C., so they could be with Terry at

Nathan Phillips Square. They hired a limousine that, unsurprisingly, Terry wouldn't get into.

> There is something new at Nathan Phillips and University Avenue — there's joy. It's this celebration. There are so many people; this is the beginning of "we're in this, we're part of this." He mentions in Scarborough, "This has to go on without me." And Doug, watching this and saying, "Whoa, this guy is changing." There's this feeling, a physical transformation. By that I mean, "What am I seeing? Oh, I'm here with all these people. What are we experiencing together?"

December 8, 1980: Leslie Scrivener receives an award from the Canadian Cancer Society for her diligent reporting on Terry throughout his Marathon. Her weekly column, "Running With Terry," enabled the nation to experience the incredible journey together. It is presented to her by Ron Potter, Ontario campaign chairman.

Photo by Michael Stuparyk via Getty Images

Leslie doesn't remember much detail of the days in Southern Ontario. There were so many journalists, interviews, events, and speeches. Terry did a lot of events on top of his twenty-six miles every day because he realized that this was it. It had blown up. He had to stay strong because the momentum had built, and he was getting all the attention on his cause that he had been hoping for. But these stops in Southern Ontario took him out of his way. Calculating the 3,339 miles he completed, had he not made the detours and the extra stops in towns, he would have made it to the border of Alberta and B.C. Almost home. Terry was doing everything he could to raise awareness and money to help research. And he did get frustrated sometimes, wondering why people weren't doing absolutely everything they could, like he was.

Leslie was out in B.C. with family when she saw the news coverage of the Marathon ending in Thunder Bay.

> It was like the bottom had fallen out. There was something so good and pure, and it had emptied out. All that hope and possibility. Terry's on an airplane crossing the country that he should have been running across. And he's in a hospital bed [in] the same place where he was three years before. How can this be? How unfair.

She thought it so generous that Betty had called her and invited her up to the hospital to see Terry, though she felt awkward among his friends.

> Everybody's healthy and strong and there's Terry, the strongest of them all. Before there was sort of sunlight and vitality and youth and vigour, and he's still wearing his T-shirt. People like him needed to be in the world. If he had lived, we wouldn't have this emotion, but we would have this outstanding person in the world who could, from his experience, provide us inspiration and this energy.

Leslie's biography, *Terry Fox: His Story* (1981).
From the editor's collection, McClelland & Stewart, 1981

The decision for her to write her book, *Terry Fox: His Story*, came about naturally. Terry called her and said, "If someone's gonna write the book, it might as well be you." Recounting the memory, Leslie laughs openly, shaking her head, "He had a way with words."

She had many visits to the Fox home, sitting and talking with Terry on the sofa so she would be able to tell his story. Betty, ever the protective mother, would check in to make sure Terry was okay and not being pushed too far.

Leslie was also at the Fox house on Christmas Eve, 1981, and was invited to partake in the family tradition of taking a swig from a giant bottle of alcohol. After Terry had had his fill of everyone playing around, he headed off to bed, walking down the hall with his sweater in his hand. That was the last time she saw him.

Terry died at about 4 a.m. on June 28, 1981. Leslie was personally invited to the funeral by Betty and was not required to cover the story in the paper. She grieved with the rest of the country.

> It was just so great to be there as an ordinary person. I truly, truly believe that he was a rare and outstanding person. I believe that in my bones. I think about him every day. I don't run anymore, but if I'm walking, I do the, like, "next pole" [goal]. It's become a part of my life, to set those small goals.

GLADYS WILLIS
Canadian Cancer Society volunteer in Port aux Basques

Sharon and Paula — the granddaughters of Gladys Willis — welcome me into Paula's home for our chat, expressing the same hospitality that their grandmother had shown Terry. They are excited to talk about the stories Gladys shared about Terry and her support for him when he ran through Port aux Basques, Newfoundland.

Gladys was heavily involved with the CCS at the time, volunteering and hyping up the whole town in support as Terry drew near. She wanted to be the town that raised the most money per capita for him. There were ten thousand residents in Port aux Basques and surrounding areas, and if everyone could give a dollar, that would raise $10,000.

> Sharon: She was on the town council, so she had a lot of contacts [and] knew a lot of people. A lot of people

Doug Alward and Terry stand outside their van at Gladys's house in Port aux Basques, Newfoundland.
Courtesy of the Willis family

respected Nan. Whenever Nan tried to get anything done, she had all these followers. And she was a small little lady. She had one straight leg — she was crippled as well — and when she spoke, everyone listened.

Gladys used her connections to go to the media and build up buzz for Terry. By the time Terry arrived, the town had reached their fund-raising goal.

It was arranged that Gladys would meet Terry and Doug up the road. Terry was excited to meet the woman who had achieved his goal of raising one dollar per person. He had been running, and his stump was bloodied, so Gladys offered him and Doug her cabin. Paula and Sharon, who were young teenagers at the time, remember some people waiting by the cabin and clapping as he went by. Their nan walked alongside him, with her limp matching his.

Once he had his nap, cleaned up, and had a snack, they went to the town hall to present Terry with the cheque. The sisters remember there being hundreds, if not thousands, of people there to cheer for Terry as he headed to the ferry after the ceremony. Terry wrote in his journal that night:

> We stayed in Gladys Lodge during the break and I signed her wall! Then I took off again. People were gathering for a motorcade that was to leave from the Visitors Bureau. We were 1 and ½ hours ahead of time so I rested. We got to the Bureau and then from there ran to the Port aux Basques arena. Here I did my speech then back out to the Bureau and then did my last 3 miles to the ferry terminal. It was great to get here! We raised $10,000 in Port aux Basques which is fabulous!

Terry also left a note behind on their cabin wall: *Marathon of Hope Run. Dear Gladys, Thank you so much for your beautiful effort. It's people like you who make my run worthwhile and a success. Terry Fox, May 6, 1980.* They cut out that portion of the wall, and it is with their family to this day.

Although they were young, Paula explains how he has impacted their family for generations, and Sharon thinks the experience feels even more impressive now than it already was.

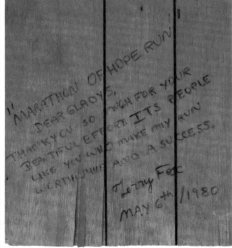

Terry signed a section of Gladys's wall on May 6, 1980.
Courtesy of the Willis family

Paula: We always got involved with the Terry Fox Run and Foundation after that. And then you talk about generations, because when our kids went to school, they were doing it, too. So, we would always tell them the story about how Nan [helped him]. And then through our work, we would help with the Terry Fox Run, so it's been a part of us for a long time.

Sharon: Because we were kids, I was blown away. Like, how could anybody do this healthy, let alone as sick as he was? It was very empowering that if someone so ill can do what he did, what am I doing with my life? It got a lot of people thinking. He was a great role model. I know there's probably lots of these stories right across Canada. You rethink, "Maybe I should do more volunteering. Maybe I should do something." Treat people with respect, too, because you get that back. And that was easily evidenced in Nan where all she had to do was ask and start things and everybody just kind of [jumped to it], but that was her personality.

The Marathon achieved its goal of raising research funds and awareness of cancer, and Paula reflects on the very personal way this has impacted her.

Paula: I think back in the '80s, you knew of someone that was touched with cancer, but you look how many years down the road it is now and there's so many. There was no cancer at that time that we knew of in our family — but then our grandfather ended up getting cancer later on and he passed away. Our mother and her two brothers, they all had cancer and passed away. And then me as well, I had breast cancer, so I had a bilateral mastectomy, and I had colorectal cancer at the same time. Two different ones. And that's extremely rare. And I believed [in hope]. I trusted it, something inside me. I feel like that's what he would have gone through as well. You gotta have that mentality and the hope.

You think about the bigger picture here and what Terry's message was trying to be, and I think that's why it's still strong to this day because there's so many people impacted by that and what he went through to try to get that message out. There's hope out there. Like, "Don't give up. Keep going, keep that strength. We're stronger than we can be." And you gotta believe. You gotta have that hope.

Hope but also courage, Sharon adds.

> Sharon: A lot of inner strength, because if you don't have a lot of willpower, you can't master that. And how does one build that hope? It's got to be inside somewhere for it to come out, and you need a support system. It takes a whole community, not just one person, to make a change. That's how hope grows. It's almost like laughter. It's kind of contagious.

Their family was devastated when they heard the run had ended, but they saw how it sparked the nation. Everyone adopted his hope and tried to raise even more funds. When Betty and Rolly retraced Terry's run on the tenth anniversary of the Marathon, they visited the cabin and Gladys.

Mrs. Willis was extremely excited last year when Terry's parents, Betty and Rollie Fox came to visit her. They met at the cabin, a special place for the owner, where Terry left a thank-you message and his autograph. Mr. and Mrs. Fox were retracing Terry's steps for the 10th annual Terry Fox Run.

Gulf News clipping of Betty and Rolly Fox visiting with Gladys Willis in 1990.

From Saltwire, *Gulf News*

Paula: I was there this day at the cabin when Nan was there, when they came to visit, she went through the day, how they met. Nan was very excited. She went through everything with them. And she even had a picture of him [with the signed wall behind] in a little photo frame. I think they were so proud of what Terry accomplished and how he touched people in such a huge way, not even realizing it ten years before, and then coming back and meeting people that went through it. I think they were amazed. I really do.

GWYNETH INSTON
Volunteer for the Marathon of Hope

Gwyn requests I meet her at the Port Credit Yacht Club where her family keeps their boat. Her energy hits you before she's even close, and she greets me with a firm, excitable handshake and an electric smile.

Gwyn first became involved with the run after she had heard Terry speak at the Royal Botanical Gardens in Hamilton. It was an emotional and heartfelt speech, and she was awestruck. Shortly after, she was in London, Ontario, visiting her best friend and heard he would be in town giving a speech at the local Holiday Inn. Her friend was working, but Gwyn decided to go on her own to try to get Terry's autograph. It was packed like sardines outside the hotel, and she thought she had missed him, but then she saw a young man with a Terry T-shirt on. It was Terry's younger brother, Darrell, and they hit it off immediately, spending the next three days together.

We went to the movies, and we went to a really beautiful craft show in Victoria Park.

Gwyneth and Darrell pose for photographer Gail Harvey in Northern Ontario.
Photo by Gail Harvey

We had dinner with Terry and a bunch of people at some restaurant, and it was really fun. Then they were heading back to Toronto, and Darrell was like, "I want you to come to Toronto." I'm like, "Yeah, okay, I can do that."

That was the start of their relationship, and it grew on the run. After so much time, Gwyn doesn't remember the exact details of towns or dates, but she assisted them where she could. She did laundry, shopped for groceries, fixed dinner or snacks for Terry, and helped collect donations from the people who lined the roads. At times, she was driving the fundraising car and followed behind Terry.

They're like, "Yeah, you drive for a while and collect money." And like, I've got a cop there, and I'm like fifteen. I've never driven ever. People would throw their money into the car. I'd have the windows down, getting pegged by money, and it was great. And then I'd have to pick it all up later. It would be all over the car. It was just so funny, I'm like, "Oh my God," shoving it in those boxes.

I knew it was a great moment to be living in. I'm like, I'm really gonna just take this and run with it because this is pretty darn special. This is a big deal. This is gonna make a difference. Like I knew at fifteen that this was going to be something. Another crazy fun day that we're gonna experience, another marathon we're gonna run. It was almost too much to really think about: "You're running another twenty-six miles? Are you kidding me? Nobody does that." And, oh, with one leg, by the way.

I remember I would cook him things and do his laundry and entertain him with my wit. He was always nice and

Gwyneth smiles from the window of the fundraising car during the Marathon of Hope.
Photo by Glemena Bettencourt

very respectful. We did a lot of joking around. We were like eight-year-olds most of the time. Pranksters. If you could prank, that would be great. Terry was up for anything fun.

Gwyneth goofs off with Terry at a crew dinner.

Photo by Glemena Bettencourt

On Terry's time off from running, that was what he needed — the support of people with whom he could just be a kid and be himself. Gwyn left the group in Sault Ste. Marie when she got the call that her mother had fallen ill and was going to the hospital. But Darrell and her kept in touch, and three days after Terry had to end his run, she was on a plane to stay with the Fox family for three weeks.

> I took it all in. I really did, like I came into this home, and, you know, shit's hitting the fan, and I'm just gonna be here in any capacity that I can to help. And then there's the telethon — we were in Terry's room, and we're watching it on the TV. We're all just hanging there together, and he was just watching it like, "This is great." I don't remember him talking a lot. But he was definitely taking it in.

Both Gwyn and Darrell had gone to the station and manned the phones for the telethon, doing whatever was needed to help. She went out to visit the family a few more times before Terry died, and she exchanged many letters with Darrell when they were apart. Gwyn says being on the Marathon of Hope was a special time in her life.

> That is when the word "awesome" is the proper use of the word, instead of everybody using it for this or that. Awesome. Like the parting of the Red Sea: awesome. Terry doing a marathon every day: awesome.

And when she needed strength, Gwyn would think of Terry.

My son got really, really sick. He almost died. I was thinking, "You need to try harder. You have to. You gotta keep fighting." And he was fighting for his life. I thought about Terry during that time because I needed somebody to lift me up at that point. I was not good. I think I was crumpled at the elevator, underneath beds at the hospital. And so I think about Terry. "Push yourself. Keep going. Come on, come on, come on."

MARLENE LOTT
Volunteer for the Marathon of Hope

I sit with Marlene in her living room, her home situated in a middle-class neighbourhood in Newmarket. With her greyish-blonde hair and Julia Roberts–megawatt smile, she shines and brightens considerably as she shares her story. She was seventeen during the Marathon of Hope and was one of the lucky few who not only met Terry but had him stay at her house with her family. Her family learned about him like most people — watching the news.

> I just thought, oh my God, this is incredible. And this man . . . this is such an incredible excursion, and it's gotta be hard. He has people with him, and they must need a place to stay, and they must need help. I just wanted [to find] anything I could do to help.

She knew he'd be at City Hall and told her dad she wanted to go down-town and meet Terry so that she could offer help when the run came near their home. She wrote a letter to Terry and put it in a bouquet of roses to give to him. She reads out her first rough draft of it to me, the one she still has, embarrassed a little by her choice of words.

> "You're the most courageous and ambitious person I know. I admire you immensely. You must have a hundred times the guts and self-confidence that anyone else has to take

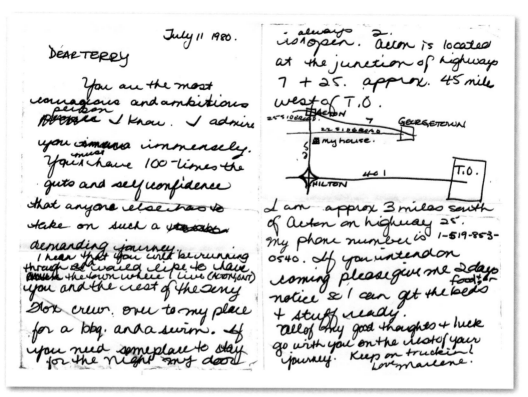

The rough copy of the letter that Marlene gave to Terry, offering her home as a resting spot.
Courtesy of the Lott family

on such a demanding journey. I hear you will be running through or near our town where I live. You and the rest of the Terry Fox crew could come over to my place for a barbecue and a swim. If you need some place to stay for the night, my door is always open." And then I say where we're located, blah, blah, anyway: "If you intend on coming, please give me two days' notice so I can get the food and beds and stuff ready. All my good thoughts and luck go with you on the rest of your journey. Love, Marlene."

Marlene had drawn a map to their house in Acton and ended it with the line "Keep on truckin'." She raises a hand to her face as she rolls her eyes and hides a blush, saying, "I don't know if that made it into the good copy. It's so cheesy. It's like a 1970s hangover!" At Toronto's City Hall, she was overwhelmed by the crowd.

It was packed, of course. I wanted to give flowers to Terry, and I was trying to get through, and I couldn't get through.

There was media and lots of other people kind of near where he was. But I saw Darryl Sittler standing a little bit off to the side, and I was a big Maple Leafs fan at the time. I thought, "I know him!" So over I go, and I'm like, "Darryl! Darryl! I need your help. I have this letter for Terry and flowers." And he says, "No, I'm not giving it to him. You're giving it to him. You go, you push, you climb."

And she did, getting close enough to tap Terry and personally hand him her flowers and the letter. When she returned home, she was unsure if she would hear from him, but her parents reassured her. "Don't be disappointed. I'm sure he gets lots of letters. He's a very busy guy. He's got to run a marathon every day, you know." And then the phone rang.

He was so humble and apologetic and kind. The first thing he said was "Is this Marlene?" "Yes." "This is Terry." And I'm like, "Okay . . ." and he said, "Thank you so much for your letter, that was really kind and I'm *so* sorry I couldn't call you sooner. [Marlene laughs.] I had to go fly in a helicopter to Niagara Falls, and then I have to throw a baseball at the baseball game." [Marlene laughs harder.] And then he says, "That would be really nice for us to come to your home when we're running nearby. Thank you so much." And I said, "Of course, and don't worry, I know you guys probably need a lot of rest, so we won't tell anybody, and you can just come and get a good rest." And then he said, "You know, I'd actually like to ask you if you would like to come along and help out."

He asked her to meet him the next morning at the van at City Hall, where he would continue on his run. There are few people who can understand the feeling of being a part of the Marathon, and Marlene explained that the energy of supporters was palpable. She still gets excited recounting the energy, her hands wide and shaking in front of her.

People were lining — stopping their cars right in the middle of these highways — *throwing* money. We were trying to run right near him, behind him, and grab the money. They were, like, windows down, trying to shove the money out of the cars, yelling for you to come get it. And just *cheering* him on. I mean, it was incredible. The power of it. It had never been done, right? I mean, now there are marathons to raise money for all kinds of stuff. But this was such a unique experience and such an incredible story. And to feel people, everybody, just so wanting to help and so excited and so willing to give. It was amazing. And that's probably what helped him get up and keep going every day, right? Because he was not alone. Like, yes, he was alone; he had to do it. But there was such a wealth of love. It was unbelievable. I've never experienced anything like that since then.

They travelled along the lakeshore and stopped at a diner, the area full of people as Terry ate inside. Another crew member came to get Marlene and took her inside to meet Terry and join him while he ate, and she remembers it being easy and natural, just two young adults meeting for the first time and enjoying lunch.

Her dad, Martin Lott, would routinely shuttle her to the van in the early hours of the morning and then pick her up again at night along the Marathon route. One evening in Hamilton, after all the events, Terry felt like a steak, so they snuck out of the hotel and went to a steakhouse. She glows as she shares how happy she was that night and how friendly they were together.

My dad shows up and he's like, "Hello, excuse me you two. Don't you have to run a marathon tomorrow?"

Martin Lott, Marlene's father, shakes Terry's hand at their home in Acton, Ontario.
Courtesy of the Lott family

217

[She laughs, her smile wide and scrunching her nose.] Which is kind of hilarious. My dad is quite a character.

When they went further out to London, it was too far for her dad to drive her, so she stayed home in Acton.

> Every once in a while, he would call at night and just chat about the day, how he was feeling and that kind of thing. And then they curled back around towards Stratford, St. Marys, Kitchener, Highway 7. And so that's where we rejoined. My dad would shuttle me and pick me up at night and help. The van would go a mile and then Terry would either run by or he would come in, and he would have an orange or some water or he'd get cooled down or eat a chocolate bar, change his T-shirt maybe.

The Lott's home was now nearby, and the group spent time with her family, staying once overnight. Marlene describes it as typical teenagers enjoying their summer break: having ice cream, hanging out, and sitting in lawn chairs on their large property while her dad prepared steaks on the back deck. The boys would also play basketball, swooshing the balls through the hoop above the garage. But Marlene's time eventually had to come to an end.

Bill, Terry, Patrick, and Doug play basketball in the Lott's driveway.

Courtesy of the Lott family

After [they] came through Acton and stayed with us, things were getting really stupid. People were calling and saying, "Are you dating Terry Fox? Are you this or are you that?" No, we were helping on the run. There was no funny stuff going on. Then there was some discussion that happened that I think involved Bill Vigars and my dad and myself and Terry, and I remember we made kind of a pros and cons list of continuing versus stopping. Nobody wanted people to have this wrong idea because that was not the purpose of the run, and we didn't want it to be distracting [from] the focus when it shouldn't be at all. I was just being a friend and wanting to help somebody who was doing an amazing thing. So, then we decided that I would stop. I remember that being really hard.

Marlene and Terry enjoy steak at her home in Acton, Ontario.

Courtesy of the Lott family

The two weeks Marlene spent on the Marathon of Hope were very special to her. It changed her and it didn't feel possible to go back to a normal life.

I remember going back to school. As teenagers do, they're very egocentric, and their problems are so huge — their hairdo, their whatever. I just remember feeling so removed from all of that and really knowing what was important. It stuck with me always. It puts everything in perspective.

Life is wonderful. But life is also hard sometimes. I've come to realize working in the school board that there's so many hardships in people's lives, right? Young people having a tough go of it for different reasons; their parents having a tough go of it. It just makes you feel like it's so important to be kind to people. You don't know what's going on in their day and what's going on in their life.

Marlene couldn't have known just how much she would need to draw on her time with Terry, giving her and her family hope and strength in their most difficult moments.

In 2020, my youngest, Aidan, was diagnosed with lymphoma. He was twenty years old. In 2016, my husband

219

had glioblastoma, brain cancer, and he passed in 2017. So many times during my life, the experience that we had together comes forward. I know I had the smallest window into it, but I appreciate that — I can't even express how much I appreciate that experience.

As for the annual Terry Fox Run, Marlene is heavily involved and brings all her photos to share with everyone.

Every year in September, we have the Runs at school, and when the posters come, sometimes in the pictures, the way he's smiling in his eyes [is] just how he used to smile. I feel like, "There you are."

EDNA TEMPLETON
Former Gravenhurst town councillor who hosted Terry for an afternoon

Edna's daughter, Jane, greets me at her home in Gravenhurst, Ontario. She is a petite woman with short hair and a face that shows she is a take-charge kind of person. She worked with the chamber of commerce for many years, and her mother, Edna, was a councillor for the township of Muskoka Lakes when Terry came to Gravenhurst. Edna was also a busy-body, so, of course, she offered up her house as a place for Terry to rest.

She tucked him into *my* bedroom. I was the lucky one. Terry had his rest, she put the laundry in, and then — because she's a marketer, very social woman — she called Camp Pinecrest, which is our biggest camp here. She called all sorts of other people and said, "Terry Fox is here." So, they kept coming. She would go into the house and then she'd come back and say, "Shhhh! Be really, really quiet." And they did. They were really quiet.

Jane shows me a photo of the crowd gathered outside their porch due to Edna's rallying. Years ago, Edna gave an interview to a local TV station, and it was recorded on tape. Jane is ready with the VCR remote and only has to press play. The camera focuses on Edna's face as she sits outside and begins telling her story of the day.

Terry signs autographs at the Templeton home while Edna surveys the crowd.

Courtesy of the Templeton family

> I was working in a shop and some men came to see me and said that Terry Fox was running through Bala, but they needed somewhere for him to rest, and did I know anywhere? Well, I said, "He can come to my house. It's big, and it's empty, and it is quiet." So, the day of the run that he came through, I was down at the lake for my usual morning swim, and he ran by the house. And I thought, "Oh, my goodness, it's too early." So, I called out and told him it was too early, and they said they'd be back later. So, as usual, I came home at noon, waited until they brought him. They came in the van, and I showed him the bedroom. They came right upstairs, took the pillows and put it under his foot, and left in the van. Told me what time they'd be back. So immediately I got on the telephone, and I phoned Camp Pinecrest, and then I phoned several people and said that Terry Fox was here, if they'd like to come and see him when he came out.
>
> Somebody called me and said could they make a banner. Oh, I said, "Sure. Make a banner." So, they brought the banner that you see in the picture, and it says, "Way to go, Terry!" And they strung it up on the veranda. Before they left, they [asked] was there anywhere they could take his laundry, and I said just give it to me and I'll do it, which I did, of course. So, when they came back, they went right upstairs, got Terry out of bed, brought him down, and I

Terry is surrounded by the awaiting crowd at the Templeton home, signing autographs.

Courtesy of the Templeton family

gave him a big hug. And they went right down the steps into this huge crowd of people and signed autographs. In the meantime, the two fellows who were with him passed all through the crowd the baskets and collected money. And that was the last I saw of Terry Fox.

Ten years after Terry's Marathon of Hope, during Rolly and Betty's tour of his route, they stopped to see Edna, who was very proud to host them.

It happened to be a very hot, hot day. I was going to make them tea, but it was too hot. So, we sat out on my lawn under an umbrella, and I made them lemonade and served them cookies. And in the meantime, we invited people to come and meet them. And my husband was here at that time, and he introduced the people to Mr. and Mrs. Fox. They were absolutely charming, and she gave me Terry's book [by Leslie Scrivener], and also wrote me a lovely letter. I didn't realize how wonderful he was until I read later all about his thoughts, which are in his book that his mother gave me. Why he wanted to do it, why he did it. And it was one in a million things that anybody would do. I don't know another person that would do that with his life, for the sake of other people. It's one of the most important days of my life. What Terry was doing for the cancer victims became a big thing in my life. I often think about it.

Jane says her mom was probably ninety-five when she did the interview, but her memory of that moment in time was as sharp as ever. She shows me the letter and other memorabilia of the run, and then she shares we are going to go to that very house where the crowd had waited so patiently. Someone else owns it now, but he knows its history and will happily open his door to us.

Bala is a sleepy town of cottagers who left the bustle of the city and tend to drive slowly and leisurely. As we pass by buildings, she regales me with their stories and waves to everyone we pass by, who all wave back with a smile. We arrive at the side of a large house that faces the water, with ducks wandering the shore. As we turn to the veranda that was

Betty and Rolly visit the Templeton family during their 1990 tour of Terry's Marathon route.

Courtesy of the Templeton family

captured in the photo, Jane waves her hand over the vast yard, saying the crowd had all gathered here, crammed in together, and the banner had been put up across the top of the veranda. We walk up the creaky steps to the second floor and pause at a window. From there, you could see the front lawn, and Edna would have been able to monitor the crowds.

Then she shows me the room and beams with pride, recalling how this was her room that now has the notoriety of being Terry's nap spot. Sadly during Terry's visit, she had been somewhere else, which she says still makes her "doggone angry."

> God knows [how he did it] — I mean he must have been in pain. Obviously, the kid was in pain. It would have been so much easier just to stay at home with his siblings. I often think, too, with him as a kid, he must have been gobsmacked to see people cheering him and screaming for him. And you know, so excited for him. Like how does the kid handle that? A lot of adults can't handle that, you know?

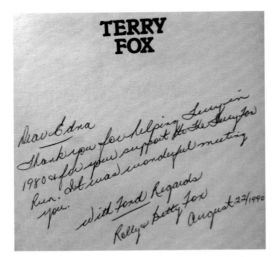

Betty's note to Edna in 1990, written inside the cover of *Terry Fox: His Story*.

Courtesy of the Templeton family

The sheer determination of that young kid, and not even always regarding cancer. My youngest daughter has an unusual syndrome, and she often refers to Terry Fox. She's forty-five now, but she was born with this, and she'll say, "He did it. I can do it." That kind of perseverance and determination and everything.

PETER & JUDY REBELEIN
Bakery owners who made Terry's last birthday cake

I arrive at The Bakery in Gravenhurst, Ontario, and one of the employees calls for Peter as I enter the shop. His wife, Judy, comes out and brings me to the back for the interview, where they've taken down the two framed newspaper clippings of Peter making Terry's birthday cake and Terry cutting into it. These are the only images they have of that moment. Peter walks over and shakes my hand enthusiastically. He is an affable fellow with dancing eyes and combed-back white hair. We chat among the baking racks as he begins to recount his story.

> Peter: It's pretty interesting how the whole thing started. We're sitting there eating supper, the news is on, and all of a sudden here's this kid that wants to run across Canada. He's got cancer, lost a leg, and we started looking at him, like, "Hmm, yeah, good luck with that one." Then a couple months later, he's in Halifax and you go, "Oh yeah, you know, he's got determination. Not bad." Next thing, he's in Quebec. Next thing, he's in Toronto. Next thing, he was going up Highway 11. Wow.

Then they found out Terry was coming into town for his birthday and needed a cake to celebrate, and they weren't given much notice.

> Peter: Just a couple of days! Mike Lipinski, the guy in charge of our chamber of commerce, he comes up and he goes, "Hey can you do me a favour?" I said, "What's that?" He said, "You know Terry Fox? Well, he's outside of town, he's coming in on his birthday. Can you make him a cake?" And I go, "Okay, how big?" He said, "Just put one hundred, one hundred and fifty people."
>
> I didn't really know how to do it. Like, I never made something that big before. Plus, I was running the place, and I had a restaurant next door and I was like, "Wow." It required a lot of ingredients.

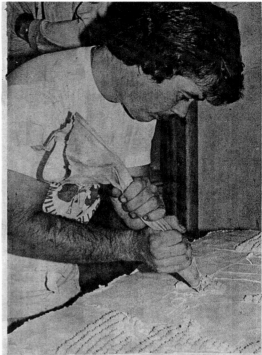

PETER REBELEIN is certain that he has never decorated a cake as big as the one he did for Terry Fox's birthday. He began with a map of Canada - which he drew from an atlas. Here he is adding the blue icing that marks the oceans. He then marked in Terry's route - and his location - Gravenhurst.

July 28, 1980: *Gravenhurst News* article about Peter's birthday cake preparation.

From Gravenhurst News

> Judy: It was all baked in the back of the bakery there, put on a big table. I think the biggest problem was is it gonna turn out? I mean, when you think about that much cake mix, mixing it together, putting it in the oven, is it gonna bake okay?

Peter thought of the design and figured there was only one obvious choice.

> Peter: It was a map of Canada, from coast to coast, and then I drew a red line from where he started, and then along Highway 401, and then the course from there up Highway

The finished birthday cake.
Photo by David McCoy

11 to Gravenhurst. I put it in the back of my little car on a big sheet of plywood. It had to be a half inch of plywood because it was heavy. You don't want to drop that!

The cake weighed about 70 pounds. Peter dropped it off, and it was his wife, Judy, who headed into the arena to deliver the cake. Peter chose to return home to be with their kids who were still young at the time, as the arena was going to be packed full of people.

Judy: They had a stage set up on the rink for him to get up on, and that's where he was introduced and talked. They had different people talking about what he'd done and how far he'd gone, and everybody who's in the crowd was just loving it. And then they said, "Here's this cake." And we all sang "Happy Birthday." Then he said, "Well, everybody come down and have a piece." So, everybody was tripping on down and going to get their cake, and all the little kids that were there. And I went down, kind of held back.

There's a lady next to me and she said, "Did Pete make the cake?" And I said, "Yeah, he did." She said, "Wow. This is exciting." And then she yelled out, "This is the lady that made the cake!" And I'm going, "Well, yeah, it was made in our bakery [but it wasn't me]." But then Terry looked over and he said, "Well, come here!" So, I went up, and he shook my hand and he said, "Thank you very, very much. It's a lovely cake. You did a good job." And I said, "Well, you are just the sweetest boy I've ever met. You're just so humble and so sweet, and so appreciative of what anybody does for you." I was just blown away. I'm thinking in my head, "You are such a hero to folks around here, and you're thanking us? We should be thanking *you* for what you're doing."

Peter crosses his arms and shifts his weight. He draws a finger under his eye, caching a tear as he comments on the intent of the run and the continuing legacy of Terry Fox.

Peter: It's still going on, it's still happening. Are we any closer to a cure? I think we're getting a lot closer. He did a big part of it. All the time I think of him. Every year when this goes on, the Marathon and all that, it's all mentioned, and you know what? I feel proud. I really do. I was there. It's always there. It's my hope feather, it's my badge, I'm proud of it. He was also unselfish, because he knew what he was doing wasn't gonna benefit him at all. Everything he was doing was to benefit others. And that's a lot.

It was Terry's last birthday, and he was made very happy by the town and how they embraced him. Judy says Gravenhurst is still fully behind Terry Fox and will always support him.

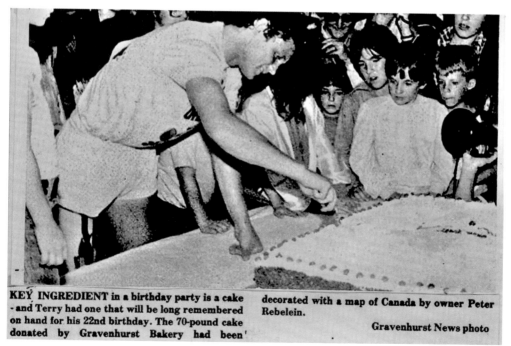

KEY INGREDIENT in a birthday party is a cake - and Terry had one that will be long remembered on hand for his 22nd birthday. The 70-pound cake donated by Gravenhurst Bakery had been decorated with a map of Canada by owner Peter Rebelein.

Gravenhurst News photo

Terry cutting his birthday cake.
From *Gravenhurst News*

Judy: Everybody was thrilled to have met him and thrilled to know that this is what he was doing. It started right away when we knew he wasn't going to make it and things were going downhill. Then when he passed, they started right that first year having a Terry Fox Run. Every year we have these Terry Fox Runs, and we always supply all the doughnuts for that, so they all get doughnuts for the Terry Fox Run. We've always stood behind anything that anybody's doing for him.

And these pictures are hanging in the store. People say, "Oh, this is Terry Fox. Tell us about him." So, people that don't really know the whole story, we tell the story of him coming through Gravenhurst, and how it was his birthday when he was here, and we made a great big cake for him.

DOUG VATER

Fox family spokesman and creator of the Terry Fox Hotline, the first fundraising office

Doug is already standing in the lobby of the Inn on Long Lake when I arrive. It was a long drive for him, but I was thankful he was able to meet halfway in Nanaimo, B.C. He is wearing a light trench coat and his "Dear Terry" T-shirt and carrying a briefcase with him. Very Inspector Gadget. He is excited to share what he calls his blessed life, and as we sit in the lobby, he opens his briefcase filled with newspaper clippings and photos, ready to tell the tale.

Doug first heard about Terry after he had left Newfoundland, and Doug followed any news that he could find about Terry all the way into Ontario. He could see the rising excitement and decided he had to get involved, so he opened an office in Port Coquitlam that he called the Terry Fox Hotline and began what was the first fundraising office. He got a secretary and put a call out for volunteers — and he got plenty of them. They put up a big map on the office wall and started tracking Terry's progress. Next, they started collecting donations by making little boxes with Terry's picture on them and placing them all

Doug and a loyal volunteer in the Port Coquitlam fundraising office.
Courtesy of Doug Vater

Doug's fundraising sign in Port Coquitlam, British Columbia.
Photo by Doug Vater

over the city. He set up a bank account, and all the funds funnelled directly to the CCS. That one office raised over $200,000.

Doug did get out to see Terry on the run one week before it ended. He had a Terry Fox flag that Terry hadn't seen before and presented it to him the evening after his very emotional speech in Terrace Bay, when Greg Scott was with him on the run. The next morning, Terry asked Doug if he could give the flag to Greg, and Greg happily accepted.

Before Doug returned home, Terry gave him a bunch of things to take back with him that people had given him on the run. On Labour

Terry gifts Greg Scott a Terry Fox flag on August 27, 1980. Doug brought the flag for Terry while visiting the Marathon of Hope.

Photo by Doug Vater

Day, he walked into the Foxes' home to drop off those gifts, and Betty was on the phone. She had just received the news about Terry's cancer returning.

She dropped the phone and said, "I need to get to Thunder Bay." That's where I took over. I literally had to have planes waiting, and I got them out that night. I took them out to the airport, and they got there.

Doug became the spokesman for them, handling their communications and filtering messages to Terry's parents so they could manage all the requests.

I was approached by people around the world wanting to get a hold of Betty and Rolly Fox. I was approached by the 700 Club and from other groups wanting to interview Terry. Nobody could [get in touch with them] because they were sheltered at this time, and I sheltered them, too. I protected them that way.

Doug was a daily visitor at the Fox house. So much so that Betty would joke, "Why aren't you at home with your wife?" Doug would have chats with Terry and help Betty handle the bags and bags of mail that were coming to the house.

One cheque was made to *Terry Fox* only and could only go to Terry Fox, and I passed him the cheque. I think it was $2,500. He said, "Give it back. It has to go to cancer research." And that's Terry. That's the Terry we're talking about.

Doug would take Terry out to basket-ball games and other fun events while he was still well enough, but Betty wouldn't let Terry drive. However, when they got further out of view, they would switch spots and Doug would let him drive, just the two of them.

His friendship with the Fox family blossomed, and he was even Santa Claus at the Foxes' annual Christmas Eve event. This was Terry's last Christmas. He was also the one to arrange Terry's trip to the BC Lions game when the team wanted to dedicate the game to him.

September 13, 1980: Terry stands for applause while attending a BC Lions game dedicated to him and his Marathon of Hope.
Courtesy of the Terry Fox Centre Archives

Everything's organized and then I phone Betty and she says, "How is Terry coming in?" And I said, "I've got a limousine coming to pick them up." She said, "Terry, won't get in a limousine." So I had to drive out there and pick him up in my Cadillac. The traffic was very busy; however, as soon as we met the first policeman, I informed him that "I have Terry Fox in my car," and they escorted us into the stadium.

Doug has always kept the Fox family's confidence and trust. Like everyone, he was amazed by Terry's courage and strength and the example he set. He still uses lessons from Terry in his daily life.

I was out for my walk; I had walked too far, and I got weak coming home. I sat down a couple of times, and then I remembered Terry. Terry used to look up at the next signpost. And he would walk to that. And that's what I did. I remembered Terry so I walked to that signpost. Then I looked to the next. And that's how he did the run. Signpost to signpost.

LLOYD ROBERTSON
Canadian national news anchor from 1970 to 2011

Lloyd answers the door to his split-level Markham home in a community with manicured lawns, a tennis court, and a small pond, home to geese, ducks, and swans. He says hello and I hear the deep, distinctive voice that has rang through so many Canadians' dinnertime. His eyes are steadfast and smiling, holding your attention as they did on the screen, and you know you can trust him.

Lloyd walks me to his living room, explaining that his wife will be home soon, and we can have some cookies and tea. We sit down and he begins by asking *me* the questions, which shouldn't be surprising from a lifelong journalist. He tells me of the early years of his career up to when he was on the news desk at CTV, and when the name Terry Fox was first uttered at the daily coverage meeting.

> I remember we were sitting around, deciding what to do. Newsrooms are newsrooms, and someone says, "Some kid with one leg is going to run across the country." And we said, "Oh yeah? How's that going to work?" There was some skepticism at the beginning. It was one of those things where you've got newsrooms across St. John's, Halifax, in New Brunswick, Montreal, et cetera. So, we alerted them just to keep an eye. You never know; see how it goes with this kid. But nobody had much faith that it would become much because it was just some kid trying something. So good luck to him.

After about three days, an editor from one of the Maritime bureaus called saying they had to start paying attention because crowds were turning up and coming out to watch Terry. They hadn't been covering it; people were just coming out through word of mouth. So, they thought, maybe something is happening, and they did one report on him in the Maritimes. Then Terry got into Quebec, and the premier, René Lévesque, commented on the story, followed by Prime Minister Pierre Trudeau. Lloyd began to realize that this kid was becoming a phenomenon.

But why, you know? What was going on here? And it was almost as though we didn't have time to ask that question. Because it just built so quickly. It just began and it rolled. And all of a sudden, he's in Toronto. And by this time, we're covering [him] like two or three nights a week. Certainly historic; every week. Every, every week.

Terry was going to be in Nathan Phillips Square in Toronto, and Lloyd went down to see him in person. On such a busy day, they only spoke briefly; but being close to him in that moment, Lloyd says he could tell how determined Terry was to finish his mission — he was going to go through with it no matter what obstacles were in the way.

When Terry had to stop the run in Thunder Bay on Monday, September 1, 1980, CTV decided to dedicate Sunday night, the most coveted night on TV commercially, for a telethon to help him raise money. It all came together incredibly fast. The idea was pitched that Thursday, cleared on the Friday. On Saturday, they brought it all together, and Sunday, September 7, they were on. Lloyd was sitting at a desk, getting ready to host the show.

I remember thinking, "How the hell am I gonna open this?" because a kid is going back to be treated for cancer, which has returned. How am I going to

A Globe and Mail article from September 9, 1980, shares the exciting tally of donations from the CTV telethon, hosted by Lloyd Robertson.

From the Globe and Mail

Terry Fox delighted as telethon pushes total to $10 million

NEW WESTMINSTER, B.C. (CP) — Canada's national hero continued his struggle with an old foe yesterday, heartened by a coast-to-coast outpouring of millions of dollars that will help others fight the same battle.

Officials at Royal Columbian Hospital reported that marathon runner Terry Fox got a sound night's sleep despite the excitement of a national telethon on Sunday that boosted the total collected in his name for the Canadian Cancer Society to more than $10-million.

In fact, he turned in early. Drowsy from the chemotherapy he is undergoing to combat lung cancer, Terry went to sleep about an hour before the five-hour telethon had run its course.

Until then, he had sat upright in his hospital bed surrounded by a small circle of friends and led the cheering as the pledges mounted.

And how the money rolled in.

Flabbergasted officials of the cancer society struggled yesterday to tally the pledges, which ranged from nickels and dimes from piggybanks to personal cheques for thousands of dollars bearing the signatures of well-known businessmen. One restaurant chain vowed to raise $1-million through its nation-wide string of hamburger stands.

U.S. entertainers Glen Campbell and John Denver, ballet stars Karen Kain and Frank Augustyn and hockey player Darryl Sittler contributed their time, talents and cash.

Cancer society officials now say a conservative estimate of the Fox fund is $10.5-million — $2-million raised by Terry alone in his half-completed run, $1-million each from the B.C. and Ontario governments and $6.5-million pledged in the telethon — most of it by ordinary Canadians.

Terry ended his run at Thunder Bay on Sept. 1 when doctors determined that the cancer had spread to his lungs.

Doctors say he is responding well to treatment and may be allowed to return home to nearby Port Coquitlam next week while continuing treatment as an outpatient.

In Manitoba alone, the Sunday television special resulted in pledges totalling $232,438. In two hours, $100,000 was raised; it took 18 hours to raise that much on the Jerry Lewis muscular dystrophy telethon.

As part of Terry Fox week in Winnipeg, rookies from the Winnipeg Jets of the NHL will play an exhibition tomorrow against a junior team, with all box office proceeds going to the cancer society.

Before their game last Sunday, the Winnipeg Blue Bombers football team promised to donate half the money for all tickets sold above 25,000. The attendance was 25,784, meaning about $3,600 for the society.

Last Saturday, stock car drivers at the Winnipeg Speedway passed their helmets around the crowd to raise $1,600.

In Montreal, hundreds of viewers called CFCF-TV directly Sunday night and letters with donations have been flooding into the city's cancer society office after the station aired the Fox telethon without including a telephone number for pledge calls. A fund-raising bylaw had forced the decision.

"The switchboard went bonkers," a CFCF-TV spokesman said. "We had eight volunteers from the staff and two from the society. The board was jammed. We coped as best we could but we only have 18 lines. Bell Canada phoned to complain that it couldn't handle the calls."

A cancer society spokesman in Montreal said yesterday: "Normally we get about 12 or 13 letters a day. This morning we had a whole bag — about four or five hundred."

In Kelowna, officials of the Central Okanagan United Way campaign announced yesterday that this year's drive to raise $200,000 will be delayed for three weeks — until the Fox campaign has abated.

open it? It can't be mournful because you're continuing the mission. You're trying to raise money. Arthur Weinthal, he was our vice president of entertainment at the time, came over to me at the desk about ten minutes before I went on, and he said, "I can tell you're having a little trouble." I said, "I'm trying to figure out how to open this show. Because we've got to set a tone." He said, "I've got a phrase for you. Just put it in your mind and work around it. 'It's a celebration of courage.'" I said, "Arthur, I could kiss you." And that was how I started. I used that phrase.

It set the right tone: positive, uplifting. The Marathon of Hope was continuing on. There was a line-up of people on the show. Some were celebrities like John Denver and Lee Majors, while many others were just people who wanted to help. The phones were ringing off the hook, and Lloyd was talking to guests as they came in. People shared their own stories of battling cancer, and what cancer had done to their loved ones. It was a fly-by-the-seat-of-your-pants operation. They had a reporter outside of Terry's hospital room, who said Terry was watching and smiling. The donations averaged about $25,000 a minute. In total, over $10 million was raised during the live event. Adjust for inflation, and that would be about $32 million in 2024.

It was so fundamentally Canadian. That's the thing about it. It was heart. It was raw. And it was us because we are different. I guess you could say we're more modest, but we're still go-getters. He reminded us that we come from that gritty background. And people forget that about Canadians, because some people think we're too modest or too soft, all that. We're not. And, you see, that was Terry. He came from an average Canadian family, and that's why so many Canadians, I think, connected because they could see themselves in him in a different way. "What if that had happened to me? Would I be able to do what he has done? Would I have the same kind of grit and determination within me? Let me think about that. Let's talk

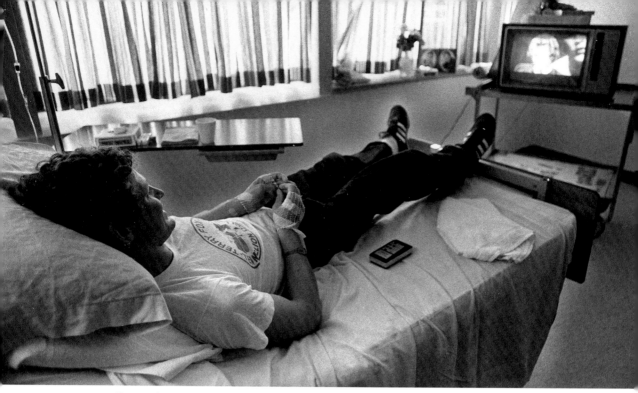

September 7, 1980: Terry smiles from his hospital bed while watching the CTV telethon organized in his honour.

Photo by Andy Clark, Canadian Press

about that with our kids." All of whom are talking about Terry. Terry this, Terry that. If Terry [were] here today . . .

When Terry died, Lloyd covered the funeral in B.C. The staff at CBC were on strike at the time, and they weren't sure if they could carry the feed from CTV. Lloyd felt it was important and spoke to the decision-makers.

I said, "I won't mention my name. I won't put myself on camera because this is too important for that. I'll identify people. I'll set a narrative tone for the broadcast, what it means to Canada." Essentially, Terry is passing, but he's passing us the torch. There was a technician with me, and we had contact with the control room in Vancouver into the network. It was a little room, and I had the monitor in front of me with the scene of the church, and then the cameras following out the casket and the hearse. I remember distinctly the steam coming off — it was a

235

July 2, 1981: Dear friends of Terry's act as pallbearers, carrying his casket during his funeral. Left, front to back: Jack and Doug Alward and Gary Zutz. Right, front to back: Terri Fleming, Ken Boldt, and Clay Gamble.

Photo by Bettman via Getty Images

hot day — and the hearse disappearing into the mist, which gave a kind of evocative narrative to the whole thing. Because, you know, I was talking about Terry and the passing of the torch and the mission of fighting cancer through his determination. It has to be carried forward now. It's up to us. And that was sort of the narrative as I closed it up.

Lloyd has been around the world, covering the news, and calls Terry one of Canada's greatest exports. When he has talked to people in other countries, some of them will mention Terry. In 1984, Lloyd was in Sarajevo conversing with the culture minister about their troubles in the Balkans. In one conversation, the minister said to him, "Yeah, Canada — Terry Fox! You have this guy, Terry Fox. We know about him. We are going to start something up here." It had only been four years, but Terry's story had already spread that far.

In 1992, Lloyd was asked by Betty to be the chairman of the Run. He spoke at the opening and was proud and honoured to have been asked. He got to know Terry through Betty, and he could see where Terry got his grit and determination from. He thinks the family has done a great job carrying the cause forward and keeping it going.

I think he inspired a giving back narrative in all of us. That is part of being a community. It's being part of a society. I mean, he led that kind of mission in people's hearts. I know I felt it, too, in writing about him and talking about him. It's simply because I think it was such a noble mission. So positive. I've done a lot of charity stuff, but this one was so close to my heart because it came through the job I was doing. And then it became personal.

Then I got involved with the mission with Betty that year as chairman, and I felt it. Anything you can do to pump this cause, because it is a great one. These days, there's so much negativity, and social media has done so much damage. It brings out that other side, that negativism, too often. So, to be able to be associated with something that is so positive, so heartfelt with people, is really a positive thing to be able to hang on to.

This monument stands in Thunder Bay near where Terry was forced to conclude his Marathon of Hope. It was designed by sculptor Manfred Pervich and completed on June 26, 1982, roughly one year after the first anniversary of Terry's passing.
From Education Images via Getty Images

July 11: Day 91 (10 miles) Today I did 8 miles in the morning. Then I did Canada AM and went to a very emotional reception at Scarborough [Civic Centre] where I did my best speech. A cute girl [Anne Marie von Zuben] with cancer gave me a [daffodil] and it broke me up. After that we went to my room where I met Darryl Sittler, a great man. Then I ran to Nathan Phillips Square. Thousands of people cheered me on.

July 14: Day 94 (23 miles) Today was a very difficult day with the wind and extreme heat. The only thing that kept me going were the people lining the roads. I was exhausted today, nearly to the point of fainting. I met 2 people today who had cancer like me, and they were both a tremendous inspiration to me.

July 20: Day 100 (20 miles) Today was a hard day because I had so many interruptions. The first mile went well but I could only do 10 because they wanted to time my arrival in Stratford. Then, in extreme heat, I did 2 miles to Stratford, where I did a speech to a large mass of people. Then one more mile when Ben [Speicher] came and I had to stop again for an hour and a half. After that I did 5 more miles and almost faint spell. We went back to St. Mary's for a beautiful reception — the whole town was out.

July 11, 1980: Terry threw the first pitch at the Toronto Blue Jays game.

Photo by Gail Harvey

July 11, 1980: Betty Fox at Nathan Phillips Square in Toronto, Ontario, holding a donations box out the window to supporters.

Courtesy of the Lott family

Marathon of hope: Terry Fox, left, who lost a leg to cancer, is running across Canada in a "marathon of hope" to raise funds for cancer research. He was given a civic reception at city hall, above, where he was greeted by his father, Rolly, at right, and the rest of his family who were flown here for the occasion.

'Showing us what courage is'

July 18, 1980: The *Toronto Star* continues to highlight Terry, with letters to the editor flooding in full of admiration and support. Pictured: Terry and his father, Rolly, stand on stage at Nathan Phillips Square.

July 11, 1980: Terry is escorted into the Scarborough Civic Centre for his speech.

Fox runs into hero's welcome from Metro throngs

By JON FERRY

Move over, Ken Taylor. Metro Toronto has just discovered a tanned, curly-haired all-Canadian hero who is 24 years younger and perhaps fitter than the showcase diplomat.

Terry Fox, the handsome, 21-year-old ambassador for cancer research now attempting to run 5,200 miles from coast to coast with an artificial leg, is every bit as much a nationalist's dream.

And every bit as modest.

Terry, feted yesterday in a jam-packed Nathan Phillips Square rally that loosed tear ducts by the bucketful, says he's not so much different from the rest of us.

He has feasted on hospitality in Newfoundland, even though he shed five to seven pounds in the process. And he's run into wild motorists and language problems in Quebec where, he says, Canadian Cancer Society officials were less than helpful.

He loves sports and Darryl Sittler — his University Avenue running companion with whom he traded sweaters yesterday.

He loves chocolate bars, junk food and carbohydrates by the carload.

But he doesn't have time for fun, frivolity or female propositions. He has to maintain self-discipline to complete the remaining 3,150 miles through northern Ontario, the Prairies, the Rockies and the Pacific coast rain forest.

Hobbled by an artificial leg that breaks down all the time, the 5-foot, 10-inch, 150-pound amputee remains stoic. "It's pain, but it isn't unbearable. It's something that I can handle."

The cancer ward, he explains, is a far tougher marathon than the one he is running. "People I saw who had cancer set an example. I've got to be strong, I can't give up."

What he sometimes feels he can't handle is all the publicity.

"People are treating me like a hero, like I'm something above other people," he told the wildly cheering welcome crowd whose reception he described as "unbelievable, unreal."

He said he wasn't doing it for self-promotion and he wasn't doing it for the money. He said he wouldn't quit — but then hastened to add that quitting wouldn't be failure in his book.

Terry, whose right leg was amputated three years ago because of a malignant tumor, started his day at 5:15 a.m. yesterday with an eight-mile jog along Highway 2 and Kingston Road in Scarborough.

One of Terry's thousands of well-wishers was 23-year-old Mark Kent, who ran 4,056 miles across Canada in 1974 as a high-school student.

Mr. Kent, who handed Terry the coaching book he used for his run, warned that the hills of northern Ontario were far more energy draining than either the Prairies or the Rocky Mountain valleys.

Terry, meanwhile, thanked the Cancer Society for its support. "They took a chance on me. I could have been a phony."

Picture, Page 5

July 12, 1980: Jon Ferry for the *Globe and Mail* reports on Terry's overwhelming reception in Toronto.

July 11, 1980: Terry stands in Nathan Phillips Square, downtown Toronto, surveying thousands of supporters in the crowd. It was the largest reception he received during his Marathon of Hope.

INSPIRATION

"Sometimes I wonder if what I'm doing is worth it — if it has meaning . . . I realized it does. Greg [Scott] rode his bike behind me today. He's only had his operation two months ago, and he's already up and walking around. He's been with us two days; I haven't heard one complaint the whole time. I'd just like to tell him he's been a tremendous inspiration to me. I thank him for coming and helping me out. You're going to be with me all the way, every step of the way, and I'll never forget it."

— Terry Fox
Speech in Terrace Bay, Ontario, August 27, 1980

DON THUR & RON KERRIGAN

Forestry officer and parole officer at the Beaver Creek Institution in Gravenhurst

While watching the media coverage of Terry running across Ontario, Don heard that the Marathon route was going up Highway 69 all the way to Sudbury. He had the idea that Terry should make a detour and come through Muskoka, as there were a lot of people in the area who would like to see him, and Don was certain they could raise some funds. He made some calls and got connected to the Canadian Cancer Society (CCS), which connected him with Terry.

Don: I remember it boiled down to "We'll change the run if you can guarantee $10,000." I said, "I can do that," because I was in charge of my own department [Forestry] at Beaver Creek. Worst case scenario, I would have to not buy anything else and figure out a way to get the money out of my budget. So, after we finished that conversation, I phoned the warden at, like, eleven o'clock at night, and I said, "They're going to change the route, come up [this way], and by the way, we're on the hook for $10,000." He just about came through the phone.

It was maybe the next day; we had a supervisor meeting at the institution. The run was going to coincide with Terry's birthday. I said, "Well, why don't we invite him to Beaver Creek, into the institution, for his birthday dinner?" So, I got back in touch with the tour.

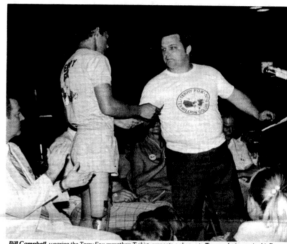

Bill Campbell, wearing the Terry Fox marathon T-shirt, presents a cheque to Terry, who is wearing his Beaver Creek T-Shirt. Bill spearheaded a drive for funds at Beaver Creek that saw the men raise more than $800 despite the fact that on three straight days on which a car wash was held, it rained. If you'd like to send money to the Terry Fox Fund, see page 4. Gravenhurst News photo.

Beaver Creek Inmates Cheer Terry Fox's Lesson in Courage

ONTARIO — Sheer guts! That's the best description for curly-headed, University student **Terry Fox**, 22, who lost a leg to cancer but is jogging his way across Canada to raise money for cancer research.

July 28, Terry arrived in Gravenhurst, Ontario and had dinner at Beaver Creek Correctional Camp, polishing off, not one, but two complete T-Bone steak dinners for which he was most appreciative. "We don't eat like this every day," said Beaver Creek Superintendent **Ted Van Petegem**.

Over the weekend, the inmates at Beaver Creek sold refreshments at two concerts in a local park. They also had a car wash and sold popcorn at the Centennial Centre, and, as a result, were able to raise about $800 for cancer research. Forestry Officer, **Don Chur**, organized a local fund-raising drive in Bracebridge and raised a further $920.

After enjoying his steak dinner, Terry told the inmates how, in his freshman year at Simon Fraser, his knee became sore while playing basketball. After the season was over, it was still bothering him so he went to the doctor and was horrified

chemotherapy. He lost his hair "but this had fringe benefits because it grew in curly." He hated wearing a wig and found that worse than the loss of his leg, he admits.

He says he is jogging across the country because he "can't forget all those cancer-sufferers who don't make it, or who live in pain from cancer treatments." He feels courage is what makes life worth living with or without cancer.

• See page 3

To accommodate the inmates, the facility had a large kitchen and dining room, so it was easy to have a table set for Terry for his birthday. Terry didn't want any fuss or media coverage; he wanted it to be a private function. He was just happy to come

September 30, 1980: an article in the *Let's Talk/Entre Nous Express* (Correctional Service Canada's newsletter), detailing Terry's visit to the Beaver Creek Institute on June 28, 1980.

Let's Talk/Entre Nous, Correctional Service of Canada, vol. 5 (18), Sept. 30, 1980, p. 1

and have a steak dinner with the inmates. The warden and the staff went to work on the logistics. Ron, a parole officer at the institution, remembers when he first set eyes on Terry.

> Ron: I was given the honour of meeting the van, and I walked up to the passenger side. I opened the door, and out stepped Doug. I felt like such a fool! Terry was driving. He got out and, the poor fella, he was soaked. I walked him down the walkway to the library area and there was an office at the end that we had set aside for Terry for whatever he needs, and as it turned out, he needed to change clothes and dry off. We went into the kitchen area where the inmates ate. It was open concept; there was a planter that separated us from the inmates basically. Took Terry in there and you could have heard a pin drop. It was just incredible. I remember his joke about his socks. And he says, "I have one sock that doesn't stink." It's funny [that] it stuck with me. The respect that the inmates had for this kid was beyond.

After the warden said a few words and Terry gave his speech, they allowed the inmates to ask some questions.

> Don: Right at the back of the dining hall, there was an inmate. He was in his late forties. He stood up, and he was going to say a few words on behalf of the inmates. He said, "I'm not proud of it, but I've been in a lot of prisons in Canada. And I'm a pretty tough con. I fought some tough cons. But I have never in my life met a person or a con as strong as you." If I'm not mistaken, everybody was cheering. It was a pretty moving tribute, I think. The fact that they met him, that they actually saw the person they were following on television — they were pretty proud. We were proud that we got to meet him. It was something like the Second Coming. And in hindsight, it turned out that it was his last birthday.

Both Don and Ron went to the fund-raising event in Gravenhurst where the rest of the town was there to celebrate his birthday with another much larger cake.

Terry receives his birthday cake with Don Thur's son at his side.
Photo by Murray Powell

Ron: He had such charisma, so humble, so polite. [And] the people in the [Gravenhurst] arena were just wanting to give everything they had. He just had an effect on people like that. I can only describe it in one word, and that was love. I think there was every kind of emotion you could imagine in that arena, but mostly joy. There were a lot of tears. Good tears, for sure. I don't think people realized how much of an impact Terry had until they actually saw it. The other word that connects people to Terry is "normal." He was a normal person. When you think about a marathon every day, and you're thinking, "Who is this Superman?" And he was the most normal kid.

Don speaks about the big running shoe that was made, a replica of Terry's Adidas running shoe, and stuffed with money. He thinks they raised about $14,000 in the arena alone and another $5,000 through selling T-shirts and other donations. Only a few months later, Beaver Creek heard the news that the Marathon had ended. It was very solemn at the prison.

Don: They embraced him, you know? The fact that they got to spend a couple hours with a person of his greatness, they accepted and took him as one of their own.

Ninety-nine percent of the Canadian population who saw him only saw him at arm's length or through the media. Here's a population of guys who you would have never ever thought would shake hands with a person like that.

Ron doesn't remember anything from the end of the Marathon and thinks he must've blocked it out — too painful to remember. His wife, Joanne, had told him that he came home and stood in their foyer crying. No one had ever affected him the way Terry had, and Terry inspired him in everything he has had to face since.

Ron: I'm a two-time cancer survivor. I went through lung cancer in 2013 or '14, and I remember sitting in that chair, looking out that window with an intravenous drip, and thinking of Terry Fox. As bleak as the diagnosis was, I never once thought that it was going to get me. Terry was responsible for that attitude.

Working as a parole officer, Ron has also shared Terry's story to inspire parolees who have needed motivation.

Ron and his wife, Joanne, with their dog, Tucker, hold their framed picture of Terry at the Beaver Creek Institute.

Photo by Barbara Adhiya

Ron: I've referenced him on many occasions with parolees. "Take a look at someone that faced adversity. Take a look at someone that did not have a good go." It would open a discussion about him, and I was always ready to talk about [his story]. When I would speak to the fellows that were down, that needed something to grasp, he was foremost, like he was the person that I would refer to — holy shit. I can't believe this. That's incredible when you think about it.

Ron takes a moment to wipe a tear from his eye. He hadn't really given this much thought before, how much his interaction with Terry has inspired him since and how much he's used him to inspire others. His face lights up, having made the connection in his mind, in his memories, and now he looks back at the bigger picture and how it all fits together.

Ron: I would just basically say that there's hope. It's not all lost. Here's a person that took the worst news possible and turned it into something that benefitted all Canadians. Nothing is impossible. I just use [him] as an example [of] someone that can overcome great odds.

ELAINE GEROW
Former president of the Havelock CCS chapter, who designed Terry's iconic T-shirt

As I drive down a side road, trying to read the address numbers on the small posts, I come upon a tall stump of a tree carved with an image of Terry Fox. Without looking further, I know I am at the right place. Elaine and her husband, Doug, are in their later years, and their daughter Melanie joins us to help her mother with some of the details. Melanie was a young girl when Terry and the group spent the afternoon at their home. He left a deep impression, converting them all into Terry Foxers. Elaine also inspired Terry, just by wearing a T-shirt she had made.

Elaine heard from the CCS that Terry was going to be coming through Havelock, Ontario, in early July. She is a go-getter, and with the support of her husband and daughter, she went to work. She had all kinds of things organized: ball games in the park, a tournament, and a dinner at the legion. The tournament idea fizzled out, and the tickets she had for the supper didn't sell, as people thought he wasn't

Elaine's original shirt from July 1980.
This artifact is now being housed in the
Canadian Museum of History in Ottawa.
Canadian Museum of History, 2015.27.1

going to stop and keep going. On the day he was arriving, she had tables set up trying to raise money.

Melanie: She had us dress up like clowns. There were balloons everywhere just to cheer him on. We were doing every-thing we possibly could to sell things and raise money. I think we had hot dog stands and popcorn while he was running through the town or while we were waiting for him. I think [we] had a band.

Elaine: We were having a supper. It was a big hall, and a lot of people couldn't get in there. I couldn't sell any tickets beforehand. But once he got here, boy. It certainly was full.

As he ran through the town, the people who had gathered to see him started crying. At the supper later on, people were trying to break the doors down to get in, and they had to call the police for crowd control.

Melanie: I don't remember what he said during his speech at the dinner, but I remember his emotions. He seemed to be overwhelmed at the number of people that were there, and the fact that there were people still trying to get in.

After Terry had run about a mile or so out of town, he came back and went to the Gerows' house to have a rest break before the organized supper. The Gerows had a pool, and the crew took advantage of it that summer afternoon. Doug and Darrell played with the kids in the pool. Since then, the Gerow kids have tried to copy the dive Doug had done, calling it the Dougie Dive. They practised it all summer and for the next few years.

Melanie says that Darrell had done a belly flop, the waves splashing onto the paper maps Terry was looking at. He was not pleased. Terry was always concerned about getting home and ensuring he arrived before winter. Having that afternoon, he had time to reflect on what was ahead of him. To go out to London, then back, was quite out of his way. He was trying to make some decisions.

> Melanie: Mom and Dad mentioned earlier about Terry sitting by the pool and looking at the maps. One of the senses that I had that day was that Terry was very serious; he was focused. We were all having fun in the pool, and I was a nine-year-old thinking, like, "Relax a bit." But we were told to leave him alone. After that day, I think I asked why, and Mom and Dad together said he was agonizing over the route. And I don't know if I've put my own memories in or not because from Havelock to go straight across Canada, it would have made a lot more sense just to go to Lindsay and North Bay and not go where all the people and money were. To me, that's Terry. He wasn't doing the run to complete it. It would have been great if he had. But he was doing it to make the maximum impact.

While Terry sat by the pool, he was talking with Elaine about her shirt.

> Melanie: This design of the map was on the front of her shirt, and then on the back it said *I'm for Terry Fox.* They worked together to design what he wanted. And then Mom went to the local shop and had them made up. Our world revolved around Terry. As soon as she heard about it, everything she did was all about Terry. That T-shirt testifies she knew he could do it. She was a hundred percent behind him. She felt he was gonna complete it.

Terry's Marathon of Hope shirt was designed by Elaine Gerow in July 1980. It became the iconic shirt that most Canadians associate with the Marathon.

Photo by Gail Harvey

They designed Terry's shirt to have the same map on the front but with the word *Marathon* curved over on top and *of Hope* curved under on the bottom. On the back, Terry chose the message *Give for Cancer Research*.

A few weeks later, the Gerows got a call from Doug asking them to bring more shirts. Terry didn't want to wear anything else, and Doug was washing out the same shirt every night. The Gerows went to Terry's birthday party in Gravenhurst and presented him with ten more shirts. It became the iconic shirt most people recognize today. Terry was later buried in that shirt, and Elaine's personal shirt has since been given to the Canadian Museum of History in Ottawa for a Terry Fox exhibit. She was glad to do it but now wishes it was still with her at home.

The family may have only had a short time with Terry, but he touched them all deeply with his strength, courage, and selflessness. They have the tree carving at the front of their property as a way of sharing Terry with everyone who passes by to keep his message alive.

Melanie recalls the day Terry had to end his run. She may have been only nine, but she remembers it vividly. Looking at her mother, she tries to hold back from crying, her voice hoarse.

Melanie: The first night that he stopped, Mom lit a candle on the table at supper and said this is for Terry. And you kept it lit every night until he passed.

JON HURST

Organizer of the Acton Terry Fox Run for forty-three years

Jon is now a widowed senior living in the south of Acton, Ontario, and was a town councillor until recently. He joins me on Zoom from his living room, wearing the newest Terry T-shirt. With his white free-flowing hair, paired with his moustache and fluffy beard, he is a dead ringer for Saint Nick. As he tells his story, it becomes clear he is also just as kind.

Jon and his family were on holiday at their cottage on Lake Simcoe when Terry ran through Acton. Not only did they miss seeing him run through their town, but they also missed when their neighbours, the Lotts, hosted him. Paying attention to when he would be

June 2023: The Terry Fox monument tree in front of the Gerows' house.
Photo by Barbara Adhiya

Terry emerges from the shadows in the early morning.
Photo by Gail Harvey

coming through their area at the cottage, they learned through radio reports that he had stopped just south of Barrie on Highway 11, which they knew was where he would start from the next morning.

Jon piled the family into their car at 4 a.m. and drove to an intersection on Highway 11 called Fennell's Corner, thinking they'd be one of a few there. Initially, it was dark and quiet, but in no time, a crowd of about forty people had gathered.

> Where we were standing, there was a little bit of a grade, and initially we didn't really see him coming. We could see the lights of the police car flashing, and then almost out of the darkness came his silhouette. And, of course, we heard the thumping of his feet on the pavement because, at that point, you could hear a pin drop. Here he is running towards us, and I'm thinking to myself, "I've got to say something really intelligent here." I was speechless. He ran by and I was just awestruck.

Jon thought Terry was an incredibly courageous kid. His family had been following his run through Leslie Scrivener's articles, and they understood what he was going through, the traffic around him, and the weather he had to tackle. They wanted to see him again, so later in the day they drove north on Highway 11 and saw a crowd stopped at a motel. Terry was having his nap inside. Jon waited, chatting with Bill Vigars, and then Terry came out and mingled with the crowd. Jon was standing right next to him but didn't say anything in the end — he was just happy to be near him. They wanted to make a donation, so Bill sold them the T-shirts he had in the trunk of his car. The whole family got one.

Jon's view of Terry on Highway 11, north of Barrie, Ontario, as he walks from his hotel through a supportive crowd.

Photo by Terri Dale

As Terry was getting ready to run, the OPP wanted him to stop because the Sunday night traffic was coming from cottage country down Highway 11. It was a two-lane highway each way, and they wanted him to stop because they were afraid of an accident. And Terry didn't want to stop. He wanted to get his miles in. So, they relented and said okay. It turned out as he started running, people were stopping in the other lane and yelling encouragement to him. And a couple of volunteers were going through the line of cars with Kentucky Fried Chicken containers, and people were throwing money in the buckets. So, the traffic was coming to a complete stop, [as] people were donating and then continuing on.

Jon is rarely without a Terry Fox shirt on and has over forty of them. When children recognize Terry on his shirt, he asks what they know about him and what they've learned in school. He looks forward to having these conversations, not just with kids but with everyone. There are always positive comments, people sharing their recollections of

Four generations of Hursts at the Acton Terry Fox Run.
Courtesy of the Hurst family

the Marathon and what Terry meant to them. Jon tells people, especially those in a battle with cancer, "You're on a journey. Terry went through it, then went on to run a marathon every day."

When the run ended and Terry returned home for treatment, Jon wanted to share his gratitude for all that Terry had done.

After he got sick, I sent a card to him and thanked him for his efforts. I thanked him for the courage he had, the example he set. To persevere. To keep going. And that was one of the lessons I thought that he had left us: when you're struggling through something, realizing that you've got to take another run at it.

That's the sort of thing that I think we learned when my beloved wife, Maxine, was diagnosed with a glioblastoma brain tumour. We knew she was terminal, that this was a diagnosis nobody survives. And so, what do you do? Well, you do what Terry did. Move forward. Live your life. Do it with hope because, as I said earlier, you don't know where this road is gonna lead you. Over the hill and around the bend. Maybe that's where the cure is. The doctor said to my wife when he confirmed her diagnosis, he said, "Your situation is terminal. No one survives this." And she looked at him and she said, "So I would be the first?"

I think Terry's story helped her to come up with that. We didn't beat it, but we gave it a wonderful run with the help of family and friends. The first time that we met with the oncologist, it was in Princess Margaret [hospital], before she started radiation. He was explaining everything to us, and we were "Yeah this. Yeah that." He stopped, and he said, "Do you two understand what I'm telling you? Do you realize what the situation is?" We said, "Yes, we understand completely what's going on. We're ready to move forward on our journey." And I think we learned that from Terry.

Jon admires that Terry didn't do it for personal gain or for fame but for others. When Terry went through difficult situations, he still went out and kept going every day to try to raise money for others. It's what inspires Jon every year when he organizes the Run.

Jon speaks to the runners ahead of the 2015 Acton Terry Fox Run.
Courtesy of Beverley McKnight Baddeley

It gives me pride because I'm able to give that opportunity for participation to my community. We've been pretty successful in Acton over the years. We're approaching a million dollars raised over the last forty-three years. We're at $951,000 right now. I never would have thought that was possible. But there are so many people in the community that want to be involved in the Run. Not that I've been doing anything special, because the Terry Fox Run promotes itself. All you have to do is provide the location and the information, maybe some food and drink. People show up, and they've all got stories. It just makes me really proud of my community that we've been able to carry this on for so long and continue to pursue Terry's dream.

SUSAN BRADNAM

Former photographer for the *Kitchener-Waterloo Record*

It isn't until I'm walking up Susan's driveway that I realize I know her. I had worked with her for over a decade as a photo editor for the Canadian Press, and the *Kitchener-Waterloo Record* was one of our members. We would speak on the phone a few times a week about coverage and sending in photos. She greets me at her door, a corner home with an expansive yard, and we settle into her dining room.

Susan doesn't remember when she first heard about Terry, but with

all the media coverage leading up to Toronto, she was bound to hear about him. Back then, she had been recently hired full-time with the *Kitchener-Waterloo Record*, their first female photographer, and was mostly assigned stories like tea parties. She didn't think she was ever going to have the opportunity to photograph him.

It was July 20, 1980, the day before Terry was due to arrive in Kitchener, Ontario, and Susan was on her way to photograph a teddy bear picnic in nearby Stratford. She was taking the back road when she saw his van and entourage.

Susan with her camera in the fall of 1980.
Courtesy of Susan Bradnam

I stopped, put on my gear, marched up, and banged on the door. Somebody opened the door who was a little bit older than Terry. He said, "How can I help you?" And I said, "Well, I'm Susan Bradnam, and I'd really like to get a picture of Terry." And he said, "What do you think, Terry?" And Terry said, "No, no, we're in Kitchener tomorrow. Tomorrow, you can get your picture." I said, "No, I can't because I don't have the assignment. I'd really like to get it now because then we can let everybody in Kitchener know you're coming." And the guy who was standing there said, "Come on, Terry." And he said okay. He looked like he was just exhausted because he'd just come through Stratford.

Anyway, he came out. He kind of tripped a bit, and I was feeling really bad. He stood in front of the tree, and he was kind of just glaring at me. And [the guy] said, "Come on, give her a smile." So he gave me two frames. And then he started running, and I started running after him and I said, "Wait, wait!" because I wanted to get him to say something for the picture. He said, "You don't seem to understand, I've gotta run!" And then he just took off. I just stood there and watched him go on. I thought, "Oh my God, that guy's something else. He's driven, and I hope he makes it."

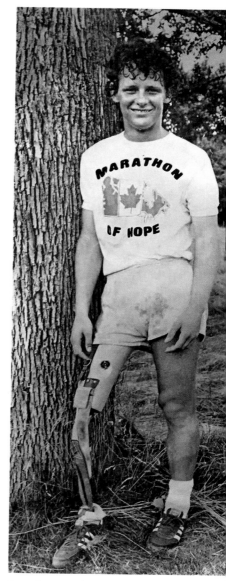

Terry leans against a tree, smiling through sweat for Susan.

Photo by Susan Bradnam

She was lucky to have caught him right there on the road on a break, completely by chance. He looked tired, sweaty, and exhausted. She felt bad having interrupted his rest period but hoped the photos would turn out.

I came back to the office, and they said, "So how are the bears?" And I said, "Oh, they were fine, but I got something on the way." "Oh, yeah, what did you get?" And I said, "I got Terry Fox. I've got two frames here." My boss said, "Well, let's see what you got." We were processing [the film]. Of course, [I'm] just like, "Please let him have a smile." I brought it out, and he said, "Oh, yeah, that's good." It ran the next day. They ran a [different] picture of him on the front page, but they put [mine] inside.

Susan only had a few copies of the image, but she's already given most of them away. She gave one to a little boy, Jacob, who lives across the street. He told her that his school had a Terry Fox Day, and when he heard that she had actually met Terry, he was blown away. He keeps the framed image in his room. Jacob then told another girl in the neighbourhood, Leighton, who was also excited to hear that Susan had met Terry. Susan walks her dog by Leighton's house every day, and she gave another print to her.

Jacob and Leighton stand proudly with Susan's photo, gifted to them after they learned about Terry Fox in school.

Photo by Ashley Roberts

It's so nice to see that in young people. I'm glad they're doing that in the schools now because we need Canadian heroes. And he certainly was an amazing Canadian hero. For a little kid like Jacob, who was in the hospital for quite a while, he looks at that guy and thinks, "Wow, he looks strong. Look at him. So strong and so masterful, and just so in charge of his life." Jacob is out every single day playing basketball. He just plays, often by himself, but he's got that kind of spirit. I bet that helped a little.

By capturing Terry in that photo, Susan prolonged his impact on the next generation, ensuring that he would continue to inspire long after he had passed. Like many others, Susan can see a little bit of Terry in us all.

> My goddaughter Emily Morgan kind of made history in St. Thomas because she had a double lung transplant when she was nine, and she lived until she was fourteen. You wouldn't have believed her. She was just teeny tiny, skinny, waiting for those lungs. And then, of course, it blew up with the steroids, but then she became this incredible [runner] — she led the Transplant Games here in London. She ran. She just lived her life because she wasn't going to take it for granted. And [Terry] was certainly like that — he just knew he had to get this done.

JOHN SIMPSON
Filmmaker and director of the documentary *Terry Fox: I Had a Dream*

After spending over thirty years living in Costa Rica, John now lives with his son, who is building a home on his property for John to live out his senior years. It's off a small road in Gravenhurst, and he greets me with an enthusiastic hello, thanking me for making the long drive into cottage country. He wants to discuss everything and anything, bit by bit, scene by scene, as any good storyteller does. It's how he saw the importance of capturing Terry's story to inspire people for many years to come.

Like so many others, it was Leslie Scrivener's columns that brought John's attention to Terry. He had read that Terry was in Nova Scotia and proposed making a movie about him to the CCS. They were dubious but said they'd be on board if he found a partner. He went to CBC, and they agreed to fund the other half. It was a small budget overall, but John could make the documentary, along with his cameraman, Scott Hamilton.

They met Terry just after he crossed the border into New Brunswick; the van was at a highway stop, parked under a tree. Doug was making Terry pork and beans from cans they had in the van.

John's cameraman, Scott Hamilton, holds a Steadicam used for running shots of Terry.
Courtesy of the Terry Fox Centre Archives

He came out. I said to him, "Hey, we're going to make a documentary of you for the Cancer Society." He didn't like a lot of interference, but if it was for the Cancer Society, [he was willing to accommodate]. And he said, "Yeah. Okay. Let's do that." I said, "Well, we'll come in every second week or something like that, follow you across country." That seemed to work okay with him, other than he said, "I won't go back so you can get more shots." He will only go straight ahead.

They began filming, John taking shots of his legs, his running stride, and longer shots down the road. He was always trying to find new ways to shoot scenes to avoid all of them being Terry running on the road, and there were many long, empty roads.

Especially in New Brunswick, there was nothing around, just this big highway. You can see farmhouses down the way, and people come down the lane to stand there to greet him. When there is nothing there and nobody around, trees and emptiness, he stopped and talked to them because I'm sure he was lonely. Say, "Hello, other human being!"

When they got to Ontario, everything changed, and those long, empty roads vanished, now filled with crowds of people hoping to catch a glimpse of him. John notes the effect Terry had on the crowd in Toronto, his own conscience and moral compass touching theirs.

> That session in Toronto was so — jeez, that was outstanding at City Hall. People were down there bawling. I can see it now; it was overwhelming. A word that I would say that you very seldom use was "blessing." What a wonderful thing was happening in their minds, in all these people, what he was showing towards others. And everybody was feeling this. A lot of these businessmen there, their eyes were filled with tears. It was very, very moving. And then they couldn't get enough money. Walking around with bags full of money. Big plastic bags. It was his innocence that people loved. They couldn't put their finger on it.

On some portions of the run, John and Scott wired Terry up for sound, hoping to record anything he might be saying to himself. But it all ended up sounding muffled, so the sound in the documentary was added post-production.

> The only sound that we really got clean was when he's going up the Montreal [River Hill on August 16]. We could hear him coughing. Then we knew something's gone wrong. That was the start of the end. The cancer had come back, and he was coughing badly. At that time, I had decided to take a break from the run. I was just starting to go on a vacation somewhere. And he went down; it all broke to hell.

John had some conversations with Terry after the run, albeit mostly surface-level. Seeing him at the hospital, John understood that Terry was really just a kid coming to grips with the truth of his situation. Looking back on it, John wonders if there was any spiritual push to this acceptance.

> He never really lost that innocence until much later. I think I flew out when he was in the hospital, and he was telling

me that he was taking chemotherapy. He said, "You think you're going crazy with the chemo. It gives you all kinds of hallucinations and all of that stuff, too. It's worse than the operation." I remember he really had a bad time at the hospital. He was upset when he found out that he couldn't run anymore. Things happen, but not always the way you planned it. I believe he did believe this is the way it is, and so be it. Not the way [he] planned it, but it brought him a whole new life and a reason for being, even though he was unaware of it.

Whether he was aware or not, Terry's life and contributions meant a great deal to others. He touched the nation, and John's documentary (released in 1981) helped spread his story and his dream to the world. Although Terry couldn't complete his Marathon, he raised over $24 million for cancer research in under a year, and people continue to run and donate in his name. People say "be kind," but here was someone who actually did it in their community, getting nothing out of it. What was so powerful was the idea that what he did was a sacrifice, and it has made a lasting impact.

GAIL HARVEY
Photographer during the Marathon of Hope, film producer of *Terry* biopic

Gail is a film director and producer with a busy schedule, but she carves out time to speak over Zoom. She has the fierceness of a woman who has battled for respect and acceptance in her industry, her dark curly hair mussed and free. She feels lucky to still talk about Terry and is grateful to have captured his spirit on film for others to feel him and experience what he did.

When Terry started his run, Gail was a photographer with United Press Canada. She was on the photo desk some nights and kept seeing the same picture of him being played in the media over and over again. She knew it was an incredible story, and she wanted to get to know him and capture more impactful shots. She called up the CCS, and they directed her to Bill Vigars. It took a few days for them to connect, but when they did, she told him she would be at Nathan Phillips Square.

The first time I saw him was when he ran down University [Avenue] — took all kinds of pictures following him into City Hall, and it was extraordinary. It was so crowded; everyone was in awe. It was electric. You couldn't believe what was happening. The streets were lined all down University.

Gail was on the stage, walking backwards through a group of photographers, and almost fell off the stage. Bill caught her, thankfully, and they've been friends ever since. Gail remembers Terry speaking to the mass of people that had gathered. To her, he was well-spoken, knew what he was saying and what he was going for, and was direct.

Gail joined the group on the run in her Volkswagen Rabbit, sometimes sitting in the open hatch while Bill drove her car, taking pictures of Terry running every day before the sun came up. There were a few days when she slept in the van, and she was there during his breaks for water and orange slices. Terry even let her into his room when he was writing in his journal at night. She tried to capture every aspect of the experience.

I took pictures of him when he was in bed with his leg off and just talked to him like, "What do you think about?" And he said, "I don't think about anything. I think about putting one foot in front of the other. That's all I can think." He was sweet and funny. I mean, he was just open. We were all so young. It was just a lot of fun. And I knew it was very important, but I think none of us recognized the magnitude of what he was going through.

Terry writes in his journal in his hotel bed; he often allowed Gail into the quiet and private moments of the Marathon.

Photo by Gail Harvey

There were a lot of events to attend outside of his run, and he often had a packed schedule. She doesn't know how he managed to do it all.

He would say, "I'm just trying to run home." He would talk about the kids and the people he wanted to help. But he was very focused on what he had to do. He didn't want anything to get in his way of being able to make a ton of money for cancer research and to just put one foot in front of the other and get home.

Canadian Cancer Society representative Jack Lambert helps a comedic Terry arrange his schedule of events.

Photo by Gail Harvey

He did have a cough the last time Gail saw him, yet it was still a shock when the run ended. She cried when she heard. Everyone believed he was going to finish the Marathon; there was no doubt. She knew he was disappointed. But she wonders if he also might have been a little happy to be going home and seeing his parents.

I know that Terry used to think of all the people that were worse off than him, all those little kids that he saw. Like, "Okay, well, this is bad, but life is like that. You just have to roll your sleeves up," kind of like what he did. Moving forward and being optimistic is always the better choice. I think that that's what people have to do. Life is not easy, and it was not easy for him to do what he did. He recognized that. He loved all the people, and he was a very sweet human being. Human beings are more powerful than we know in many ways, whether it's something that you think and [then] it happens, or you believe in quantum entanglement. Who knows? There's something

Preferring to be behind the camera, Gail's shadow stands behind Terry as he runs through Northern Ontario.
Photo by Gail Harvey

that we don't understand, something that's very magical, and I think this is one of those things for sure.

In 1982, HBO hired Gail as a photographer for *The Terry Fox Story*. Later, she would go on to produce her own biopic, *Terry*, in 2005. One day during production, she was in a coffee shop with one of the actors, studying her contact sheets of the Marathon. When the server came over, he saw the sheets of photographs and asked what they were looking at. He shared that he was carrying a Terry Fox coin in his wallet as an inspirational token.

I've been very lucky, met tons of people, but literally, Terry Fox affected me more than anyone. I would have never picked working in drama or being a director. I ended up in the film industry because of Terry Fox.

MICHAEL LEVINE
Executive producer of the biographical film *The Terry Fox Story*

Michael's office is in the historic Chelsea Shop in Toronto, a small bookish place with wood shelves on every wall. I sit across from his desk, and he explains that all the books on his shelves were by authors like Pierre Trudeau, Conrad Black, and Mordecai Richler, for whom he acted as an entertainment lawyer and literary agent for high-profile deals. As a negotiator for stories, he knew he had to give Terry Fox's story the spotlight.

It was after Terry ended the run that Michael was approached with the idea of acquiring the film rights for the story. As with any movie, it had many moving parts: funding, contracts, rights agreements, networks, and casting. HBO acquired the movie, Michael became the executive producer, and then the rights were sold to CTV. They found a young man to play Terry, Eric Fryer, who was not an actor but had also lost his leg to cancer, and Robert Duvall was cast as Bill Vigars. *The Terry Fox Story* came out in 1983.

Before Terry passed away, Michael only had one conversation with him, where he relayed how the film team admired what Terry had achieved and hoped to memorialize his story forever. Michael knew how extraordinary an act it was, that anyone would even think of such an endeavour, and felt it could inspire others.

> Number one, I'm a very strong, small L liberal. I say that my religion is humanity. My race is humanity. I've always been involved in social issues. Number two, I'm an export nationalist. I absolutely believe that [Canada has] stories that can teach the world. For example, with Charles Bronfman and Patrick Watson, we created the Heritage Minutes [vignettes on Canadian history and identity]. Well, the Heritage Minutes are not simply stories. Every one of them is laden with a value. I've always believed that we had stories to tell the world, and of all of them, Terry would rank as number one or number two.

It's rare for people to think anything is possible, as Terry did. Certain factors must come together to achieve something impossible, and strength of character is one of them.

> Some people are endowed with a character that permits them to have courage, to have empathy, to have compassion.

Terry was blessed in the sense that his character was such. Instead of saying "Poor me," he said, "How can I use my problem to help the world?"

Did Terry rationally sit down and think like a forty-year-old? Absolutely not. But he did have the intuition to say, "If I can do this run, and I can prove that my disability has not precluded me from doing something for other people, is that going to inspire other people?" It awakened something, and it also triggered empathy. I think empathy is the most important thing where you intuitively understand what motivated him without knowing any of the facts.

People could see and understand what Terry was sacrificing and the physical consequences of it. They can also see how much he achieved in the attempt. Not everyone can run a marathon a day, but people can use what Terry did as a metaphor for their own challenges.

In the Heritage Minutes, many of them are filled with hope or imagination, people thinking things up. You realize the Alexander Graham Bells, the Henry Fords, and then the Bill Gates's of the world are always running against the current. Not everybody is capable of it, but the people who are can be inspirational. So, there are three types of people: those that do it, those who inspire others to try, and then the people who don't get it. And there are lots of people who don't get it. I think people should have hope, they should have dreams, and they should try it. It doesn't mean it'll succeed. I tell everybody: I learn more from my failures than I do from my successes, always.

2012: Michael receives the University College Alumni of Influence Award from the University of Toronto.

Courtesy of Michael Levine

July 22: Day 102 (20 miles) Today was slow because of continuous delays. First of all, I was stopped at 9 miles just before Guelph. Then I ran 2 miles in did a speech to a good gathering. I did 5 miles out of Guelph, then my feet started to wobble — I began to shake and get dizzy. I had to stop and get to bed. I did 4 miles and then went to Georgetown for a reception.

July 23: Day 103 (10 miles) Today was short because of a great reception with corporate executives in Toronto. I left a good impression and did one of my best speeches. Later we met and ate dinner with Bobby Orr — the highlight of the trip!

July 28: Day 108 (20 miles) Today was a great day! I did 12 miles in the rain in the morning. Went to the Holiday Inn for a birthday party and a cake fight! Slept for 5 hours and then went out and did 8 more bringing me 12 short of Gravenhurst. I went to Beaver Creek prison for a reception and then a wonderful birthday party in Gravenhurst.

July 30: Day 110 (26 miles) Today I got up and the first 4 miles were hell. I was bothered all day by people from media worried about my stump because someone reported I was hurting myself. The next 8 miles went very nicely. It is pretty windy along the 169. Bala was a nice town. The next 9 miles went well and so did the final five.

July 23, 1980: Terry meets one of his heroes, Bobby Orr, whose hometown is Parry Sound.

Beaver Creek Cheered
• From page 1

Rain didn't dampen the enthusiasm of these Beaver Creek inmates who ran a car wash to raise money for Terry Fox's Marathon of Hope.

About 3000 people gathered in the Gravenhurst Centennial Centre to wish Terry a happy 22nd birthday. Terry was on stage, cutting a giant cake and still wearing his Beaver Creek t-shirt. When the Master of Ceremonies thanked "our friends at Beaver Creek" for their donation, the whole crowd gave a thunderous round of applause

making this one of the most touching parts of the program.

Jack Lambert, Ontario District Director of the Cancer Society, said "the generosity of the people of Gravenhurst is unbelievable. I've never seen anything like it." The town and neighboring areas had collected $17,000 in their all-out effort.

August 1980: Terry and Darrell Fox, Kerry Anne, Patrick, and Bill Vigars goof off at a rest stop in Northern Ontario.

Photo by Doug Vater

An article in the *Let's Talk/Entre Nous Express* (Correctional Service Canada's newsletter), detailing Terry's visit to the Beaver Creek Institute on June 28, 1980.

Let's Talk/Entre Nous, Correctional Service of Canada, vol. 5 (18), Sept. 30, 1980, p. 3

July 28, 1980: Terry stands on stage in the Gravenhurst arena, thanking the supporters for gathering.

Photo by David McCoy

Tues. Sept 9 '80

Dear Terry Fox,

During visits with my mother, here at Millhaven Penitentiary, I have been brought up-to-date on your run.

For all that you've done, I'm sure there is a great message for many in the same condition, as well there is a great message for others and their situations. This I know is very true. Yours are very much an inspiration to those in search of inspiration; you are very much like a symbol of good to all those who need reminding that virtuous people still inhabit the earth.

Currently doing a life sentence, I've become depressed and anxious at times, however, knowing that great individuals and humanitarians, such as yourself, are out there on the other side of the fence, my depression & anxiety are relieved.

On behalf of my mother and myself, I would like to say we've both been deeply affected by your deeds. Although I'm not too religious, I pray that if there is a God, a supreme immortal or being, that you are blessed in the heavens.

Terry, we love you.   Sincerely,
Brian Laurier

Many inmates across the country wrote letters of support to Terry and thanked him for his inspiration. In this September 9, 1980, letter from an inmate, Brian, in Bath, Ontario, he says, "Currently doing a life sentence, I've become depressed and anxious at times, however, knowing that great individuals and humanitarians, such as yourself, are out there on the other side of the fence, my depression and anxiety is relieved."

Courtesy of the Terry Fox Centre Archives

SELFLESSNESS & SERVICE

"The first twenty years of my life I had been very self-oriented. I had no concerns for anybody but my own well-being. It took cancer and helpful, loving people as yourself to realize that being self-centred is not the way to live. The answer is to try and help others."

— Terry Fox
Letter to Donna Ball, April 20, 1979

ISADORE SHARP & BEVERLEY (NORRIS) BLAIR
Founder of the Four Seasons Hotels and the annual Terry Fox Run and former director of advertising, Four Seasons Hotels

When the newspapers announced that Terry Fox was planning to run across Canada, Isadore Sharp was intrigued. Who was this kid who thought he could do the impossible? He saw that this young man was bringing attention to cancer in a way other people hadn't. People had heard of cancer, but Isadore saw Terry confronting it like no one else had.

He asked Beverley Blair in his marketing department to check out the story and see what was really happening. She reported back that he was facing difficulties getting wider attention in the early days:

Vancouver Province

Let's make Terry's run really count.

Here's how you can help make it a ten million dollar run... **for only $2.00 per mile.**

1,000 companies each pledging $2.00 per mile for Terry's cross Canada run will raise ten million dollars to help defeat cancer. We're starting this campaign with our pledge of $2.00 per mile. Terry hopes to run a total of about 5,000 miles.

Terry Fox is a 21 year old university student from Port Coquitlam, B.C., who lost his right leg to cancer three years ago. Having started in St. John's, Newfoundland, he plans to run across Canada this summer to

Vancouver to prove that cancer can be beaten. Let's help prove he's right.

You can make your pledge at any branch of the Canadian Cancer Society or by phoning Four Seasons Hotels toll free from anywhere in Canada,
800-268-6282.
In Toronto call 445-5031.
We also have pledge boxes in the lobbies of our hotels across Canada for individuals who may also wish to contribute. Every penny counts. A pledge of one cent a mile would contribute $50.00.

Please help us make Terry's run really count in the battle against cancer.

This message is being published for the Canadian Cancer Society

Four Seasons Hotels
Montreal • Toronto • Ottawa • Belleville • Calgary • Edmonton • Vancouver • Israel • United States
Inn on the Park   Toronto • London, England

April 22, 1980: The *Toronto Star* shares this ad, created by Isadore Sharp, calling on 999 other companies to follow his lead and donate to Terry's cause.

Courtesy of Isadore Sharp

Isadore: I decided we would get behind him, try to do something about it. We took out an ad in the newspapers and magazines. The ad read something like, "We, Four Seasons, are going to contribute $10,000 to his run," and in the ad I invited nine hundred and ninety-nine other companies to join us in the venture and make it a $10 million run. Well, he heard about it, and he called me I guess from some payphone on the highway. In a broken, emotional voice, you could almost feel the tears, he said, "I was just ready to throw in the towel, but at least some-body believes in me. That's all I need to keep going."

Isadore put Beverley in charge, on behalf of the Four Seasons, to help in any way they can, providing rooms and helping to promote and raise funds at their hotels across the country. The first time Beverley properly met Terry was at the Four Seasons in Montreal, where they had organized an event for Terry to give a speech. It would be one of the largest gatherings for Terry since he began his run, as most events up to that point had been in smaller cities or towns. Next was Ottawa, where they planned to release a thousand balloons off the hotel roof. Beverley puts her hand to her temple and recounts the day.

Beverley: We blew up all these frickin' balloons and totally forgot that we had to get them to the roof. So, now we're in the elevator with these balloons — I think we had to make ten trips to get the balloons up to the top of the roof — and then Terry came in, and he was exhausted. [He] took a little rest, I guess. And then we did this whole thing up on the roof. They did an interview; they had Cancer Society reps there, and they spoke. The bike guys [Garth Walker and Jim Brown] spoke, too, I think that afternoon. Then we released the balloons off the roof of the building, and they did pictures and photographs. He went from there to the Ottawa Rough Riders game where he did the kickoff. I can remember he was really nervous about doing the kickoff, but he did a great job.

Terry makes a speech at a gathering at the Four Seasons Hotel.
Courtesy of Beverley Blair

Isadore met Terry when he arrived in Toronto on July 11, 1980. He was with him on stage at Nathan Phillips Square and was excited to have put together a luncheon at his hotel.

Isadore: I held a luncheon for him, and we invited the business community. One of my greatest regrets is not taping that speech, because here is an audience of almost five hundred people and he was speaking in his regular attire, a T-shirt and shorts, with his leg fully exposed. In his hands, he held a paper clip. And as he was speaking, he was flicking the paper clip. The room was so still you could hear that click of the paper clip. He held everybody in his thrall. He knew what he wanted to say, and he spoke from the heart. And the audience, nobody even touched a coffee cup. It was just that solemn.

Beverley remembers that speech like it was yesterday.

> Beverley: Terry came into the room — along with a lot of other "blue suiters," as I called them at that time — with his dirty grey shorts, which were well worn, and this artificial leg, and there wasn't a dry eye in the house. It was just unbelievable. And he stood up at the front, and he gave a speech about how he was doing this for the kids. "I don't want anybody else to have to go through what I've gone through. And I want to see if I can get them enough money to raise for cancer research and prevent this from ever happening to anybody again." It was a great speech. He talked right off the cuff, that's what was amazing about him. One minute, he could be a fifteen-year-old, the next minute he could be a thirty-five-year-old, talking articulately to a group of Bay Street corporate presidents and CEOs. And that was really, to me, quite amazing, his ability to do that and his determination. Determination came above all else: "I'm doing this. Whether you give me a cent or not, I'm still going to do this." He was just tremendous that way. And then the luncheon was over, and protocol says that Lieutenant Governor Pauline McGibbon is to leave the room first. Well, that didn't happen. All the blue suiters got up in the room and went rushing up to Terry.

Isadore was already thinking of how to help Terry make this run into something that could continue well into the future. He watched it explode in Ontario and knew Terry should be thinking and acting now to lay the groundwork for what was to come. He was a natural businessman, and he felt he could help guide Terry into the next phase of what he started.

> Isadore: I suggested at that time that he should really be thinking [about] when he reaches Vancouver; now's the

time to put together an organization to be able to really promote it, making it a worldwide event. Terry said, "I don't really want to talk about that now." And I thought then that he knew he wasn't going to make it because he had been running with, I guess, such pain. But he said, "I'm gonna continue running till I can't." Which he did.

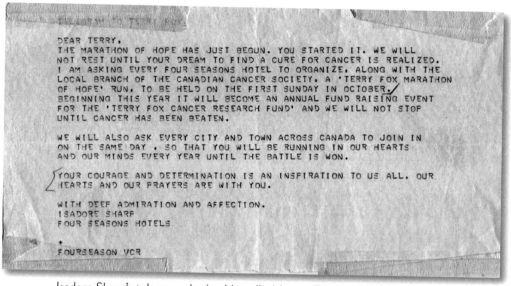

DEAR TERRY,
THE MARATHON OF HOPE HAS JUST BEGUN. YOU STARTED IT. WE WILL
NOT REST UNTIL YOUR DREAM TO FIND A CURE FOR CANCER IS REALIZED.
I AM ASKING EVERY FOUR SEASONS HOTEL TO ORGANIZE, ALONG WITH THE
LOCAL BRANCH OF THE CANADIAN CANCER SOCIETY, A 'TERRY FOX MARATHON
OF HOPE' RUN, TO BE HELD ON THE FIRST SUNDAY IN OCTOBER.
BEGINNING THIS YEAR IT WILL BECOME AN ANNUAL FUND RAISING EVENT
FOR THE 'TERRY FOX CANCER RESEARCH FUND' AND WE WILL NOT STOP
UNTIL CANCER HAS BEEN BEATEN.

WE WILL ALSO ASK EVERY CITY AND TOWN ACROSS CANADA TO JOIN IN
ON THE SAME DAY , SO THAT YOU WILL BE RUNNING IN OUR HEARTS
AND OUR MINDS EVERY YEAR UNTIL THE BATTLE IS WON.

YOUR COURAGE AND DETERMINATION IS AN INSPIRATION TO US ALL. OUR
HEARTS AND OUR PRAYERS ARE WITH YOU.

WITH DEEP ADMIRATION AND AFFECTION.
ISADORE SHARP
FOUR SEASONS HOTELS

FOURSEASON VCR

Isadore Sharp's telegram sharing his well wishes to Terry upon his return to the hospital after the Marathon of Hope. "Your courage and determination is an inspiration to us all. Our hearts and prayers are with you."
Courtesy of the Terry Fox Centre Archives

When Terry was in hospital after having to end his run, Isadore sent a telegram saying the Four Seasons would do whatever they could to continue supporting him. But Terry told Isadore he didn't want anyone to repeat what he did or to finish his run — he still had it in his mind that he would get back out there and finish it himself.

Isadore: Unfortunately, he died before that happened, and in speaking to him and his parents, I suggested, "Look, maybe if you can't do it, what we'll do is hold something each year and commemorate what you started, not like a race but an event of family runs and try to continue to raise money for cancer."

Beverley takes a moment, gazing into the distance. She blinks away tears and tells me how painful it was when Terry died.

> Beverley: I went into the Four Seasons, and I got on the elevator, and the irony of ironies, Isadore Sharp got on the elevator at the same time. We both kind of walked in together, and we just looked at each other and we started to cry. I mean, you don't see him cry very often, but the tears were rolling down his cheeks and he was very emotional. We didn't say a word. What could you say? What was there to say that hadn't already been said about this incredible young man who had some kind of inner strength?
>
> But then we said, "Okay, it isn't over. We will have a fundraising event every year, until cancer is beaten." That was Issy's commitment — until cancer is beaten. And we're not there yet. The Terry Fox Run still goes on in all those cities and countries. Then, of course, we expanded it. Betty was concerned; she didn't want it to go outside the Run, but we did come up with a thing called Terry's Team, where we got young cancer kids from all across the country to sort of run for Terry and collect money for Terry. They would collect money through all their connections and everything else. We publicized that, then we spread it to the Canadian embassies around the world.

Beverley explains to me how the Terry Fox Run began. Isadore went to Terry before he passed to discuss his idea for the Run, something everyone could participate in and continue raising money for cancer research, and to get his blessing.

> Beverley: I think he wanted to know from Terry, because Terry had sort of been adamant about the run not being continued. He wanted to know from Terry that it was going to be alright if we did this and was there anything that he might object to. And Terry was pretty open about it. I think at that point, he realized that he was not going to get back

out there to run it. But again, nobody finished his run. This was never finished. It was just a continuation in cities and towns across Canada. In honour of him.

Terry liked the idea. It was inclusive of everyone, and all money would go to cancer research. They started the first run in September 1981, three months after he passed away, and Isadore had Beverley become the director of the Terry Fox Run. Then, as the hotel chain expanded, they held runs in countries all over the world. Beverley feels it is important to also talk about the support from other organizations and the influence Terry had that people don't often discuss.

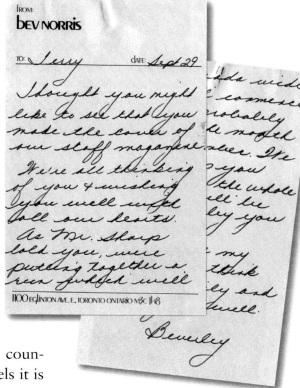

September 29, 1980: Beverley writes a note to Terry on behalf of the staff, sharing that he was featured on the cover of their staff magazine and their plans for the Terry Fox Run.

Courtesy of Beverley Blair

Beverley: The War Amps would constantly send out new legs to try out. He would report back to them, and he would try all kinds of legs. Today, kids are running on legs that were designed and developed in conjunction with Terry Fox and his running across Canada. I mean, the first leg that kid had to run across Canada was — I don't know how he did it, to be honest with you — an old clunker. Now, they're thin and streamlined and tailored to take the jogging and the bumps, and everything else. That in itself is another feat that he accomplished, and these young kids today that do have these artificial legs can be thankful that they now have a leg that functions a lot better than it did when Terry first started out running.

Isadore's connection to Terry is a deeply personal one, having lost a young son to cancer in 1978. Christopher Sharp, the third of Isadore's four sons, was seventeen when he was diagnosed with melanoma. Isadore understood what Terry had endured and the toll it takes on the body and on a family.

> Isadore: We had recently lost our son. This much has been accomplished since then, but even at that time there were many people who *did* survive. The cancer our son had was terminal. The doctor said the survival rate was two percent. But that does mean two people out of a hundred *do* survive. So, there's always that hope you can hang on to. Terry, at that time, was a survivor.

Many may not realize that Terry had undergone chemotherapy for a year and a half and was able to be one of the early recipients of a new drug. One made possible because of research. Being a survivor,

Isadore rallies a crowd at Wilket Creek Park, likely the third year of the Terry Fox Run, in 1984.
Courtesy of Beverley Blair

he didn't have to go on his Marathon of Hope. He could have run for himself, becoming a Paralympian and competing on the world stage. But he didn't. As a cancer-free survivor, he decided to be selfless and raise as much money as he could, all in service to others. Isadore believes as long as there was research continuing, there would be hope.

> Isadore: That is the most important aspect of what he [meant] to so many people: hope. What that message was doing was giving kids like himself a day of hope versus a day of despair. That gift of "never give up and always have that hope" as a positive rather than negative.

BREEDA & MARTHA McCLEW

Former national director of the Terry Fox Foundation and vice president of community and school programs for TFF

Walking up to the home of Breeda McClew, I am struck by the beauty of the over one-hundred-year-old trees whose branches stretch to inter-mingle as a canopy over the street, and the sunlight peeks through the filigree of leaves. The street is lined with some of the older houses in Toronto, each with sweeping front lawns and sculpted shrubbery. Breeda answers the door, wearing her "Dear Terry" T-shirt. She grabs my hand and leads me into her home, positivity and joy radiating out of her as she speaks to me about how grateful she is that Terry changed her life and her family's. The McClews are devout supporters of his cause, with three members going on to

Mike McClew, Martha McClew, Betty Fox, Breeda McClew (middle of bottom row), and Terry Fox Foundation volunteers.

Courtesy of Martha McClew, Terry Fox Foundation

work for the Terry Fox Foundation and her husband, Mike, participating in the Terry Fox Run every year.

   Their introduction to Terry began with dinnertime one night in
1980. Mike was going around the table asking their four children
what they did that day, and their daughter Martha answered. She said
she had seen this man put his leg — not his proper leg — into the
ocean and that he was going to run across Canada. Being a child, they
thought perhaps she had been mistaken. Watching the evening news,
they saw the same coverage of Terry dipping his artificial foot into the
Atlantic Ocean. Inspired, Mike told the family they would follow his
journey, and they looked every morning in the paper but were sad to
see that he wasn't being adequately covered.

   And then they heard he was going to be in Toronto that July. Breeda
was outside the Four Seasons with her two sons — eight and eleven,

July 11, 1980: Breeda in the crowd as Terry runs down University Avenue in Toronto.
Photo by Ron Bull via Getty Images

who were complaining about the boiling-hot weather — packed into the crowd of people, waiting to catch a glimpse of him.

> Breeda: We were all engaged, looking at him and wondering how he could do this. How could he do this in the middle of summer with the humidity? How could he run?

One of Martha's biggest regrets was not going to the Four Seasons Hotel when her mother went to see Terry. Years later, Martha was going through photos at the Foundation's national office and came across a photo of Terry leaving the Four Seasons. She took a closer look and realized her mother was in the picture, cheering him on. Breeda shares what that moment, captured on film, was really like.

> Breeda: Terry comes out the door of the Four Seasons and walks down the path onto Avenue Road to run down University Avenue. My first thought was that he was so handsome with all his curly hair. And his good leg was strong and tanned. I didn't even actually notice his artificial leg. As he came down, we were waving, and he just shyly waved back to us, and then he went out on the road. And of course, I've never been able to tell the story without crying. He started to run in this intense heat and humidity with this leg. It was only at that very moment that I really saw the hardship of his run. I'd seen him on television but at that moment, I said, "How can he do that?" He had already run from Scarborough that morning. I started crying. Not just crying, bawling. I didn't mind. The children were saying, "You're embarrassing us." But it is a moment in my life that is there every single day and will be there till the day I die. It was a miracle moment for me that this young man would give his life for a cause. Not just for him, but for others.

Breeda had been a nurse in England and had seen firsthand what people with cancer suffer through, both adults and children. When she saw what Terry was doing, she asked herself why she was not also doing something. In 1985, once her youngest was in school, Breeda decided she *would* do something. The staff overseeing the Terry Fox Run at the Canadian Cancer Society (CCS) hired Breeda as a postal code clerk to prepare donation pledge sheets for tax receipts. She would also excitedly tell everyone she met about Terry and his mission.

Seeing how enthusiastic she was, when the Ontario Terry Fox Run coordinator resigned, Breeda was asked to take on the position. Both her daughters, Katharine and Martha, had been involved with the Run for years at this point. Breeda didn't think she was capable of doing the job.

> Breeda: Katharine said something to me that really made me feel I could. She said, "You have to do it because the Run needs someone with a soul." And so that touched me, and the need to do it for Terry. And I thought, "I'm going to try." It was that word *soul* that spoke to me. That's where I thought I had Terry. That's where I thought he was, in my body, in my soul. I took it on, and I loved it for twenty-eight years.

Breeda went on to become the provincial, national, then the first international director of the Terry Fox Run for the Foundation in 1996, spreading Terry's message across borders.

Mike, Breeda's husband, comes around the corner of the living room, leaning on his cane, and asks Breeda who I was and what she was doing. He is a large man with a full face and a mischievous look in his eyes. Mike suffered a stroke a few years ago, but his memories of Terry are fresh and sharp. When he was a partner with Ernst & Young, he convinced all the people who worked on Bay Street to join the cause and get involved.

> Breeda: He gave lunches and invited the other corporations, and they would all come. It raised massive amounts of money. But not only that, they came to the Run. That was the beautiful part of it. They came to participate, not just give them money. They came to participate in the memory of Terry.

Mike describes the early days to me, his cheerful nature and bellowing voice bringing the scene clearly into my mind.

> Mike: The best times were the early days when we had a run [in] downtown Toronto. Everybody came here at five o'clock in the morning. We all had bagel and eggs, and the place was jammed with people. And then we go off and we finished at Upper Canada College. We ran through Forest Hill, all the rich places, so we screamed and yelled!
>
> We used to have rows of tents with people selling things, selling T-shirts. We had the bands that came and then we had the fire trucks that came with all the firemen and showed off all that regalia. Yes, it was quite a show!

The McClews became known as the Terry Fox family, doing all this with their own money. Their front lawn was even filled with large signs that said *Terry Fox* in big letters as a way of sharing Terry's story with those in her neighbourhood.

> Breeda: Anyone that passes, I go out and I talk to them and tell them, "Do you know about Terry?" Some people don't, and I tell them the story. I'd say to them, "You know, Terry wasn't always perfect, of course. But he never gave up. When you find things difficult, will you be like Terry? Will you try to be like Terry?" "Oh, yes, yes, yes!" [Breeda smiles, with her hands clasped together at her chest.]

In the first few years after Terry died, she says that people thought the whole thing would fade out and people would forget and move on. She was not going to let that happen. She often accompanied Betty Fox on trips to events, and the two soon became close friends. Betty shared with Breeda how the experience in the hospital changed Terry. How the doctor would come in to speak to another family, and he'd hear the doctor say they had a twenty to thirty percent chance of surviving. He could hear the children talk with their parents and said it was at that time that his heart grew larger.

Betty (third in from left) and Breeda (far right) in Bangladesh for the Terry Fox Run in 1997.
Courtesy of Martha McClew, Terry Fox Foundation

Breeda: At the end, his mother said, "I have come to believe, now, that he was sent to us for a purpose." I think it took a long time for her to come to that. She was an amazing woman. She was determined. I was in Ontario at the time, and I went to schools with her. She would speak at five schools, and she was as good at the fifth as she was at the first because she was so determined that her son [and what he did] was not going to be forgotten. She always tried not to cry. I admire that so much about her. When she had a day that was tough for her, she would always say, "This isn't a good day for me." And that brought everybody closer to her. She was just so honest about everything. She never exaggerated about Terry. She would say he was a pain in the butt at times, but they were very close.

In 1989, Breeda hired Martha to come work at the Foundation when she finished university. Martha jokes with me that her mother never lets her forget it. She is now the VP of community and school programs and event fundraising, and has been with the organization for over thirty-four years.

> Martha: Betty and Rolly, Terry's family, are obviously the whole reason the Run continues. When I look at my mom, I see the reason the Run thrived. She and my dad saw the need that Canadians had to connect to Terry, and who better than his mom? And so, they made sure she was involved in everything. That's why the Foundation and the Run are an incredible reflection of who Terry was to this day.

Through their fundraising work, Betty and Breeda became close friends.

Courtesy of Martha McClew, Terry Fox Foundation

Martha thinks she connected so deeply to Terry because she had never seen anyone so selfless. She clearly saw that he was not doing it for himself, running for ten hours a day to help someone else, and he never stopped.

> Martha: It's an enormous task. I used to go out to speak at schools as part of my job, and I was grateful when our program got bigger, and we were able to hire people, because I would cry when I talked to children. I would look at them and think they were so reflective of Terry. Here were these children and teenagers who hate running and yet who understood the concept of helping someone else, and that's because of Terry. Terry is a face that is so accessible, regardless of your age. This little kindergartener raised $600 because he had gone home and said to his mother, "We're raising money for a Fox with one leg." [Terry] would so love that.

As Martha has changed over the years, what she admired in Terry has changed with her. It changed again when she had children and continues to change now. But overall, her admiration has only grown. Working for a non-profit organization can be challenging, but the spirit of the Foundation mirrors Terry's own calling to help serve others.

> Martha: We talk about "Terry Foxers" a lot and that they are very committed to the cause. I don't want to judge people because they may not feel this passion necessarily for Terry. But at the same time, when you are working every single day with people who have come to your organization because they believe in Terry, they were inspired by him, or they lost someone to cancer, you have to put that spirit back into the world. What Terry believed in is compassion. My God, like how he was able to hear those stories from people who just stopped him on the road to say "My son just died" or "I lost my mom." How he kept going day after day, listening to stories and trying to keep himself focused and healthy. If you don't give that back to people, they are disappointed. They are truly disappointed because they see the Foundation as a living reflection of Terry. It's a big responsibility, but it's a glorious responsibility.

When the pandemic hit, Breeda and Mike were isolated. Once they could see visitors from their porch, they would wave, their visitors shouting from down the driveway. Breeda feels these past few years have been hard on people and that there are so many people who could use Terry and his inspiration right now.

> Breeda: It's badly needed, and in the world we live in today, hope is missing. We need someone to give us hope that we can achieve our dreams, and we can achieve them with determination. Never giving up; just keep going. That's what young people, old people, or middle-aged people all need to do. There is no greater inspiration, in my opinion, than Terry Fox.
>
> Someone was asked, "What made him different from the rest of us? What was it about him that really touched

our hearts and minds and souls?" I can remember I wrote down [their answer] from this article: "Terry Fox took us deeply into the soul to show the magnificent beauty of human potential. A gifted few have taken us there with music. Others have paved a way with words. But Terry Fox took us there with courage, one step at a time."

How did Terry get up every morning, run another marathon, and show compassion to so many people, experiencing their raw emotions all day?

Martha, Mike, and Breeda McClew in 2023 at the unveiling of the Legacy Art Project in Toronto, the latest Terry Fox monument to be erected.

Photo by Barbara Adhiya

Martha: It was a weight, but it didn't drag him down. I think he kind of cloaked himself with those stories and they propelled him on. What moves me so much in the schools on Terry Fox Day [is that] we don't offer free shirts; we don't offer incentives. There are no flights to Jamaica for raising the most money. There is nothing except that sense that you did something good. You changed the world, probably — it's not too grandiose to say that. I found a quote [by John Bunyan] years ago I still like to use: "You haven't truly lived until you have done something for someone who can never truly repay you." You may never meet somebody who will benefit from that. And yet that spirit lives. It was lit by Terry. Will it burn brightly for many of those kids? Yeah, it'll take them to their next place in life, whether that's a Terry Foxer, or an environmentalist, or whatever they care deeply about. But they will care deeply, and they'll see that that is possible.

GLEMENA BETTENCOURT

Marathon of Hope volunteer and organizer of the Terry Fox Run in Richmond Hill for forty-three years

Glemena waits for my arrival at a small café in Richmond Hill, Ontario. She sits in an oversized brown leather armchair that seems to envelop her tiny frame. She is wearing a Terry T-shirt, and on her calf, clearly visible, is a tattooed image of Terry.

In 1980, Glemena was nineteen years old when she read a small blurb without a picture in the *Toronto Star* about a young man who was going to try to run across the country with only one leg. She was captivated. She went searching for information and couldn't find much until Leslie Scrivener's weekly column started, and every Friday she would run to the newspaper box to see where Terry was.

> When he was running towards Ontario, I started trying to fundraise in Toronto. I had this little fishbowl, which I still have, and I took that little fishbowl everywhere I went, knocking on doors. This was even before he got to Toronto. I would go and empty over a hundred dollars onto the desk of the Canadian Cancer Society, and I did that every day. Then one day, they finally said, "Well, wait a minute, where are you getting this money and who are you?"

Glemena smiles out the window of the fundraising car during the Marathon of Hope.

Courtesy of Glemena Bettencourt

This got the attention of the North York unit of the CCS. They set up a twelve-day fundraising event with Glemena working with the management at different malls. In those twelve days, she raised $30,000. That's about $116,000 as of 2024.

> They all allowed me to set up a little booth. The North York Cancer Society would give me all these pamphlets

to give out, so it looked legit, I guess, because I'm just some kid asking for money.

Glemena knew there was going to be a huge crowd at Nathan Phillips Square in Toronto, so the day after that event, she decided to go to nearby Mississauga and stand on Lakeshore Boulevard. She waited for a few hours, the crowd around her ten people deep on both sides of the road.

> And then all of a sudden, lights flashing and Terry's curly hair, bobbing up and down, came over the crest of the hill — that's a memory you never forget — and got closer and closer. I kind of ducked out of the crowd and started running parallel with Terry on the outside. Then Terry decided to go into this restaurant to have a break, and Darrell and Bill came outside looking for volunteers. I basically jumped out of my sneakers, and they picked me. And I was the first runner behind Terry.

They had asked her to run with him for three miles, but it ended up being over ten and just about killed her. She didn't get to meet him, and she thought maybe that was the end of her Terry experience. He continued on to London, Ontario, and she still went around collecting money and bringing it to the CCS. Then one day, Lorrie Goldstein, a journalist, called her at home and asked to meet her.

> He said, "I have a great big surprise for you. I'm going to take you to meet Terry." He took me to the Four Seasons Hotel [in Toronto] and I couldn't believe it. It was the best day of my life. All I can remember now is Terry coming out of a room where he had just met Bobby Orr because he had a great big grin on his face — that famous grin — and he was really happy. And Lorrie Goldstein stopped him in the hallway and introduced me, and then that picture of me and Terry — I was kissing him on the cheek — was taken.

Glemena gives Terry a kiss on the cheek.

Courtesy of Glemena Bettencourt

As the run carried on through Georgetown, Brampton, and Richmond Hill, Glemena continued selling T-shirts and collecting money. She lived near enough that she could drive every day to where the Marathon crew was in Southern Ontario until they went up to Parry Sound, and her mother told her not to go any further.

The last time I remember sitting with Terry and talking with him was in Parry Sound where I gave him a belated birthday gift because I was not there in Gravenhurst. I found him to be a little bit shy. And of course, he had just run a marathon anytime I saw him, or he was focused on what he did for the day. I learned really quickly just try and stay away and out of that area. I knew what his purpose was, and I didn't want to be in the way of that. It was nice that I got that moment at that picnic bench that day for sure. He was also coughing a little bit, at that time, in Parry Sound. And we had talks about him not feeling great. But at our age, we were just talking.

I can't put a finger on it. There was something about him that you just believed everything. You believed in him. Not for one second did I ever think this guy's fake or he's cheating. I don't know how to describe it. There's something about him that you wanted to be around. Not so much physically touch him or anything like that but just to see him and be around him.

It gave me a focus of something good. Because to be honest, I'd really been going down [a suicidal path]. It was like a fork in the road for me. I wanted to do good things. And I believe it saved my life to this day.

Like the rest of the country, Glemena was shocked when she heard that the run had ended on September 1, 1980, and once again, she wanted to get right in there and help.

Glemena gives Terry a birthday present in Parry Sound.
Courtesy of Glemena Bettencourt

> When I heard that he had to stop his run, I was driving at the time. I almost went off the road, I was like, "Oh my God." Somehow, I got my way into the telethon. My job there as a volunteer was to escort Anne Murray or whoever was there, Darryl Sittler, from the dressing rooms to the stage. And it was quite a long walk down the little corridor. So, I got a chance to talk to everybody as I walked through. I still have the pass they gave me. And you know how I got in there? I just went to the studio the day of, and I said, "I want to volunteer. What do I do?"

Glemena has continued to support the cause in any way she can and is determined to keep Terry's story and memory alive. Every year for the past forty-three years, Glemena has organized the Terry Fox Run in Richmond Hill. She participates in events and arrives with Terry T-shirts to sell. In 2008, she participated in the Tour of Hope, when Terry's original Marathon van was refurbished and taken across Canada, and she felt firsthand how difficult doing this kind of work can be. She couldn't imagine what it had been like for Terry each day.

> People would come up and just kind of grab your elbow and start crying, thanking you for the work you're doing to keep Terry's memory alive or whatever it is, and then telling you the story about their child or somebody that's got cancer or has died of cancer. It's so much to cope with. But I [only] did that for a moment in time and it affected me deeply.

The Terry Fox tribute statue at Ransom Park in Richmond Hill, Ontario.
Photo by Barbara Adhiya

At one point, Glemena noticed that the city had no tributes honouring Terry.

> I didn't expect the statue. First of all, I just asked. I went to the council, and I said, "We don't have a city street, a park, nothing named after Terry Fox." They did their

thing, and they came up and said, "We're gonna give you a statue." I'm like, "Alright, I'll take it!" So, when the artist was sculpting and everything, I would go to his studio all the time in Toronto, and I would bring all my memorabilia because the artist really liked to feel Terry to help him work. We'd pin all these pictures up all over the studio and I would spend hours there with him. I'm so proud of that statue. It looks so much like Terry.

After consultation with Glemena and other residents, Radoslaw Kudlinski's realistic statue of Terry was unveiled in Ransom Park on September 12, 2015, on the thirty-fifth anniversary of the run.

I love going to the statue; I call it "Tea with Terry." I just sit there with my Tim Hortons tea — so Canadian — and people that come to the statue to visit Terry, I always start talking to them. And always they tell me their stories. I used to clean the park until the town told me I couldn't anymore; True story. They said, "You don't do that anymore, we do that."

Marlene Lott and Glemena reunite in 2023 at a Terry Fox event hosted by Craig Jarvis at the Royal Canadian Yacht Club.

Photo by Barbara Adhiya

Glemena tilts her head with a quirky smirk and shrugs her shoulders. Terry has clearly inspired a full and happy life of volunteerism and community service. Although cancer has touched her family as well, Glemena has hope that continuing Terry's mission to raise money for research will help save more lives.

MARY HARDISTY
Former OPP officer who escorted Terry in Northern Ontario for the Marathon of Hope

Driving up to Stayner, Ontario, it is a clear summer's day when I meet with the Hardisty family. With the sights, sounds, and smells of small-town Ontario, the route itself is a balm for city stress. This is also what it feels like to spend an afternoon with the Hardistys.

Both Mary and Steve are retired OPP officers. Their daughter Lisa works with seniors, and their son Raymond is a champion, having battled leukemia, who lives an animated life long after his doctors predicted a future of only two years. This is a family that lives and believes in service to others, knowing the blessedness that comes from overcoming life's challenges.

Like many others, Mary had first seen Terry on TV, dipping his leg into the Atlantic Ocean. She remembered the reports of him being almost run off the road a few times in Quebec.

The OPP was dedicated to ensuring Terry's safety throughout Ontario, escorting him each day of his Marathon.
From the Canadian Press

The OPP had made it very clear that once he hit Ontario he was going to be escorted [by them], and I thought, well, that's a pretty good idea. I never really gave it any thought, like I knew he was in Toronto and knew he was around the area. I just went in for a midnight shift, and there was a note there: "Please meet Terry Fox down at the Lake Joseph Motel at 5 a.m." And I thought, "Oh, wow, isn't this neat."

She went to the motel in Bala and waited, then saw Terry come out the back stairs, followed by the rest of the group.

Whoever spoke to me said, "We go first and then them. We stop quite often." I said hello to Terry very briefly, and away we went in the dark. And there was nobody. It was so odd. There's one section; it's Highway 141–Highway 69, and it goes up on a really big curve and incline. And the 141 goes to Roscoe and there was nobody out there. I found it fascinating just what he's doing. And big transports are the only ones on the road at that time — *beep beep*, and he just put his hand up, just kind of acknowledged, and kept going. But yeah, it was slow going, very slow, especially because of the landscape.

Mary stayed in her car, even during the breaks. It looked like such labour, watching him run twenty-six miles a day, and he looked like he was in pain. A natural protector, Mary had to hold back on her instincts while driving behind him.

It might have been about maybe 7:30 a.m. and I thought, "Ugh, just get in the cruiser." He seemed to be really strong. It was just painful to watch him. I think I was with him until about 10:30 in the morning.

When we finished up, when I was being relieved, that's when I went over to the van, and he was just coming out. He'd finished his break and I just said, "Terry, it's been a real great honour to meet you, and I wish you all the best

293

with your marathon. I'll be keeping an eye and see how things are going." Just sort of chat like that and shook hands. But you could see he was very focused.

Later that day, Mary got to see him as a spectator, cheering along the road as he ran by.

Terry runs past Parry Sound's town sign in Northern Ontario.
Photo by Mary Hardisty

I was going to head south to my parents' place, which is south of Windsor. He was just getting to the town of Parry Sound to the turn-off, and it was wall-to-wall people. I ran down and I tried to get a spot and get a picture. And I got that photo with him by himself with the "Home of Bobby Orr" sign.

I was happy to see the crowd that was there. I thought that would kind of rejuvenate him a bit because, I mean, there's nobody out there and it's dark and everything else. I know he was meeting with the Orr family that day in Parry Sound, and Bobby was a favourite [of his], I think. [And people] were cheering and whistling, and that would give him some momentum. It was a good crowd there, even though Parry Sound was kind of a little town.

Not long after, Mary was attending police college in August, and it was through an instructor that she learned that the run had ended.

> I mentioned then to my platoon that I just escorted him, like, five weeks ago. And they said, "Oh my God!" These were Toronto cops, and they were really impressed. The whole class, I was the only OPP officer and the only female. It was a very sad time to hear that. I was thinking it was going to be just a temporary blip. It just seemed unreal that it was gonna be the end of the Marathon. It started out so quietly and then it gained such momentum, especially when we hit Ontario, every big shebang in Toronto. And then to make it to Thunder Bay, almost getting to the Manitoba border. It was just unreal that it had come to such a quick end.

Mary didn't have any experience with cancer at that time. She was twenty-two, the same age as Terry. She and Steve got married, had kids, and then cancer struck their family.

> I knew how nasty cancer was, but I didn't really have any personal connection. No one in the family had it or anything at that point, but that changed very quickly. Nine years later, there are lots of words in our vocabulary, like platelets and antigens, that we didn't have before.

Their son, Raymond, had leukemia and underwent a bone marrow transplant when he was just five years old. Mary's husband, Steve, shares that it was Terry who gave Raymond strength.

A young Raymond Hardisty smiles proudly wearing his Terry Fox shirt at a Stayner Collegiate Terry Fox event.
Courtesy of the Hardisty family

Raymond didn't know he was fighting cancer. We didn't tell him. It was "This is what we have to do today." And he'd be getting a shot, or they'd be taking fluid out of his back, all of these different things. It's just one day at a time. Terry getting up, and doing what he was doing, one day at a time, one step at a time, and everything else. He was just in my head.

Raymond recalls when he became aware of Terry.

I think it was like two or three years after my transplant. I saw Mom's photo on the wall, and I'm like, "Mom, who's this?" She said, "This is Terry Fox. I escorted him through Parry Sound, and he had cancer just like you." And she would say that the cancer had gone so far that they had to amputate his leg and "see in the photo there. That's an artificial leg." I think I was about seven when she told me.

Terry has been intertwined throughout their lives. One time, as Mary drove Raymond to camp, she realized she was on the same strip of road where she had escorted Terry — twenty years to the day. And this time, her son, who had fought cancer and lived, was beside her. Mary has hung pictures of Terry around their house, and she even carries a photo in her wallet so she can see him every day. He has served as a reminder and an example of service to the Hardisty family, and they have carried that forward: Mary and Steve as officers, Lisa in her work with seniors, and Raymond in his fundraising for SickKids. He has raised around $130,000 since 2008, and he celebrates the day of his transplant every five years.

Steve, Raymond, and Mary visit with Fred Fox on August 31, 2022.

Courtesy of the Hardisty family

DR. RODNEY OUELLETTE
Senior researcher and founder of the Atlantic Cancer Research Institute

Rodney joins me on a Zoom call from Moncton, New Brunswick, on Canada's East Coast. He is sitting in his office, the wall behind him covered in framed degrees and certificates. His eyes are kind, and he speaks with an even, comforting tone. As he talks, he rocks side to side in his chair in rhythm to the story he is telling.

In 1980, Rodney was in grade ten at the Louis J. Robichaud High School in Shediac, New Brunswick. The students had heard stories of Terry Fox, how he was running across Canada on an artificial leg, and they knew that spring in Atlantic Canada was not easy. It was cold and miserable, and it rained a lot. They were told he was going to come to the school to speak.

Dr. Rodney Ouellette stands at a microscope at the Atlantic Cancer Research Institute.

Courtesy of the Atlantic Cancer Research Institute

> He spoke about cancer and his battle with cancer. He spoke about losing his leg and then wanting to do something so that others didn't have to suffer the same fate. I don't remember how long he spoke, probably about fifteen to twenty minutes. I was shy, but I remember quite a few questions to Terry were regarding his leg. Running a marathon on one leg, nobody had done that before. So [they were] trying to understand how he could run twenty-six miles each day. And he talked about the preparation that he needed to make sure that the remaining part of his leg didn't get blisters or sores.

Rodney thought he may want to pursue a career in the medical field but didn't have a concept of cancer, as he didn't know anyone who had it or died of it. Later that same year, his grandfather died from the disease, and it dawned on him that cancer could happen to anyone or anyone close to them.

[I was] asked if it was something that had kind of convinced me or changed my mind in terms of career direction. I can't say that it was specifically, but maybe subconsciously, there were these key elements in your life, and as you age, you start going down a path to become a researcher or a physician. These are probably things that weigh in the balance one way or another.

When Rodney was going through his post-secondary education, Terry's legacy became more and more apparent. The name "Terry Fox" was coming up everywhere. He remembers when Memorial University opened the Terry Fox Cancer Research Laboratories in 1989 with Terry's mother in attendance. Then in the mid-'90s, after receiving his MD and PhD in molecular and cellular biology, Rodney was asked to be a representative of New Brunswick on the governing council of the Canadian Institutes of Health Research (CIHR).

1998: The Atlantic Cancer Research Institute team stands in front of their building being constructed.

Courtesy of the Atlantic Cancer Research Institute

When I joined the governing council of CIHR, I became quite close with Victor Ling. Victor was on the CIHR governing council at that time, and he was VP of research at B.C. Cancer at the time. So, a few years later, when the Fox family and the Foundation decided to create TFRI [Terry Fox Research Institute], Victor reached out to me. I think we were no longer on CIHR, or we were ending our terms at that time. He asked me to be part of the interim working group that set up TFRI. For me, that was like an automatic "Yes!" I mean, anything that has to do with Terry Fox, count me in. And so, we set up the TFRI, and then every year I have participated in the research conference. Anytime I'm asked to do something for the TFRI or the Fox Foundation, I feel I have to give back. That's my way of keeping the vision alive to try and move research forward in any way possible, either through fundraising organizations that enable the research or actually doing the research.

Rodney believes it was a blessing in disguise that Terry didn't quite realize what he was in for when he started the run, having to face the terrain and cold, wet weather of the East Coast.

I think I know how he felt in the sense that maybe he didn't realize what a challenge it would be when he started. And I think sometimes that's a good thing. You grow through the challenge, and you become mentally and physically tougher to fight through it. If you would have known from the get-go, here's the pain and the steady beat of what you need to do day in, day out, from daybreak to sunset, I think that would scare anybody. So, I think he had to have more hope than understanding of what it really involved. He was certainly committed, and he felt passionately about this. Fortunately, he probably didn't know the height of the mountain he had to climb to get through it. That's my opinion.

Having to deal with challenges and setbacks, then getting up to try once more, is something Rodney sees often in his field of research. When the trials don't lead where the team wants them to go, it isn't always a bad thing — but it is frustrating.

> When you have a good idea, and it seems to be working, seems to be relevant, then you apply for funding, and most of the time the answer is no. So that's challenging, too. You reflect upon what the reviewer said and what you can change. Then you start writing again, and you reapply. So, there is a lot of failure involved in what we do. And even the most successful researchers will probably say the same thing. There's a lot more failures than successes.

A research assistant studies cell culture at the Atlantic Cancer Research Institute.
Courtesy of the Atlantic Cancer Research Institute

The concept of a marathon is often used in everyday language when talking about relationships, careers, recovery, or getting through challenges in general. There are good days and bad days, and to succeed at something, the long-term vision has to be approached one day at a time. As both a doctor and a cancer patient, Rodney understands what Terry had to go through and what his mindset was to keep going.

> With patients who have cancer, for the longest time I tried to put myself in their shoes. Early in my career, I did participate in patient care, trying to understand what they're going through. For us as physicians, you kind of become immune to the individual situation because you have to keep a certain level of distance while being empathetic. But then it can happen to you, and I had to live through two cancers: one in my early fifties, and then one just a couple of years ago. You always say it happens to somebody else, but then it can happen to you, and that becomes another mini marathon in your life. Then there are the steps where you get through surgery or whatever treatment that you're going through, and then you want to get back to where you were in terms of physical abilities, and so on. You can't rush it; each day goes by, and there's not much difference than the previous day, but it may be marginally better. And then the next day, it gets a little bit better [again]. So, it's kind of a marathon as well.

Rodney has not only dedicated his life's work to cancer research, I comment that he is also a cancer survivor.

> Well, cancer [combatant], let's say. I think I've survived the first one. The second one? Well, we'll see.

CRAIG JARVIS
Philanthropist, volunteer, and president of the Legacy Art Project in Toronto

Craig Jarvis was twenty years old when Terry ran his Marathon of Hope. He huddled in his dorm room during his first weekend of university, glued to the TV. Craig wasn't a Terry groupie, which is what he calls himself now, but he did follow the story in awe of Terry's accomplishments. Lloyd Robertson was hosting the telethon on CTV, and the sadness and disbelief he felt when Terry stopped running turned to hope when Lloyd announced they had raised millions of dollars that evening.

He also believes in the power of inspiration. At the age of forty-two, a cancer diagnosis changed his life, and Terry's story gave him hope, courage, and gratitude.

> I'm very lucky to be here. I had stage 4 bladder cancer [and] spent a year on different types of chemotherapy. They removed my bladder, and then another six months of chemo and drugs. So it was two years. Every day and every week is a bit of a struggle for me. I'm no longer afraid of death. I've had a good run and feel blessed.

Now Craig gives back as much as he can. About fifteen years ago, he became involved in all things Terry, helping the Fox family keep the dream of a cure alive. In May 2007, he met Darrell Fox for the first time, when Darrell was speaking at a charity event in Calgary held by ScotiaMcLeod, the wealth management firm where Craig works. Craig was struck by Darrell emotionally sharing his experience with his brother during the Marathon, and the two formed a friendship. Soon after, the Marathon of Hope van was found, and Craig helped get the van back to the family.

> [Darrell] was coming to Toronto a few months later and he called me before he came. He said, "We found the van. The original Terry Fox van." The van was being used by a family in London for the past twenty-seven years. The parents had it as a family camper van. Then the kids had this rock group, and they travelled all across North

America. Put on hundreds of thousands of miles on it. And those Ford Econolines, they used to last three or four years. Then Ford refurbished it, had it all in pieces. They did a fabulous job when they brought it back.

Once it was refurbished, Craig suggested they do a cross-country tour, driving the van through Terry's whole planned route, starting in St. John's, and there would be a Fox family member on board at every stop. It was called the Tour of Hope. Craig reached out to all his contacts and said that at every stop, there had to be an event. It wasn't always a formal event, but his colleagues and friends agreed, and they paid for it all.

Seen here deconstructed and then completed, the Marathon of Hope van was refurbished in 2008.

Photos by Glemena Bettencourt

They had events from farmer's fields to a private dinner in Winnipeg, Manitoba. They had forty [to] fifty stops across Canada starting in May 2008 to the fall in Victoria, B.C., and the van travelled the same route that he planned. Thousands of people saw it. We raised half a million dollars for the charity, but more importantly, it was the thousands who came out.

Craig was also integral in getting the Terry Fox musical together, working with the family, the writer, and the composer, and then bringing it together with a production company. It was a passion project for him, and *The Marathon of Hope: The Musical* (2016) ran for two years in Ontario to warm reviews.

His latest philanthropic adventure is the Legacy Art Project Toronto (LAPT) at the city's waterfront. It was created to build a permanent public

The LAPT statue at Toronto's waterfront. Designed by Jon Sasaki, it is three abstract pieces that, when viewed from the correct angle, show Terry running on his Marathon of Hope.
Photo by Jon Sasaki

art installation in honour of Terry Fox, led by Geri Berholz, founder of Future Possibilities for Kids, and journalist Leslie Scrivener. They had hoped to have the installation on University Avenue, which Terry ran down on July 11, 1980, but it would have been too difficult to construct, and their first proposal was turned down by the City.

Leslie and Geri approached Craig for assistance, who was happy to help but couldn't be on the committee as he was already busy with the musical. However, he knew people who worked for the City, so he inquired about the process and what was needed to gain approval. Former Toronto mayor John Tory advised him that there was a whole department to handle art installations, as many people make requests for statues or art to honour someone, and that there was a strict checklist and process to achieve approval.

> Fortunately, they have this land on the waterfront that was quietly available for a good cause, and they thought this was a good cause. But they had to put it in front of city council to vote on. So, they put it in front of city council in 2018, and they voted unanimously to give us the park based on all the protocols and doing a very thorough application.

Craig and his wife, Judy, had spoken about how, during the pandemic, parks became so important. People needed a place to go, and they really wanted this park to inspire people. They decided to put forth a large amount of money as a personal donation to the project, hoping it would spur other people to give generously. For Craig's sixtieth birthday in January 2021, he asked for donations from their friends, and in March of that year, he held meetings with the BIA, which donated as well, and the City of Toronto matched those funds. Next, they approached Waterfront Toronto, which is made up of the city, provincial, and federal governments, which also agreed to support the project.

Gala attendees view designs for the LAPT statues of Terry in January 2019.
Courtesy of Craig Jarvis

One of the
Legacy Art
Project's
statues at the
waterfront
in Toronto,
Ontario,
features Terry
before his leg
amputation.
The installation
was unveiled
in September
2023.

Photo by
Barbara Adhiya

Judy felt it would be necessary to have mock-ups of the park to demonstrate to people what they would be donating to. They turned to art consultant and expert Rebecca Carbin, principal of Art + Public UnLtd, and put out a call for submissions. They received forty, and the jury selected five finalists.

These five mock-ups were presented at a gathering at the Fort York Visitor Centre in January 2019. A couple hundred people attended and gave their feedback, and the winner was announced in March. Designer Jon Sasaki and DTAH won with their installation titled *We Are Shaped by the Obstacles We Face*. It is a curved, landscaped path obscured by granite slabs. They look abstract, but when seen from the west end, the iconic silhouette of Terry in mid-stride appears in the space between the slabs.

The Fox family liked the concept but felt it needed more, so Craig stepped in to find out what they wanted to see improved. He was having lunch with Darrell Fox when Jon shared another idea.

> Jon Sasaki said, "Here is something I'd like to show you," and he had the statue of Terry sitting down, with *both* legs. It was very emotional for Darrell and the family. They always wanted a statue with Terry with both legs, but they never asked. It brought it to life because this is Terry's journey as a young man before he set out on his Marathon of Hope. The path is a crooked path going through the three large pieces of granite. It symbolizes the obstacles that he had, but also the obstacles we all have in life.

With Terry now sitting at one end, the message of the installation was strengthened. In the spring of 2023, they finally started breaking ground, and they held the official opening on October 5 later that year.

> My involvement with everything Terry has brought me much inspiration and joy. What really excites me is seeing the next generation so passionate for the cause. I am just one of thousands who are focused on helping our great Canadian hero. Thank you, Terry.

August 26: Day 137 (26 miles) Today was a very good day. Did 13 in the morning and 13 at night. Greg [Scott] and his parents came. We ate in Terrace Bay. I swam in a lake with Greg and the others after.

August 27: Day 138 (26 miles) Today I had a good run in the morning, 13 [miles]. The afternoon, my ankle started to hurt again. Greg rode his bike behind me for about 6 miles and it has to be the most inspirational moment I have had! At night we had a beautiful reception in Terrace Bay. I spoke about Greg and couldn't hold back the emotion.

August 29: Day 140 (20 miles) Today was a difficult day. I didn't sleep last night and was wiped before I started. Exhausted and fatigued all day long. I feel sick tonight.

August 31: Day 142 (23 miles) Today was alright. Started late and it was cold for the entire morning. 12, 11 [miles]. Nothing else happened.

September 1: Day 143 (21 miles)

Total 3,339 miles

August 26, 1980: Terry rests after swimming in Terrace Bay, Ontario.

Photo by Boris Spremo via Getty Images

Lung cancer finishes Fox's Marathon of Hope

NEW WESTMINSTER, B.C. (CP-Special) — Runner Terry Fox came home yesterday after ending his Marathon of Hope, but not the way he or his thousands of well-wishers had hoped.

As a chartered plane carrying the 22-year-old British Columbian arrived from Thunder Bay, Ont., he was taken directly to hospital in this Vancouver suburb to begin a second, grim battle with cancer.

This time, it was lung cancer. Three years ago, cancer forced the amputation of his right leg above the knee.

The Fox party eluded reporters and officials of the Canadian Cancer Society alike when the plane was diverted to a different part of Vancouver International Airport.

The stricken runner was placed aboard a waiting ambulance and sped away.

Mr. Fox had dreamed of limping triumphantly into Vancouver late this year, but his coast-to-coast marathon to publicize the fight against cancer came suddenly to an end when doctors in Thunder Bay diagnosed cancer had spread to his lungs.

Holding back tears as he lay on a stretcher, Mr. Fox told a hastily assembled press conference in Thunder Bay just hours after undergoing tests: "It was an unbelievable shock. I really didn't think this could happen."

Mr. Fox had raised $2-million for cancer research since he began his cross-country marathon in St. John's on April 12.

"If there's any way I can get out there again and finish it, I will," the runner said from a stretcher outside the cancer clinic in Thunder Bay.

"I'd like to thank all the people out there behind me who have helped me and I hope they will continue in the provinces I haven't been to and in the provinces I've been to already."

No details were released on how far the cancer has spread or what action will be taken. Mr. Fox said more tests and treatment would be conducted in B.C.

Mr. Fox was first taken to hospital in Thunder Bay on Monday and was thought to be suffering from stomach flu after running 31 kilometres (19 miles) that day. He said he first noticed something was wrong in the afternoon when he had trouble breathing and began coughing and choking.

Barbara Kilvert, spokesman for the Canadian Cancer Society, said the cancer diagnosis "took us completely by surprise. We had had no reports of ill health at all. We're desperately upset about this. The

FIGHT — Page 2

September 3, 1980: The *Globe and Mail* shares the sad news with the nation that Terry's Marathon of Hope was ended due to the return of his cancer.

From the Canadian Press / *Globe and Mail*

A message of hope for Terry: 'Fight it, my friend'

Terry's parents, Rolly and Betty Fox, and his constant companion, Bill Vigars stare almost in disbelief as Terry's stretcher is loaded onto aircraft.

Sittler says he'd help finish run for Terry

Terry doesn't want pity just a chance to finish his run

I'll never give up Terry vows

(top) March 4, 1981: Pope John Paul II sends well wishes to Terry after his cancer returned. (bottom) June 28, 1981: Queen Elizabeth II and Prince Philip send condolences to the Fox family after Terry's death in 1981.

Courtesy of the Terry Fox Centre Archives

September 2, 1980: Terry prepares for transport from Thunder Bay, Ontario, to the Royal Columbian Hospital in British Columbia.

From *Toronto Star* Archives via Getty Images

September 3, 1980: A full page of the *Toronto Star* dedicated to the ending of Terry's Marathon of Hope, with articles written by Leslie Scrivener, Paul Dalby, and Peter Rickwood. Within one article, Darryl Sittler says, "I think it would be a terrific idea for some of us to finish off the marathon for Terry if that's what he wants."

EPILOGUE
THE FUTURE AS
TERRY HOPED

MICHAEL MAZZA
Executive director of the Terry Fox Foundation

I meet Michael over Microsoft Teams on a Monday morning. He is in his office at the Terry Fox Foundation (TFF), a framed picture of Terry with a police escort behind him visible over his right shoulder. He is dressed sharply in a suit and black-framed glasses and has a bright, friendly demeanour.

As executive director of the TFF, Michael shares that the focus of the Foundation is to inspire people to understand the power of philanthropy and how philanthropy can effect change. By the end of 2023, TFF has reached around $900 million through fundraising. The funds are given to the Terry Fox Research Institute (TFRI), allowing scientists to explore the unexplained and big ideas that may involve higher risk and discover the answers to their complex questions. TFRI is overseeing a new system that promises to revolutionize the diagnosis and treatment of cancer patients.

When Terry ran, his wish was to find a cure for cancer through more research. As scientists began to understand cancer, they learned that there were over two hundred types with different genetic drivers and behaviours. They may have made progress over the decades, and survival rates have increased from twenty-five percent to over sixty-five percent, but there is more work to be done. And because institutions

Michael Mazza, executive director of the Terry Fox Foundation.
Courtesy of Michael Mazza, Terry Fox Foundation

and organizations are responsible for their own information and data, they are largely not being shared for research purposes. This wasn't necessarily because of institutional egos or different healthcare systems in each of the provinces, but due to regulations that ostensibly protect the privacy of patients. But data is needed to drive innovation, and if a solution can't be achieved individually, then it's better to work together — much like the Marathon of Hope.

> Precision medicine is about the right treatment, right patient, right time. But to get there, you need a lot of information. Today, we have over thirty-two institutions and hundreds of Canada's best researchers, who are all working together to share the information. It's moving away from "breast cancer is breast cancer" [to] how is that cancer composed? And what cancers is it similar to across our country? If we understand that — if this cancer is like that cancer, and this cancer was successfully treated by doing A, B, C — then we can take the guesswork out of how to treat *your* cancer. We can say, "We're going to treat your cancer like this because we know it's been

effective for other cancers that are similar to yours." It's whole genomic sequencing [coupled with] all the clinical health information. Past patients help current patients, and current patients help future patients.

Most patients feel as Terry did, not wanting others to go through what they have gone or are going through. Terry showed that one person can inspire, and one person can create change, but it takes all of us to make it really happen. Canada has universal healthcare, with everyone helping each other through their taxes, but healthcare is funded provincially, with each province having its own protocols and institutions. It is also paramount that personal health information stays private. With everything being done differently across the country, privacy couldn't be guaranteed.

> It was the simplicity of the solution. If everyone collects data in the same way, then we don't have to move it. So, each institution can maintain their responsibility for ensuring the privacy, but we can then create platforms that all of the researchers and clinicians will be able to access that information across the country. The issue was [that] we couldn't get away from who owns it, who runs it, and how do we centralize it to we [all] collectively own it, we all maintain it, and we just create access points.

What researchers see has all been anonymized, with personal parts of the data secured behind each institution's firewall. Now, if they organize and process it in the same way, others can have access to that information. A national advisory committee decided what information will be required, and though they may not know what they need today, it's important they do whole genomic sequencing so that what they collect will be completely accurate and permanent. That information from that patient today will be relevant ten, twenty, fifty years from now. There are two hundred criteria on the clinical data inputted and attached to the whole genomic sequence.

What this means, in the simplest of terms, is they can take the samples from a tumour, sequence those, and then compare the genetic changes across the data system. They will be able to see who has had a similar tumour and how it was treated. Some treatments may have been successful and others less successful, and researchers will be able to see that and provide the best treatment plan to your oncologist based on that tumour's molecular characteristics and how it was treated previously. When the data from each treatment is inputted into the system, it builds the data for future patients. The more data gathered, the more quickly cancers can be identified and diagnosed, and tailored approaches to treatment provided — which drugs, how often, which chemotherapy or radiation, and for how long.

A researcher conducts tests in the Terry Fox Research Institute lab.
Courtesy of Michael Mazza, Terry Fox Foundation

Right now [in December 2023], we have three thousand cases that have been fully sequenced. About seven hundred have attached clinical data. That number will start to approach the three thousand, which is twenty percent of what we want to accomplish by March 2026. So, March

2026, we want to be at fifteen thousand. In the spring, we are going to start doing some research queries, cross-institutional, where they will start to utilize that three thousand to pull up new information that they didn't have access to before. So, it's immediately beneficial.

Within five to ten years, the TFRI hopes that a patient's physician can put their information in the database to devise optimal treatment. Michael says it will probably be ten-plus years when this is a reality for every patient. The amount of data pulled is massive and takes up to half a terabyte. Artificial intelligence and machine learning will assist in pulling up cases that are similar, so researchers and doctors have the information they need quickly. With advances in technology and data sharing, they can have a mass of information that can be sifted through to narrow down what can be effective and, just as importantly, what is *not* effective for treating a specific type of cancer and what matches the criteria of the patient needing treatment. It saves time by removing the guesswork of trying one treatment, watching it fail, and trying another.

Scientists at the Terry Fox Research Institute in 2022.

Courtesy of Michael Mazza, Terry Fox Foundation

From Terry's Marathon of Hope in 1980 to the TFF's fundraising to the TFRI earning the trust of the medical community and taking the lead on this project — this is Terry's vision of research being used to help others avoid suffering the same fate that many have in their battles with cancer.

> I think Terry might have been surprised to learn of the lack of coordination in research, and he would have been thrilled [by this]. You live by what you learn. I think Terry's values lead us, and he believed we can all do something. And I think those are the guiding principles by which this project comes together. Nobody is more important than anybody else, but collectively we're way better [off] than we are as a collection of individuals. I think it would be right up his alley, and he would have said, "You should have done it from day one!"

Only by working together will we do the impossible.

ACKNOWLEDGEMENTS

We'd first like to express our love, support, and admiration to all those who have fought, are fighting, or are supporting those in the fight against cancer. We hope that this book has brought some positivity and encouragement to your journey.

The story behind the creation of a book is often just as interesting as the book itself. In this case, that rings very true. Throughout the process, speaking with over fifty individuals, we were constantly amazed by the small, often magical moments that occurred. Strange coincidences, small-world surprises, and outright unbelievable discoveries had us frequently saying that Terry was guiding us through the process, nudging us in certain directions. Thank you, Terry, for everything you have done and continue to do in your mission to cure cancer. We are grateful beyond words.

Thank you to every person who shared their story with us, helping create a beautiful image of Terry and his life. Each anecdote, tear, and photograph were so thoughtfully entrusted to us, and we are humbled to be the ones to share them with the world. While we wish we could create a never-ending book, we could not include every story due to a pesky page count. We would like to especially thank those whose stories were not featured in the final product: Yvonne Fox, Joan Gibb, Jeremy Gilbert, Greg Hart, Donna Hilsinger, Ken MacQueen, Cheryl McCargar, Bradley Moss, Brian Norris, and Bill Strong. Your stories were important to the production of this book and a fuller understanding of Terry. We are so grateful you took the time to speak with us.

Unfortunately, several months after we interviewed Dick Traum, he passed away at the age of eighty-three. In his interview, he was incredibly kind, thoughtful, and generous with his time. He is truly an inspiration — to Terry, and to many. Our deepest condolences to his family, friends, and the team at Achilles International.

This book was made possible by a number of individuals. We'd like to first thank the Sprott family, Jennifer Cryderman, Leo and Margaret Couprie, Getty Images, and the *Globe and Mail* for their generous support. As demonstrated within these pages, it is this type of selflessness that drives change. We would also like to extend our gratitude to Gail Harvey for the use of the incredible photographs that she took throughout the Ontario portion of the Marathon of Hope. She captured the side of Terry described to us, and we're so thankful to her for preserving his personality through these images.

Throughout the creation of this book, multiple team members were impacted by cancer, creating an even stronger sense of purpose and urgency to this project. In 2023, the Canadian Cancer Society reported that an estimated forty-five percent of Canadians will be diagnosed with cancer, and twenty-two percent of Canadians will lose their life to the disease. Thankfully, progress in science and research continues to bring us better treatment options and a clearer path to a cure. So, on behalf of every individual facing a cancer battle, we'd especially like to thank you, reader, for picking up this book. Fifty percent of the proceeds are going to the Terry Fox Foundation and their continued mission to beat cancer.

ECW Press &
Burman Books